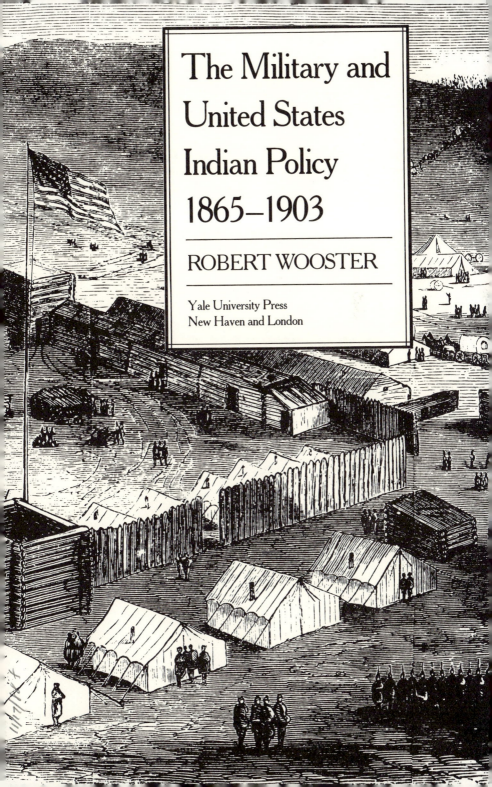

The Military and United States Indian Policy 1865–1903

ROBERT WOOSTER

Yale University Press
New Haven and London

Designed by Nancy Ovedovitz and set in Garamond No. 3 type by Rainsford Type, Ridgefield, Connecticut. Printed in the United States of America by Halliday Lithograph Corporation, West Hanover, Massachusetts.

Library of Congress Cataloging-in-Publication Data

Wooster, Robert Allen.
 The military and United States Indian policy, 1865–1903.
 (Yale Western Americana series ; 34)
 Bibliography: p.
 Includes index.
  1. Indians of North America—Wars—1866–1895. 2. Indians of North America—Government relations—1869–1934. 3. United States. Army—History—19th century. 4. Indian warfare.
I. Title. II. Series.
E83.866.W66 1988   973.8   87–14234
ISBN 0–300–03972–7 (alk. paper)

The paper in this book meets the guidelines for permanence and durability of the Committee on Production Guidelines for Book Longevity of the Council on Library Resources.

10   9   8   7   6   5   4   3   2   1

To Mom and Dad

Contents

Maps

Acknowledgments

An author's greatest satisfaction comes in thanking those who helped make his book possible. The initial suggestion for this book came from Paul E. Isaac while I was an undergraduate at Lamar University. Several professors at the University of Texas provided encouragement. John E. Sunder, my dissertation advisor, was always ready to help: his sage advice and easy comraderie made my work much more pleasant; he more than anyone else helped to refine my hazy ideas into a finished product. Lewis L. Gould generously offered his wise, professional counsel as well as a number of research notes and hints.

Other groups and individuals also assisted my efforts. A number of sources at the University of Texas, including the Dora Bonham Fund, the Clara Driscoll Fellowship, the Graduate School Research Fund, the University Fellowship Committee, and the Colonial Dames Scholarship provided financial assistance. John Lamphear made a number of important suggestions on the military aspects of the subject. Robin Doughty and L. Tuffly Ellis took the time to read the manuscript. Howard Lamar gave me a sympathetic ear and some insightful hints during a memorable morning break at the Barker Texas History Center. Meighan Pritchard, formerly of Yale University Press, performed yeoman service as manuscript editor. As a graduate student, I enjoyed the distinct pleasure of working for James A. Michener as he wrote his novel, *Texas*. His insight, experience, and deep devotion to education had a profound impact on my career. During this period I had the good fortune to work with John Kings and Lisa Kaufman. I learned much about scholarship, writing, and life from these unique spirits, and I hope that some of their special expertise wore off on me.

Corpus Christi State University funded the maps during a time of fiscal crisis. Chrystal Steffens typed the bibliography and handled assorted clerical tasks. Patrick Carroll has been particularly helpful as a friend and advisor.

A number of persons deserve special mention. Robert Benedittino and David Barber provided solid friendship. Sally Graham and Jim Boyden helped celebrate the good and overcome the evils that bedevil every scholar—I owe them a particular debt of gratitude. David Gates, as always, was a friend and confidant.

My wife, Patricia Thomas, carefully edited the manuscript. Her sage counsel and loving support on this and other projects has been invaluable. The advice, encouragement, and love of my parents, Ralph and Edna Wooster, can never be matched. As always, I only wish I could say it better.

Abbreviations

AAG	Assistant (or Acting) Adjutant General
AG	Adjutant General
ASP:IA	*American State Papers: Indian Affairs*
ASP:MA	*American State Papers: Military Affairs*
JMSIUS	*Journal of the Military Service Institute of the United States*
LC	Library of Congress
LS, AGO	Letters Sent by the Office of the Adjutant General
LS, SW	Letters Sent by the Secretary of War Relating to Military Affairs
NA	National Archives
OR	*The War of the Rebellion: A Compilation of the Official Records of the Union and Confederate Armies*
SI	Secretary of the Interior
SI, AR	U.S. Secretary of the Interior, Annual Reports
SS	Secretary of State
SW, AR	U.S. Secretary of War, Annual Reports
UT	University of Texas at Austin

Introduction

In 1893, Frederick Jackson Turner proclaimed the close of the American frontier to his colleagues at the American Historical Association meeting. This speech, which offered a fresh view of American history, established Turner's reputation, and he went on to become the preeminent American historian of the early twentieth century. In addition to arguing that the frontier explained the uniqueness of the American character and acted as a "safety valve" for American liberty, Turner maintained in a series of books, articles, and speeches that sectionalism was fundamental to American development and life. Eager students and disciples, most notably Ray Allen Billington, refined and added to Turner's frontier thesis and sought in particular to examine the West as a distinct, identifiable region of the United States.[1]

Critics, however, launched a series of counterattacks against the Turnerians in the 1930s, assailing Turner's overgeneralizations, his "safety valve" concept, and his tendency toward overstatement. Earl Pomeroy in particular pointed to the significance of imported cultural traits rather than geography in affecting frontier life. Pomeroy also rebuked western historians for limit-

---

1. A good selection of Turner's essays may be found in Turner, *Frontier and Section*. For Billington, see Billington, *America's Frontier Heritage*.

ing their interests and examinations to things purely western and
for failing to recognize the enormous importance of outside influences. Stressing the need to integrate the West into a wider context, Pomeroy noted the federal government's importance in
western affairs. Seizing the initiative, scholars like Howard Lamar conducted a series of studies that examined this federal influence on the western states and territories.[2]

Not only the American West but the United States as a whole
between 1865 and 1900 has been the subject of intense study.
Attacking the tendency of earlier scholars to dismiss the Gilded Age
as a "great barbecue" marked by scandals and unabashed profiteering,
historians like H. Wayne Morgan have attempted to point out the
political and economic growth experienced during the period. Others
have reevaluated the presidents of this era, arguing that these men
were more than simply political buffoons or puppets manipulated
by cagey, unscrupulous underlings and people with wealth and
power.[3]

Related to discussions of both the Gilded Age and the West are
the issues of Indian policy and the army. Again, historians have
recognized that these affairs rarely fit neat stereotypes. As Francis
Paul Prucha and Robert Utley have explained, the Indian-chasing
cavalry of popular myth represents only a small portion of the army's
role in the West. They have also noted that the army's treatment
of Indians was too complex to be explained by the sole motive of
extermination. On a strategic level, Russell Weigley and others have
dealt with post-1865 military practices largely in terms of the Civil
War. Weigley argues that generals, conditioned by their Civil War
experiences, sought to apply doctrines of total war against hostile
Indians.[4]

2. Taylor, ed., *Turner Thesis*; Pomeroy, "Reorientation of Western History";
Lamar, *Dakota Territory*.

3. Morgan, *From Hayes to McKinley*. See also Gould, *William McKinley*, and
Doenecke, *Garfield and Arthur*.

4. Prucha, *Broadax and Bayonet*; Utley, *Frontiersmen in Blue*; Weigley, *American
Way of War*.

Countless books and articles have documented the western conflict between whites and Indians after the Civil War. To adequately understand these clashes, however, it is necessary to analyze the problem within the larger context of the politics of the Gilded Age, the role of the federal government, and the American military tradition. As such, this book is divided into two parts, the first outlining in a thematic fashion the major problems and issues facing the army, the second describing the army's western experiences between 1865 and 1903.[5]

The first chapter describes the American military after 1865, concentrating on administrative problems, the army's varied responsibilities, and the special difficulties posed by western Indians. Chapter 2 gives brief portraits of the army's senior Indian fighters after 1865, stressing the cultural constraints within which they worked. The third chapter focuses on the regional and national political problems which further hindered the development of consistent policy. Using the framework established in the first three chapters, Chapters 4 through 6 analyze the western campaigns. The conclusion explores America's post-Civil War Indian conflicts in the light of broader military experience, paying special emphasis to the connections between these wars and the colonial wars of other nations during the latter third of the nineteenth century.

Throughout this work, I will concentrate on the military's futile attempts to construct a consistent policy aimed at controlling the conflicts with western Indians. Focusing on the War Department's overall military efforts in the post-Civil War period, and more

5. For extensive bibliographies of the Indian-white conflicts, see Utley, *Indian Frontier*, 295–306; and Hutton, "Indians' Last Stand." On overall strategy: Marshall, *Crimsoned Prairie*, is inadequate. Much better is Utley, *Frontier Regulars*, although Utley is more concerned with the army's experience and performance in the West than in strategy. Among the more general studies of military strategy, Weigley, *American Way of War*, 153–63, is not as strong on the Indian wars as on other eras of America's military history; Huntington, *Soldier and the State*, is good but now somewhat dated; Williams, *History of American Wars*, 303–16, is solid but brief, as is Millett and Maslowski, *Common Defense*, 232–49.

particularly on high-ranking government and army officials, this book will discuss specific weapons, treaties, and battles only as they pertain to the larger picture. To a lesser extent, I will assess the army's role in the near extermination of the buffalo, as well as the connections between the nation's experiences with its own indigenous cultures and its later strategy toward guerillas and insurrectionists during the occupation of the Philippines.

While noting the importance of the frontier environment to army policy-makers, I would like to stress the influence of the federal government on western affairs. The importance of post-1865 politics in the formulation of the army's Indian policy is also clear. Although the politicians and issues of Reconstruction and the Gilded Age deserve serious attention, few individuals of national prominence cared a great deal about Indian affairs. And while acknowledging that the strategies employed in the Civil War have some similarity with large-scale operations against the Indians, the vastly different political, environmental, cultural, and tactical conditions found in these conflicts make sweeping generalizations about their direct connections extremely tenuous.

The army's Indian policies after 1865 should not be considered entirely in light of Civil War experiences, and labels of terror, annihilation and extermination, though applicable in certain instances, do not adequately describe military actions against Indians in the latter nineteenth century. The elements affecting military policy during the period were much more complex than is generally acknowledged. A wide variety of issues, including politics, perceptions of the western environment, railroad building, international relations, clashes between the War and Interior departments, personal disputes, and misconceptions among whites about Native Americans all influenced the military's operations against Indians after 1865. While the goals of subjugation, removal, and acculturation remained constant, the means by which they were to be achieved differed markedly throughout the last half of the century. This interplay of factors sheds new light on the much-debated subject of Indian-white relations.

The United States Army was truly a "child of the frontier."[6] The army, organized in the early days of the republic to protect pioneer settlers from Indian attack, was called upon to perform increasingly difficult tasks throughout the nineteenth century. Yet the regular military establishment grew slowly and proved unable to maintain a consistent presence along the nation's vast frontiers. High-level military officials rarely focused their full attention on Indian warfare, an omission that further compounded the difficulties of the frontier regulars. And although many Americans voiced their opinions on Indian relations, comparatively few studied the issue with any particular intensity. Consequently, the army, composed of poorly-paid enlistees and officers of uneven abilities, was often the federal government's sole agent in the trans-Mississippi West.

The small regular force faced many difficulties in the pre–Civil War West. Its primary objectives included protecting settlers, defending emigrant routes, and occupying new territory. The army also tried to shield smaller Indian tribes against attacks by more powerful tribes or, in a few cases, from threats by whites. Its chief problems stemmed from the wide disparity of Indian groups it dealt with, the vast distances and expanding boundaries it was supposed to guard, and a Congress and citizenry reluctant to increase military spending.[7]

The military had made some progress in the West prior to 1865. The army gained at least superficial knowledge of western Indians, many of whom differed greatly from the more sedentary groups previously encountered in the East. In addition, it established the basic organizational and administrative structure that would function in the West after 1865. A number of forts were constructed, but only rarely were they consciously designed as part of a comprehensive defense system. Finally, whereas offensives against certain

6. Prucha, *Sword of the Republic*, 394.

7. To illustrate the effect of intertribal disputes on Indian-white warfare, see Ewers, "Intertribal Warfare." For a more complete study of pre-1860 strategy, see Wooster, "Military Strategy in the American West, 1815–1860," 256–62.

tribes were recognized as necessary, experience had largely discredited the idea that roving columns should replace stationary posts as the basis for frontier defense.[8]

Government and military planners had proposed a variety of means through which the army might control hostile Indians. The creation of a geographic barrier was a commonly voiced solution. While still dominant in North America, England had tried to create such a permanent frontier line along the Appalachian Mountains in the Proclamation of 1763. Secretaries of War Henry Knox (1789–95) and Timothy Pickering (1795–96), General James Wilkinson, and soldier-explorer William Clark hoped to establish a line of forts just ahead of western settlement. In the early 1800s, President Thomas Jefferson thought the Mississippi River a suitable border.[9] Some years later, Secretary of War Lewis Cass (1831–37) wanted to construct a military road supported by a series of fortifications from Fort Towson along the Red River to Fort Snelling, on the Mississippi River—what he believed was the permanent line of division between whites and Indians. His successor, Joel R. Poinsett (1837–41), proposed a double line of fixed posts along a similar position. As settlers moved further west, some military officials believed the "Great American Desert" was inhospitable to whites and presumed that a permanent Indian frontier might be created along the edges of arable land. Secretary of War Jefferson Davis (1853–57) was certain that white settlement had reached its limits in western North America; he suggested that several permanent forts defend this

8. Utley, *Frontiersmen in Blue*, 341–46. For Smith's views, see Smith to Freeman, July 19, 1853, in Crimmins, ed., "Freeman's Report," 215.

9. Knox to Washington, Dec. 29, 1784, *American State Papers: Indian Affairs* 1:534–35; Pickering to Committee on the Military Establishment, Feb. 3, 1796, U.S. Congress, *American State Papers: Military Affairs* (hereafter cited as *ASP: MA*) 112–13; Wilkinson to Hamilton, Sept. 6, 1799, Syrett, ed., *Hamilton Papers* 23:377–93; Osgood, ed., *Field Notes of Clark*, 188; Prucha, *Sword of the Republic*, 84–85.

line, which he envisioned to be near the 98th meridian. The next secretary of war, John B. Floyd (1857–61), reached a similar conclusion, though he pressed for a larger number of smaller-sized garrisons.[10]

Perceptions of the American West played a large part in these developments. Secretary of War John C. Calhoun (1817–25), an avowed expansionist, had envisioned the territory gained in the Louisiana Purchase as a region of future prosperity. He believed the potentially most productive areas needed to be occupied by whites and thus pushed for more military appropriations.[11] By contrast, Secretary of War Charles Conrad (1850–53) deemed the New Mexico Territory a barren desert not worth the cost of defense. Following the reports of Lt. Col. Edwin V. Sumner, Conrad urged that settlers be moved out of the worthless area to regions where cheaper, more effective protection might be provided.[12]

A number of people proposed plans for western defense. Noting that the federal government's weak line of forts had failed to prevent Indian intrusions, many officials believed that military offensives were necessary to overawe hostile tribes. Such punitive expeditions achieved only mixed success. Columns led by Josiah Harmar and Arthur St. Clair suffered shocking losses in a series of fights along the Maumee and Wabash rivers in 1790 but were somewhat avenged by Anthony Wayne's victory at Fallen Timbers four years later. William Henry Harrison and Andrew Jackson inflicted further defeats upon Indians during the War of 1812. William Clark concluded that Indians must be set against each other: "encouraging [sic] of War among the Indian Tribes, is *cruel*," he wrote, "but the

10. Wooster, "Military Strategy in the Southwest, 1848–1860"; Report of Davis, Dec. 1, U.S. Secretary of War, Annual Reports (hereafter cited as SW, AR), 1856, 5–8.

11. Calhoun to Jackson, Mar. 6, 1819, Jameson, ed., *Calhoun Corr.* 153–54; Calhoun to Smyth, Dec. 29, 1819, *ASP: MA* 2:33–34.

12. Report of Sumner, May 27, SW, AR, 1852, 23–25; Report of Conrad, Dec. 4, ibid., 5.

situation of this Country has been such, that I found myself compelled to promote a War amongst the Indians."[13]

Several secretaries of war agreed that offensive operations were necessary. Calhoun and Cass strongly favored these expeditions, as did their successors of the early 1840s. They hoped that strong military columns dispatched into Indian lands might intimidate the tribes and bring them to the peace table. Yet as warfare continued to plague America's frontiers, active campaigning west of the Mississippi became increasingly violent. Charles Conrad wanted to launch offensives intended not merely to intimidate but to strike directly at the Indians' homelands. The scarcity of troops hampered Conrad's efforts, but an 1855 increase in army manpower made offensives more practical. Davis and Floyd organized several powerful campaigns, the latter eventually recognizing the value of infantry as well as cavalry raids.[14]

The disposition of available manpower was an ever-present question for military authorities. General Alexander Hamilton wanted to concentrate the frontline garrisons as circumstances permitted but stressed the importance of maintaining a strong force in reserve. President George Washington supported this proposed reserve, although he disagreed on its proper location.[15] Arguing that the army was too dispersed, Secretaries of War James Barbour (1825–28) and Poinsett sought to collect a strong reserve at St. Louis. Davis agreed that the troops were too spread out; he proposed that many tiny

13. Clark to Graham, Aug. 28, 1817, Carter and Porter, eds., *Terr. Papers* 10:301–3.

14. Calhoun to Atkinson, Mar. 27, 1819, Jameson, ed., *Calhoun Corr.*, 159; Calhoun to Long, Mar. 8, 1819, Hemphill et al., eds., *Calhoun Papers* 3:639–40; Calhoun to Cass, Jan. 14, Feb. 25, 1820, ibid., 4:573–74, 684; Calhoun to Atkinson, Dec. 19, 1820, Carter and Porter, eds., *Terr. Papers* 15:684–85; Report of Cass, Nov. 29, 1833, *ASP: MA* 5:170; Report of Cass, Nov. 30, 1835, ibid., 627; Conrad to Sumner, Apr. 1, SW, AR, 1851, 125–26; Conrad to Smith, ibid., 117–18; Report of Harney, Sept. 5, SW, AR, 1855, 49–51; Report of Floyd, Oct. 5, ibid., 1857, 3–5; Floyd to Nichols, July 9, ibid., 1860, 60.

15. Hamilton to Washington, Sept. 9, 1799, Syrett, ed., *Hamilton Papers* 23:404; Washington to Hamilton, Sept. 15, 1799, ibid., 417–20.

frontier posts be abandoned in favor of larger forts along the edges of civilization. Although these advocates of concentration presented strong theoretical cases, in actual practice the army remained widely scattered during the pre–Civil War era.[16]

Recognizing the nation's opposition to a large standing army, most policymakers sought to increase the efficiency of existing forces. Secretary of War William H. Crawford (1815–17) spent most of his two years in office reorganizing the high command in an effort "to rid the army of old women and blockheads, at least on the general staff."[17] John C. Calhoun, also wary of the strength of opinion opposed to a large permanent establishment, advocated an "expansible" army with a high ratio of officers in the standing units. Volunteers could flesh out the skeletal force of trained officers in case of emergency. Calhoun hoped, as did Cass in a later period, that a more proficient force might mask the deficiencies stemming from its small size.[18]

Virtually everyone associated with strategic policy recognized the need to reduce transportation costs. Advance frontier outposts were often built at the heads of navigation of major rivers, and army expeditions followed water routes whenever possible.[19] But most war secretaries also strove to improve land transportation and allowed troops to be used in building roads and bridges. Going a step further, Lewis Cass envisaged a major military road built parallel to the frontier. The road, as the centerpiece of Cass's proposed western strategy, was intended to deter Indian attacks. Yet Cass's successor, Joel Poinsett, wanted the transportation arteries to run perpendicular

16. Report of Barbour, Nov. 28, 1826, *ASP: MA* 3:330; Report of Poinsett, Dec. 30, 1837, ibid., 7:777–78; Poinsett to Linn, Jan. 11, 1839, National Archives, Letters Sent by the Secretary of War Relating to Military Affairs (hereafter cited as LS, SW), 20; Report of Davis, Dec. 1, SW, AR, 1853, 5–6.

17. Crawford to Gallatin, Sept. 22, 1813, Adams, ed., *Gallatin Writings* 1:583.

18. Report of Calhoun, Dec. 12, 1820, *ASP: MA* 2:188–91; Spiller, "Calhoun's Expansible Army."

19. Wooster, "Military Strategy in the Trans-Mississippi West," 258–59. See also Hill, *Roads, Rails, and Waterways.*

to the frontier, connecting western outposts with supply bases to the East. Later military leaders saw railroads as the army's answer to the transportation and communication problems. Jefferson Davis's role in securing one million dollars for a series of railroad surveys is well documented; less publicized were the earlier efforts of Gen. Edmund P. Gaines and the subsequent work of John Floyd.[20]

Despite such schemes, pre–Civil War leaders never developed a consistent, long-range military strategy against Indians. Admittedly, changing frontier conditions made such planning difficult. The continual turnover of personnel in the War Department also contributed to the lack of clear policy. But the secretaries of war, with the exceptions of Calhoun, Davis, and perhaps Poinsett, were themselves men of indifferent abilities. Often selected for overtly political reasons, they betrayed a critical lack of imagination and originality. Their advisors frequently had similar shortcomings. Even such able generals as Winfield Scott found power struggles and personality clashes within the army more absorbing than the elaboration and execution of Indian policy. The army's difficulties in the Second Seminole War, during which a few thousand Indians tied up stronger regular and volunteer forces in Florida for seven years (1835–42), were almost predictable in light of such internal controversies.[21]

The nation's overall Indian policy suffered from similar problems. British and colonial American officials had wanted to bring the

20. Nelson, "Military Roads for War and Peace"; Prucha, *Sword of the Republic*, 185; Crawford to Jackson, Mar. 6, 1816, Bassett, ed., *Jackson Corr.* 2:235; Report of Calhoun, Jan. 7, 1819, Hemphill et al., eds., *Calhoun Papers* 3:461–72; Cass to Senate Committee on Military Affairs, Feb. 19, 1836, *ASP: MA* 6:150–52; Report of Poinsett, Dec. 30, 1837, ibid., 7:777–78; Gaines, "A Plan for the Defence of the Western Frontier," Feb. 28, 1838, House Doc. No. 311, 25th Cong., 2nd sess., ser. 329, 1–12; Report of Davis, Dec. 1, SW, AR, 1853, 23; Davis to Sandridge, Jan. 29, 1856, LS, SW, 37:347–49; Floyd to Pope, May 5, 1857, ibid., 39:49–52; Floyd to Shields, Mar. 16, 1858, ibid., 40:96–97; Floyd to Brown, June 9, 1858, ibid.: 251.

21. Cunliffe, *Soldiers and Civilians*, 136–44, has a good account of these disputes.

benefits of Christianity to the Indians. The central government under the Articles of Confederation and the new constitution hoped to convince Indians to follow standards of behavior acceptable to white Americans. To most leaders these altruistic motives did not seem inconsistent with the more tangible goal of securing title to tribal lands. While seeking on the one hand to "civilize" the so-called savages, they sought at the same time to exploit the Native American for his land and resources. Few recognized the contradictions inherent in this position or admitted that racism would prevent the proper execution of all but the most careful plans. Still fewer were willing to give the subject their full attention. To those in power, other questions of government, economics, and society appeared much more pressing than the Indian issue.[22]

In the absence of alternative solutions, Thomas Jefferson's plan for removal became a cornerstone of federal Indian policy. Claiming that the process would benefit both whites and Indians, he and other leaders argued that the nation's frontiers could best be protected by removing Indians from settled areas. While some whites sought to ease the displacement process, this policy, conducted poorly and without proper appropriations or foresight, inevitably led to enormous suffering. Even removal became subject to divided government jurisdiction; in 1849 the Office of Indian Affairs was transferred from the War Department to the newly created Department of the Interior. Because the War Department retained control over military removal of Indians to reservations, this transfer divided authority over the Indian problem into two departments, making each even more susceptible to the claims of special interest groups and further hampering attempts to develop a consistent policy.[23]

The same year, Commissioner of Indian Affairs Orlando Brown proposed that Plains Indians should live on clearly defined reservations free of unauthorized white intrusions. Some tribes were to be removed to these designated areas, thus continuing earlier policy.

22. Berkhofer, *White Man's Indian*, 134–66.
23. Ibid.; Sheehan, *Seeds of Extinction*.

The army was to police reservation boundaries. Military officials of the 1850s warmly embraced the reservation system, although the extent of the army's legal and moral jurisdiction in reservation affairs remained unsettled for decades.[24]

The option of using force to deal with Indians in the United States was seldom questioned. It was generally conceded that those tribes that challenged the government's authority had to be crushed before they could be taught the virtues of Anglo-American civilization. Yet the changing shape of the frontier, the instability and dearth of creativity in War Department leadership, and the absence of interested, competent advisors prevented the development of lasting military strategy or policy in the trans-Mississippi West before the Civil War. Few prominent officials found this particularly troublesome; most realized that Indians posed no real threat to national security. As no emergency existed, neither army officers nor government officials found it necessary to work out comprehensive doctrines to be used in dealing with Indians.

24. Trennert, *Alternative to Extinction.*

Chapter One
The Military after 1865

After the mighty Union armies defeated the eleven rebellious Confederate states, most of the weary veterans soon began readjusting to civilian life, but a few soldiers remained in a regular army that faced a military situation far different from that of the Civil War.[1] For the next four decades, scattered in more than two hundred small posts throughout the country, America's armed forces struggled to define and implement a general policy applicable in vastly differing environments and against widely dissimilar Indian tribes. The military's primary task was to cope with Indians, but other developments—Reconstruction, civil disputes, international problems, and

1. Glatthaar, *March to the Sea*, 180–82; Weigley, *History of the United States Army*, 262.

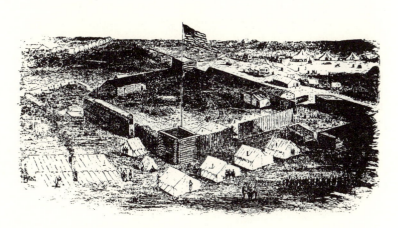

natural disasters—prevented the army from focusing its full attention on Indian affairs. In addition, the army's confused command structure compounded the quandaries facing military officials. Even when the War Department had addressed these concerns, the unique military problems posed by hostile tribes in the West made effective policy-making difficult.

In 1866, the most pessimistic officers in the United States Army did not predict the varied duties their troops undertook in the years to come. Most assumed that their men would patrol the nation's western frontiers as the regulars had done before the Civil War. Instead, a large number were assigned to duties unassociated with Indian service—for example, reconstructing the eleven Southern states, which was the most significant drain of all these tasks on army manpower. For twelve years considerable numbers of regular troops protected unpopular civil governments, ensured federal authority, and attempted to enforce new voting regulations in the defeated Confederate states. In 1867, these occupation duties involved almost 40 percent of the army; as late as 1876, 15 percent of the entire army was still billetted to the South.[2]

The task of watching Mormons also diverted the army's attention from Indian affairs. The army, having sent an expeditionary force under Col. Albert Sidney Johnston into Utah in 1857, continued to worry about the possibility of armed resistance by Mormons after the Civil War. Many officers thought that Mormons discriminated against Gentiles and encouraged Indian opposition to the central government. One feared that "the Mormons alone could now gather more men capable of bearing arms than you could muster in your whole army, and that in the Switzerland of America." Although the majority of army men did not share this extreme view, the War Department remained wary of Brigham Young's followers and sent

2. SW, AR, 1867, 436–74; 1868, 732–67; 1869, 152–71; 1870, 66–87; 1871, 88–105; 1872, 104–19; 1873, 58–73; 1874, 70–85; 1875, 42–57; and 1876, 142–57.

troops periodically into Deseret to display the "moral influence" of the United States government.[3]

Garrisons at federal arsenals and seacoast fortifications further reduced the strength of the Indian-fighting army. The figures do not match those for Reconstruction duties, but the number of troops involved is significant. From 1865 to 1875 roughly 11 percent of the army guarded arsenals and coastal forts in the eastern United States; 13 percent did so from 1875 to 1885.[4] The attention given seaboard defenses increased after 1885, when a special board, consisting of Secretary of War William C. Endicott, four army officers, two naval commanders, and two private citizens, presented its recommendations to Congress. The Endicott Board called for a comprehensive system of heavy artillery, searchlights, mines, and torpedo boats to protect the nation's coasts. Although Congress never fully implemented the board's proposals, money, manpower, and attention were regularly diverted from the frontier.[5]

Other duties also demanded the army's attention. Civilian scientists, while adding greatly to the knowledge of the American West in the postwar period, frequently required small military escorts. The army also conducted its own experiments and surveys

3. Miles to Sherman, Dec. 12, 1881, Library of Congress (hereafter cited as LC), Sherman Papers, 57, reel 30 (first quotation): McCook to Adjutant General, Dec. 3, 1885, Box 17, LC, Schofield Papers (second quotation). See also Dodge to Pope, June 4, 1865, LC, Grant Papers, series 5, 54, reel 24; Townsend to Sherman, National Archives, Letters Sent by the Office of the Adjutant General [hereafter cited as LS, AGO], 42, reel 29; Sherman to John Sherman, Jan. 17, 1867, LC, Sherman Papers, 20, reel 11; Sheridan to Ord, Jan. 29, 1872, Box 7, LC, Sheridan Papers; Sheridan to Sherman, June 9, 1877, Box 17, ibid.; McCrary to Emery, June 23, 1877, LS, SW, 82, reel 75; Howard to Schofield, July 15, 1885, Box 40, LC, Schofield Papers.

4. See SW, AR, 1867–76, pages cited in n. 1, and those of 1877, 16–29; 1878, 12–25; 1879, 15–31; 1880, 10–24; 1881, 50–62; 1883, 32–43; 1883, 60–71; 1884, 58–68; and 1885, 80–91.

5. Millis, ed., *American Military Thought*, 196–207; Weigley, *American Way of War*, 169.

throughout the country, often under the auspices of its Corps of Engineers or Signal Service. One branch of the latter, for example, concentrated on meteorological observations and eventually developed into the United States Weather Bureau. In the 1880s and 1890s, the army became custodian of the Yellowstone, Yosemite, General Grant, and Sequoia national parks. Although War Department officials and army officers welcomed these added responsibilities, troops had to be detailed to the parks to protect wildlife and to suppress vandalism by hunters and tourists.[6]

The federal government also used the army to execute assignments for which no other agency existed. In the wake of droughts and grasshopper infestations, soldiers distributed surplus rations, blankets, and shoes to destitute settlers on the northern plains. Four companies of the Eighth Infantry Regiment helped maintain order in Chicago after the 1871 fire destroyed much of the city. The army also played a significant role in quelling domestic turbulence during the Gilded Age. In 1877, close to four thousand troops protected government property, opened railroads, and restored order after wage cuts sparked massive protest among the nation's railroad workers. During the mid 1880s regular units occupied Omaha, Seattle, and Rock Springs, Wyoming, when civil authorities were unable to maintain peace after anti-Chinese riots. Almost two-thirds of the army either stood on call or actively participated in the disorders of 1894, during which nearly three-quarters of a million workers went on strike in the wake of massive layoffs, wage cuts, and economic panic. On three other occasions the military intervened in the Coeur d'Alene mining regions of northern Idaho. Such tasks often interfered with the army's usual Indian duties: in 1877, for example, Brig. Gen. E. O. C. Ord warned Lt. Col. William R. Shafter to "act cautiously" along the Rio Grande until the troops delayed by that year's strikes could be moved to Texas.[7]

6. Whinah, *History of the United States Weather Bureau*, 18–60; Hampton, *How the U.S. Cavalry Saved Our National Parks*, 55–60, 80, 129, 146; Badé, *Life and Letters of John Muir* 2:294–95.

7. Ord to Shafter, Aug. 25, 1877, Stanford Univ. Library, Shafter Papers, reel

To perform their varied assignments, army officials set up a series of geographic divisions, departments, districts, and subdistricts. In theory, these administrative units functioned according to strict hierarchical order. In practice, boundaries and limits of authority changed frequently, and directives routinely failed to go through proper channels. Commanding the Division of the Missouri, Gen. Philip H. Sheridan complained that "Dept. Commanders & their officers are ordered out of my command without informing me. Important orders are sometimes given to Dept. Commanders direct & sometimes copies are sent for my information & sometimes not. In the latter case I then depend on the Dept. Commander to send me record of the surreptitious way in which directions are given."[8]

Managing Indians was only one of a series of considerations determining the geographic divisions of army administration. There were no special Indian divisions, although some departments were organized to deal with threats that a particular tribe or group of tribes might pose. Because administrative units were not set up according to regular guidelines, generals sensitive to any hint of favoritism shown a rival were often simply given commands of equal importance. Major generals usually headed divisions, while brigadier generals controlled departments. The president, advised by the commanding general, made the appointments.[9]

L.

1; Fite, "United States Army and Relief to Pioneer Settlers"; Townsend to Pope, Feb. 4, 1875, LS, AGO, 57, reel 44; Sheridan to Townsend, Oct. 29, 1871, Box 6, LC, Sheridan Papers; Sherman to Sheridan, Oct. 31, 1871, ibid.; Cooper, *Army and Civil Disorder*, 46–50, 86–89, 100–14, 128, 165, is a fine study. Older is Hacker, "U.S. Army as National Police Force." Primary accounts are in Sherman to Sheridan, Nov. 29, 1877, LC, Sherman Papers, 90, reel 45; Lincoln to Sheridan, Mar. 10, 1882, LS, SW, 95, reel 84; Drum to Endicott, Sept. 4, 5, 1885, LC, Cleveland Papers, series 2, reels 18, 38; Report of Schofield, Sept. 30, SW, AR, 1892, 45–46; ibid., Oct. 1, 1894, 57–59.

8. Sheridan to Sherman, Dec. 20, 1880, LC, Sherman Papers, 54, reel 28.

9. Sherman to Hancock, June 5, 1869, LC, Sherman Papers, 90, reel 45; Sherman to Pope, Jan. 25, 1871, ibid.; Sherman to Sheridan, Nov. 29, 1877, ibid.; Sherman to Lincoln, Mar. 10, 1881, ibid.; Sherman to Lincoln, May 4,

Departments and Divisions of the Military West, July 1, 1870

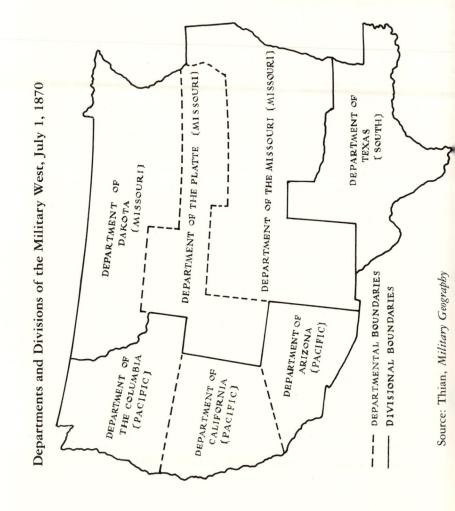

DEPARTMENT OF DAKOTA (MISSOURI)

DEPARTMENT OF THE PLATTE (MISSOURI)

DEPARTMENT OF THE MISSOURI (MISSOURI)

DEPARTMENT OF TEXAS (SOUTH)

DEPARTMENT OF THE COLUMBIA (PACIFIC)

DEPARTMENT OF CALIFORNIA (PACIFIC)

DEPARTMENT OF ARIZONA (PACIFIC)

‒ ‒ ‒ DEPARTMENTAL BOUNDARIES
――― DIVISIONAL BOUNDARIES

Source: Thian, *Military Geography*

For most of the years between 1865 and 1900, administrators partitioned the country into the divisions of the Atlantic, the Missouri, and the Pacific. That of the Atlantic consisted for the most part of the departments of the East and of the South. Additional districts, departments, and a special Division of the South were organized during Reconstruction. The Atlantic division encompassed most of the states east of the ninetieth parallel and had little to do with Indian affairs. Soldiers of the division instead served in labor disputes, held down Reconstruction posts, and garrisoned coastal fortifications, tasks that proved a constant source of irritation to them.[10]

In contrast to the Division of the Atlantic, the Division of the Missouri was associated closely with the Indian question. Generally, the Division of the Missouri included the states of Minnesota, Illinois, Iowa, Kansas, Missouri, and Texas, the Indian territory, and the territories of Montana, Dakota, Utah, Nebraska, Colorado, and New Mexico. In these regions lived the Comanche, Sioux, Cheyenne, and Kiowa, tribes that most threatened white expansion. Authorities split this key division into the departments of the Platte, Dakota, and the Missouri, with the Department of Texas occasionally shifted into another division. Most of the army remained in the Division of the Missouri.[11]

The Division of the Pacific, composed of California, Oregon, Nevada, the territories of Washington, Idaho, and Arizona, and the District of Alaska, was also a key administrative unit in carrying out army Indian policy. Apache, Nez Percé, Paiute, and Modoc tribes living in this division resisted white encroachments and challenged the government's military superiority until the mid-1880s. In order to handle more efficiently the marked differences among tribes and diversity of physical terrain encountered in the Far West,

---

1881, ibid.; Sheridan to Pope, Mar. 12, 1881, Box 59, LC, Sheridan Papers; Sherman to Sheridan, Sept. 16, 1869, LS, SW, 63, reel 60.

    10. Thian, comp., *Military Geography*, 17–19, 27–28.

    11. Ibid., 23–25; Wade, "Military Command Structure," 13–21.

officials created the departments of California, Arizona, and the Columbia. Yet, as in the Atlantic division, troops stationed in the Division of the Pacific also performed functions that had no relation to Indian affairs: breaking up labor disputes, protecting national parks, and manning coastal fortifications.[12]

In theory, clear and consistent instructions from Washington guided divisional commanders, who in turn advised their departmental subordinates on the best means of implementing army policy. This idealistic routine rarely became practice because of the intense rivalry between staff and line officers. The War Department included ten staff bureaus: the Adjutant General's Office, the Inspector General's Department, the Judge-Advocate-General's Office, the Quartermaster's Department, the Subsistence Department, the Ordinance Department, the Corps of Engineers, the Medical Department, the Signal Bureau, and the Pay Department. The commander of each was a brigadier general. Line officers usually remained with their regiments in the field; staff officers served on bureaus and almost always lived in major cities.[13]

Staff chiefs, with their disproportionate share of high-ranking officers and political influence, possessed virtual autonomy and generally operated outside the commanding general's authority. Other staff members, positioned at department and divisional headquarters but assured of support from their powerful Washington-based superiors, gained effective control of logistics on lower levels as well. One officer noted the "total separation of the Staff Corps from the Army" in 1876. Jealous regulars bemoaned their inability to secure supplies for field operations and complained bitterly that their staff counterparts received unfair and undeserved privileges. The staff-line controversy hurt morale, reduced efficiency, and hampered efforts to coordinate policies established in Washington with events that occurred in the West.[14]

12. Thian, *Military Geography*, 26.

13. Weigley, *History of the United States Army*, 290–91; Utley, *Frontier Regulars*, 31–34; Cosmas, *An Army for Empire*, 16–26.

14. Schofield to Sherman, May 8, 1876, LC, Sherman Papers, 43, reel 23

Conflicts stemming from the poorly defined division of authority between the offices of the commanding general and the secretary of war proved even more serious. Regulations gave the commanding general control over affairs defined as military and the secretary authority over staff and fiscal matters. But fiscal control could be used to influence troop operations through distribution or diversion of supply; no specific regulations prevented the war secretary from intervening directly in territorial departments. The army thus functioned without a clear understanding of which office set routine policy.[15]

The problem was not new. Before the Civil War, Gen. Winfield Scott and Secretary of War Jefferson Davis had argued vehemently about their respective powers, and Scott was unable to prevent Davis from assuming effective control over the army. Gen. Ulysses S. Grant and Secretary of War Edwin M. Stanton had arranged an informal, workable system during the Civil War, in which Grant sought to have all orders from the secretary of war routed through the general-in-chief's office. Upon becoming president, Grant issued instructions which further served to ameliorate the situation. He then, however, went on to appoint his friend and former chief of staff John A. Rawlins as secretary of war. Rawlins promptly convinced Grant to restore the former procedure by which the secretary of war could give orders.[16]

(quotation); Cosmas, *An Army for Empire*, 16–26; Utley, *Frontier Regulars*, 32–33; Sherman to John Sherman, Mar. 4, 1876, LC, Sherman Papers, 42, reel 22; Sherman to Pope, Apr. 24, 1876, ibid., 90, reel 45; Schofield to Sherman, May 29, 1879, ibid., 50, reel 26; U.S. Senate, *Cong. Rec.*, 45th Cong., 3rd sess., VIII, pt. 2, 1758.

15. Weigley, *History of the United States Army*, 291; Utley, *Frontier Regulars*, 29–31.

16. Weigley, *History of the United States Army*, 192–94; Grant to Stanton, Jan. 28, 1866, LC, Stanton Papers, reel 10; Grant to Stanton, Jan. 29, 1866, in Sherman to Belknap, LC, Sherman Papers, 92, reel 46; Grant to Sherman, Sept. 18, 1867, ibid., 21, reel 12; Sherman to Grant, Mar. 26, 1869, ibid., 90, reel 45; Sherman to Grant, Sept. 2, 1870, ibid.; Grant to Stanton, LC, Stanton Papers, reel 10; Hart, *Sherman*, 412.

Rawlins died in 1870 after only a year in the War Department. His replacement, William W. Belknap, was determined to assert direct civilian control over the military. Ironically, Belknap had commanded a division under William Sherman in the Civil War, and the two had once been good friends. Despite their former affinity, the newly appointed war secretary infuriated his commanding general and old comrade by issuing orders without consulting him. Finding the situation intolerable, Sherman stormed out of the capital in 1874, transferring army headquarters from Washington to St. Louis. Although Sherman remained the army's senior officer, he was virtually powerless to control his various bureau chiefs, whose offices remained in Washington. Only when Belknap resigned to avoid impeachment for illegally selling post sutlerships did the impasse resolve itself. Sherman returned to Washington in 1876; future secretaries did not challenge his authority.[17]

The issue of authority surfaced again in 1882, when Sherman retired in favor of Philip Sheridan. Sheridan sought a final solution to the question by extending his authority to the staff bureaus, but Secretary of War Robert T. Lincoln fended off his inroads. The problem was not resolved until 1903 when, following an earlier plan suggested by Gen. John M. Schofield, the commanding general's position was abolished in favor of a chief of staff who advised the secretary of war. But the festering conflict had in the meantime compounded the military's already difficult situation in the post–

17. Sherman to Belknap, Aug. 17, 1870, LC, Sherman Papers, 28, reel 15; Sherman to Sheridan, Apr. 1, 1871, ibid., 90, reel 45; Sherman to Belknap, Dec. 2, 1874, ibid., 34, reel 18; Sherman to Belknap, May 8, 1874, ibid., 37, reel 20; Sherman to John Sherman, May 29, 1874, ibid.; Sherman to John Sherman, Dec. 29, 1875, Mar. 4, 1876, ibid., 42, reel 22; *Army and Navy Journal*, July 4, 1874; Hutton, *Phil Sheridan*, 296. Some in the army opposed Sherman's move to St. Louis. See Sheridan to Sherman, May 26, 1876, Box 11, LC, Sheridan Papers; Sheridan to Ord, July 17, 1874, ibid. Scattered information on the Belknap resignation is in "Official Documents, 1876–1879" and "Official Correspondence . . . 1876–1879," in LC, Belknap Papers.

Civil War era and had severely impaired efforts to construct a consistent strategic policy.[18]

The supremacy of civilian authority over the military meant that government officials, politicians, and civil leaders influenced the army's plans regarding Indian affairs. With his prestige and powers of appointment, the president could set the tone for overall military strategy. Army officers often applied their own interpretations to his statements, but the president's ultimate authority remained unchallenged. The practical effects of presidential dominance depended on the individual in the White House. Grant, for example, attempted to establish rudimentary guidelines for Indian policy; others, notably Andrew Johnson, expressed little interest in the subject.[19]

Presidential appointees, especially the secretaries of war, state, and the interior, also helped shape policy. The interior secretary, with cabinet-level influence and control of the powerful Office of Indian Affairs, could effect radical changes to army proposals concerning his "wards." His subordinate, the commissioner of Indian affairs, maintained strong political connections as well. Both the secretary and the commissioner could request or prohibit military action on reservations.[20] Not to be overlooked was the State Department, whose authority in Indian affairs stemmed from the in-

18. Weigley, *History of the United States Army*, 287–88; Goff, *Robert Todd Lincoln*, 126–27; Weigley, "Military Thought of John M. Schofield"; William H. Carter, "Creation of the American General Staff: Personal Narrative of the General Staff System of the American Army," Senate Miscellaneous Document No. 119, 68th Cong., 1st sess., II, ser. 8254; Matloff, ed., *American Military History*, 346–48.

19. For studies of Grant's Indian policy, see McFeely, *Grant*, 305–18; Waltmann, "Circumstantial Reformer," 323–40.

20. Townsend to Pope, July 25, 1865, LS, AGO, 40, reel 27; Sheridan to Terry, Feb. 8, 1876, Box 58, LC, Sheridan Papers; Sherman to Sheridan, Nov. 11, 1878, LC, Sherman Papers, 91, reel 45; Sherman to Sheridan, Oct. 26, 1879, ibid.

ternational aspects of Indian activity along both Mexican and Canadian borders.[21]

Civilian influence on the military extended to congressmen and private individuals. With its power of the purse, Congress dictated the extent of military action. By limiting or granting appropriations, House and Senate members controlled the feasibility of military operations. Citizen's associations such as religious groups of all denominations, pacifists, and Indian rights organizations waged public campaigns that further restricted the army's available options. These groups, asserting that moral instruction and training could reform tribal customs and eliminate "barbarism" among Indians, sought to limit the role of the military in forming Indian policy.[22]

Fortunately, the groups able to influence military behavior changed throughout the period. Because a wide variety of sources were involved, no single group or ideology gained long-term dominance. While this constant flux led to inconsistencies in government and military policy, it prevented the disastrous results that might have occurred had extremists among Indian-haters or civilizers controlled military actions.

Within these constraints, the army's general officers took an active if often ineffectual role in setting the course of the government's military policy toward western Indians. The commanding general

21. On the State Department and the Canadian border, see McCrary to Secretary of State, Sept. 3, 1879, LS, SW, 85, reel 78; Lincoln to the Secretary of State, Jan. 18, 1882, ibid., 95, reel 84; Tweedale to the Secretary of State, Apr. 12, 1883, ibid.; Lincoln to the Secretary of State, Apr. 12, 1883, ibid., 102, reel 87; Keoton to Commander of the Dept. of Dakota, May 3, 1886, LS, AGO, 77, reel 56. On Mexico, see Foster to Ord, July 16, 1877, Aug. 28, 1878, Bancroft Library, Ord Papers; Crosby to the secretary of state, Mar. 6, 1882, LS, AGO, 96, reel 84; Sherman to adjutant general (hereafter AG), May 2, 1882, LC, Sherman Papers, 95, reel 47; Endicott to the secretary of state, June 28, 1887, LS, SW, 117, reel 100.

22. Report of Sherman, Nov. 10, SW, AR, 1876, 24; Sheridan to Sherman, May 31, 1878, LC, Sherman Papers, 48, reel 25; Welsh, "Indian Question"; Walker, "The Indian Question"; Schurz, "Present Aspects of the Indian Problem"; Mardock, "Alfred Love."

sometimes met with the president and the secretaries of war and the interior to outline proposed actions. Division and department commanders held private meetings with senior government officials and testified before congressional committees.[23] These discussions were held only on an irregular, case-by-case basis, however, and were never part of a continuing policy-making process. As such, the recommendations of division and department commanders on general Indian policy frequently carried little weight, and civilian guidelines limited their military options. Yet in a few circumstances the persistence of army men paid off, allowing the regulars to conduct major offensives free from outside interference. However arbitrary the impact, the army's involvement in making Indian policy at least afforded its senior officers a better understanding of what civilian authorities wanted.

Within the limitations imposed by these diverse civilian influences and structural problems, the army sought to formulate a workable, effective Indian policy. The army's duty, of course, was to implement government plans. Yet the vague or impractical nature of these instructions frequently allowed the army a great deal of leeway. Thus, despite the structural limits of his office's authority, the commanding general retained great influence over policy-making in the army. Four of the Union's most distinguished Civil War generals—Grant, Sherman, Sheridan, and Schofield—held the office in succession until 1895, when Nelson A. Miles, also a Civil War veteran but more renowned as an Indian fighter, took control. For the most part, division and department commanders respected the abilities of the commanding generals and sought their advice even when not required to do so. Through both personal and official

23. Belknap to Sherman, Nov. 28, 1873, LC, Sherman Papers, 36, reel 19; Sheridan to Belknap, Oct. 26, 1875, Box 58, LC, Sheridan Papers; Sheridan to Sherman, Nov. 13, 1875, Sherman Papers, 41, reel 21; Sherman to Sheridan, July 19, 1879, ibid., 91, reel 45; Testimony in House Rpt. No. 384, 43d Cong., 1st sess., 1874, ser. 1624; House Misc. Doc. No. 64, 45th Cong., 2nd sess., VI, ser. 1820.

correspondence, commanding generals influenced the policies carried out by subordinates.[24]

The commanders of the Missouri and Pacific divisions stood next in the much-abused army hierarchy regarding Indian affairs. The chiefs of the department of Texas, Arizona, California, Dakota, the Missouri, the Platte, and the Columbia followed. Lesser officers seldom received the chance to become involved in the official policy-making process. Their superiors demanded action, not theory, and few army men introduced new concepts on Indian policy through professional journals or papers. Still, circumstances sometimes forced them to swiftly interpret hazy instructions while in the field, thus making them de facto policy initiators in many instances.[25]

The policy-making process was surprisingly flexible. Especially significant were the annual reports submitted by the commanders of each administrative unit. These documents included reviews of the year as well as recommendations and plans for the immediate future and were published as part of the congressional serial set. These reports described army reactions to specific disputes, but only rarely addressed the overall problems of policy. Reports dealing with more specialized conditions were also filed, but on an irregular basis.[26]

The official nature of these reports prevented officers from fully tracing the development of military doctrine regarding Indians.

24. Sherman to Miles, Feb. 9, 1878, LC, Sherman Papers, 90, reel 45; Sheridan to Sherman, Dec. 12, 1879, ibid., 51, reel 26. Note also Sherman's letters to Augur, Feb. 11, June 27, 188 , Feb. 9, July 4, 1885, Ill. State Hist. Library, Augur Papers.

25. Utley, "The Frontier and the American Military Tradition," in Tate, ed., *American Military on the Frontier*, 9.

26. For examples of an official report's importance, see that of Pope, Feb. 25, 1866, House Ex. Doc. No. 76, 39th Cong., 1st sess., 12, ser. 1263, 1–15. Responses are in Grant to Sherman, Mar. 12, 1866, LC, Sherman Papers, 18, reel 10; Grant to Sherman, Mar. 14, 1866, LC, Grant Papers, series 5, 47, reel 21; and Report of Sherman, Nov. 5, SW, AR, 1866, 20.

Most senior army men, who often had in common a West Point education and Civil War combat experience, preferred to work less formally. Generals tried to inspect their areas of command to better understand the terrain and to remain in personal contact with subordinates. Senior officers generally allowed their subordinates operating in the field a great deal of latitude as long as they acted within basic policy guidelines. All realized that the general-in-chief in Washington or the division commander in Chicago could not comprehend a complex situation in the parched Texas Panhandle or in the snow-covered Black Hills of Dakota as well as a responsible officer on the scene could. Commanding the Missouri division in 1876, Sheridan admitted to Brig. Gen. George Crook, in charge of a field column in the Dakota Territory, that "I am too far away to order or even suggest." Sheridan's instructions to Crook three years later were not uncommon: while seeking to provide "general supervision" concerning troop disposition within Crook's Department of the Platte, Sheridan authorized his subordinate to make final decisions.[27]

The general-in-chief and division commanders thus set forth broad geographical, political, and military guidelines but removed themselves from the detailed planning for operations against hostile Indians. There is no evidence to suggest that they discussed strategy with subordinates on a regular basis. In peacetime all correspondence slowed, and plans were made on an ad hoc basis rather than according to established routine. During emergencies, leaders kept in much closer contact with their officers through telegrams and personal meetings.

Department commanders, acting within these limitations, controlled actual operations. According to circumstance and personality

27. Sherman to Rawlins, Sept. 21, 1866, House Ex. Doc. No. 23, 39th Cong., 2nd sess., 6, ser. 1288, 16; Sheridan to Crook, July 16, 1876, Box 58, LC, Sheridan Papers (first quotation); Sheridan to Pope, Oct. 3, 1879, Box 59, ibid.; Sheridan to Crook, May 15, 1879, Box 42, ibid. (second quotation).

some took the field themselves, hoping their experience and leadership would inspire success and ensure national prominence.[28] Others preferred to remain in the rear, where they were able to inform leaders of separate columns of their respective positions and remain in closer communication with other regions. From such a communications center, the department chief could also speed proper reinforcements and supplies to his operational leaders. If the head of a department took the field himself, or if the campaign included more than one department, the divisional commander relayed information and wrestled with supply problems. Vast distances and woeful communications systems, however, usually prevented effective coordination of separate columns. As one veteran reported, the officer in the field "was immediately thrown upon his own resources. He had to think, plan, and act for himself and for the welfare and safety of his command."[29]

The relatively small number of army officers involved in outlining general policies reduced divisiveness over broad decisions. Although the army's policies changed repeatedly, most participants understood the reasoning behind the shifts. Immediately after the Civil War, the army's major concerns were defensive. Unsure of how congressional reductions and southern resistance to Reconstruction would effect the number of troops available for western duty, military officials focused on the passive protection of settlers and the emerging transcontinental railroads. Yet they soon realized the ineffectiveness of immobile defense along the Indian frontiers. White expansion across the continent had to be facilitated, they believed, and Indian opposition crushed. As a result, large army columns ranged across

28. George Crook and Nelson A. Miles are the best examples of department commanders who took the field consistently.

29. Sheridan to Pope, Nov. 18, 1874, Box 56, LC, Sheridan Papers; Sheridan to Augur, Dec. 1, 1874, ibid.; Miles, *Serving the Republic*, 111 (quotation); Cameron to president, July 8, 1876, LC, SW, 79, reel 72; Sheridan to Crook, June 20, 1876, Box 58, LC, Sheridan Papers; Sheridan to Carr, June 20, 1876, ibid.; Sheridan to Terry, June 23, 1876, ibid.

the Plains and the rugged terrain of southern Oregon and northern California in 1867 and 1868.[30]

The offensives were halted during Ulysses S. Grant's first term in the White House. Convinced of the military's inability to resolve the Indian question, Grant forbade new army initiatives and implemented a peace policy that apportioned control of Indian agencies among interested religious denominations. However, renewed frontier violence erased initial successes, and Grant himself appeared to be less sympathetic toward the Indians in the wake of a series of scandals concerning his civil appointees after 1872. As Grant's interest in Indian affairs waned, the army took the field with a vengeance. For the next seven years, it conducted major operations in Texas, the Indian territory, and the Dakota, Montana, Wyoming, New Mexico, and Arizona territories.[31]

With several notable exceptions, major Indian resistance to white expansion had been crushed by 1880. At the time, however, the military did not know that the major confrontations had ended. Wary of still another serious outbreak, the regulars continued to patrol reservation lines in an effort to prevent clashes between Indians and whites that might precipitate renewed conflicts. Large reinforcements, transported by railroad to the scenes of potential violence, subdued disaffected natives and quelled sporadic outbreaks. Consolidating past gains thus became a key object of army policies for the remainder of the era.[32]

Some concepts remained constant despite the changing conditions. The army had long recognized the importance of forts in

30. Report of Sherman, Nov. 5, SW, AR, 1866, 21; General Order No. 27, Feb. 28, 1866, Senate Ex. Doc. No. 2, 40th Cong., 1st sess., 1867, ser. 1308, 2–3; Utley, *Frontier Regulars*, 115–89.

31. Grant, Annual Message, Dec. 5, 1870, in Richardson, comp., *Messages and Papers of the Presidents* 7:109; McFeely, *Grant*, 305–18; Waltmann, "Circumstantial Reformer"; Utley, *Frontier Regulars*, 201–374.

32. Reports of Sherman, Oct. 27, SW, AR, 1883, 45–46; Sheridan, Nov. 1, ibid., 1887, 72–76; and Schofield, Oct. 22, ibid., 1889, 60–62.

providing effective frontier defense. One officer argued "that the permanent cure for the hostilities of the northern Indians is to go into the heart of the buffalo country and build and hold forts till the trouble is over." Another claimed that building forts "in their country . . . demoralizes them more than anything else except money and whiskey." From these fixed positions placed in advance of white settlement and along key emigrant trails, scouts patrolled the surrounding countryside, and troops and supplies were collected for field operations.[33]

Ideally, each fort held enough men to provide troops for field operations as well as to protect the position itself. The army favored mixed garrisons of at least four companies at each post. Cavalry was needed for active duty; infantry and artillery units could guard the fort or temporary field camps while the cavalry scouted the region. Officers believed that further reductions hurt efficiency and displayed weakness to Indians. Nonetheless, the army's limited size and wide range of responsibilities meant that smaller detachments garrisoned many frontier positions in the post–Civil War period. Even at the positions held by several companies, desertions, special assignments, low recruitment, sickness, and death limited the number of personnel available for duty. In one typical example, the surgeon at Fort Richardson, Texas, issued the following statistics for his post in June 1870: of the 32 officers belonging to units stationed there, only 22 were present; of the 415 noncommissioned soldiers, only 327 were actually present. Of those on hand, a sizable number were sick, in the post stockade, or otherwise unavailable for field service.[34]

33. Collins to Pratt, Feb. 15, 1865, House Doc. No. 369, 54th Cong., 1st sess., pt. 1, 69, ser. 3436, 98 (first quotation); Robert A. Murray, *Military Posts*, 8; Ord to acting adjutant general, Mar. 5, 1867, Senate Ex. Doc. No. 13, 40th Cong., 1st sess., ser. 1308, 83 (second quotation); Sherman to Rawlins, Sept. 12, 1866, House Ex. Doc. No. 23, 39th Cong., 2nd sess., ser. 1288, 13.

34. Post medical returns, Fort Richardson, 1870, 6; Reports of Terry, Sept. 27, SW, AR, 1867, 53; Augur, Sept. 30, ibid., 58–59; Halleck, Sept. 22, ibid., 1868, 41; Reynolds, Sept. 30, ibid., 1871, 65; Sherman to Reynolds, May 21, 1871, LC, Sherman Papers, 30, reel 16; Special Orders No. 102, May 31, 1872,

Another constant was the necessity of protecting the railroad and telegraph lines and their construction teams. "It would be a national calamity," wrote Sherman in 1867, "if the work on the Pacific rail road should cease." By easing troop transfers and supply problems and encouraging settlement, the railroads received the army's full attention throughout the period. Similarly, telegraph lines afforded officials in Washington and at divisional headquarters increased contact with subordinates. Information on the locations of hostile Indian bands could be sent quickly and reliably to nearby army posts. As a result, frontier commanders repeatedly asked for more telegraph lines and operators to improve communications.[35]

Certain principles in dealing with western Indians remained consistent as well. Throughout the period, the army sought to punish any Indians caught off reservations. While Indian agents did not always permit such action, the army dealt with offenders as severely as conditions allowed. Military leaders also stressed a desire to separate hostile Indians from those deemed friendly. Citing numerous examples of Indians leaving reservations, committing depredations, and returning to mingle with tribesmen who had done nothing, army officers tried to establish military authority over the reservations as well as over who would be allowed to enter or leave. Only with such controls, they argued, could they punish the guilty and

Wallace, ed., *Ranald S. Mackenzie's Official Correspondence*, 81; Report of Sheridan, Oct. 27, SW, AR, 1873, 42; Testimony of Sherman, Jan. 7, 1874, House Rpt. No. 384, 43d Cong., 1st sess., ser. 1624, 15; Mattison, "Military Frontier on the Upper Missouri," 171–74.

35. Sherman to Grant, May 27, 1867, LC, Grant Papers, ser. 5, 55, reel 24 (quotation); Report of Sherman, Oct. 1, SW, AR, 1867, 36; Sherman to Augur, Feb. 28, Nov. 23, 1868, June 9, 1870, Ill. State Hist. Library, Augur Papers; Sherman to Schofield, Jan. 9, 1871, LS, AGO, 53, reel 40; Schofield to Sherman, Box 49, LC, Schofield Papers; Sherman to Colton, Sept. 26, 1878, LC, Sherman Papers, 91, reel 45; Report of Sherman, Oct. 22, SW, AR, 1880, 54–56; Report of Reynolds, Oct. 21, ibid., 1869, 144; Belknap to Senate Committee on Military Affairs, Jan. 17, 1871, LS, SW, 55, reel 61; Belknap to House Committee on Appropriations, Apr. 14, 1874, ibid., 75, reel 68; Report of Miles, Mar. 4, SW, AR, 1875, 84.

spare the innocent. Punishment, in the form of military and economic retribution, was designed to be severe enough to dissuade
others from committing future acts that the government considered
illegal.[36]

Several elements of the army's tactical doctrine also remained
relatively stable during the post–Civil War period. In dealing with
Indian groups declared hostile, determined pursuit and converging
columns of troops repeatedly proved effective. As Nelson A.
Miles observed, "No man, be he white or Indian, likes to be hunted, and
if the hunt is continued it will in time unnerve the stoutest hearted."
By using several converging columns, the army hoped to corner its
Indian opponents, forcing them to battle or preventing their escape
until the lack of supplies necessitated surrender. Only then should
peace be made, military authorities maintained, believing that Indians could be civilized only after they had been stripped of their
weapons and of any desire to make war.[37]

Despite the general agreement on these precepts, officers differed
on the type of force best suited to frontier conditions. Many assumed
that cavalry provided the only effective means to catch and chastise
hostile Indians. Departmental and divisional commanders pleaded
continually for more mounted men in order to create mobile frontier
defenses, as well as to harass Indians in their homelands.[38] But

36. Crook to commander, Apache Camp, Sept. 12, 1871, National Archives,
LS, Dept. of Arizona; Sherman to Hazen, Sept. 26, 1868, LC, Sherman Papers,
90, reel 45.

37. Miles, "My Forty Years of Fighting," 796 (quotation); Sherman to Leet,
July 1, SW, AR, 1867, 67; Mackenzie to Sherman, June 15, 1871, LC, Sherman
Papers, 30, reel 16; Augur to Sheridan, June 10, 1872, Mackenzie Corr., 80–81;
Sheridan endorsement, June 19, 1872, Box 7, LC, Sheridan Papers; Report of
Sheridan, Oct. 12, SW, AR, 1872, 35–36; Report of Miles, Mar. 4, ibid., 1875,
85; Sherman to Tappan, July 21, 1876, Sherman Papers, 90, reel 45.

38. Report of Sherman, Oct. 1, SW, AR, 1867, 35; Report of Crook, Sept.
28, ibid., 1871, 78; Report of Hancock, Oct. 23, ibid., 3; Miles to Sherman,
Oct. 23, 1876, LC, Sherman Papers, 44, reel 23; Miles to Sherman, Nov. 18,
1876, ibid., 65, reel 23.

cavalry proved too expensive for all western duties. Infantry companies both garrisoned key points and caches of supplies in the field and joined in the chase themselves. Most soldiers in mountainous areas and on extended campaigns agreed with reporter John F. Finerty's observation that "man is a hardier animal than the horse." Inferior horses and inadequate training further reduced the cavalry's effectiveness. Although a few cavaliers still extolled cavalry's shock potential, mounted troops usually dismounted on the battlefield. Because every fourth man guarded the horses, effective firepower was reduced by twenty-five percent.[39]

Although the army maintained overall technological superiority in its conflicts with Indians, the problem of reconciling the twin needs of firepower and mobility plagued the regulars throughout the latter nineteenth century. Troops carried the single-shot .45 caliber Springfield rifle or carbine for most of the period but received little or no target practice until the 1880s. "Since a man could enlist, . . . serve five years and get discharged without firing his piece, not much damage was done," recalled one officer after an 1874 skirmish in the Texas Panhandle.[40] Commanders sometimes brought along Gatling guns or Hotchkiss mountain howitzers to supplement firepower, but most found such wheeled pieces too cumbersome on rough terrain. The limited mobility of this equipment reduced practical battlefield use to special circumstances, such as those that occurred during the Modoc War in 1873 and the Sioux Ghost Dance in 1890. Miles seems to have been one of the few

39. Finerty, *War-Path and Bivouac*, 74; Steele to Fry, Oct. 25, 1867, National Archives, LS, Dept. of the Columbia; Testimony of Sherman, Jan. 6–7, 1874, House Rpt. No. 384, 43d Cong., 1st sess., ser. 1624, 12–15; Testimony of Davis, Jan. 17, 1874, ibid., 163; Report of Augur, Oct. 25, SW, AR, 1870, 33; Hutchins, "Mounted Riflemen," 79–85; Rickey, *Forty Miles a Day*, 275; Hedren, "Infantry Company in the Sioux Campaign."

40. U.S. Army Hist. Res. Coll., Hatfield, Order of Indian Wars Collection (quotation); Utley, *Frontier Regulars*, 72; Sherman to Belknap, July 12, 1870, LS, AGO, 52, reel 39.

officers who employed these guns against Indian foes with anything approaching consistent success.[41]

Volunteer units sometimes accompanied the regulars on the frontiers. Citing high costs, poor discipline, and inefficiency, most army officials had long opposed the use of volunteers. General William T. Sherman maintained that volunteers should be called up only when absolutely necessary. A few senior officers, including Maj. John S. Mason, Col. Joseph J. Reynolds, and Maj. Gen. Irvin McDowell, were among a distinct minority who suggested that mounted frontiersmen be employed more frequently. Yet because of the added manpower offered by these units, they were used on occasion to help the army overwhelm Indians. Notable were the efforts of the Nineteenth Kansas Volunteer Cavalry in 1868–69 and the Texas Rangers after 1874.[42]

Indian allies were used more extensively. Advocates stressed their military value and claimed that such alliances provided restless braves with a needed dose of Anglo-American civilization. The army, authorized by Congress to enlist friendly Indian scouts, hired large numbers of Crow, Pawnee, and Navajo irregulars. These men won high praise for their superb horsemanship, tracking skills, and

41. Sheridan to Townsend, May 6, 1872, Box 7, LC, Sheridan Papers; Sheridan, endorsement, Feb. 12, 1879, Box 21, ibid.; Miles to Sherman, July 8, 1876, LC, Sherman Papers, 44, reel 23; Report of Miles, Sept. 14, SW, AR, 1891, 148–52; Frank Wheaton to Schofield, May 10, 1873, Box 9, LC, Schofield Papers; Henry to Schofield, Jan 5, 1891, Box 27, ibid.; Stegmaier, "Artillery Helped Win the West"; Roberts, "Artillery with the Regular Army," 238, 259. Armstrong, *Bullets and Bureaucrats*, is a fine secondary account. The problems of reconciling demands for firepower and mobility continued to plague the American army into the next century. See Weigley, *Eisenhower's Lieutenants*, 2–7.

42. Report of Sherman, Oct. 1, SW, AR, 1867, 35; Ord to Sherman, Oct. 25, 1877, Bancroft Library, Ord Papers; Lonnie J. White, "Winter Campaigning with Custer and Sheridan," 93; Webb, *Texas Rangers*, 312–24; Reports of McDowell, Oct. 18, SW, AR, 1866, 34; Mason, Apr. 29, ibid., 1867, 98; and Reynolds, Sept. 30, ibid., 1870, 41; Mahon, *History of the Militia and the National Guard*.

knowledge of western terrain, though some whites doubted their willingness to actually kill enemy Indians.[43]

In addition to scouting, native auxiliaries were by the 1880s performing valuable services as reservation policemen, freeing regulars for other duties and preventing unnecessary army-Indian collisions. Later officials, including Secretary of War Redfield Proctor (1889–91) and Commanding General John Schofield, favored more direct measures, sponsoring new policies that added Indian companies to most of the army's regiments. This last step never gained full favor among line officers. Some opposed it on racial grounds; others, who had supported the scout programs, argued that language problems would demoralize Indians and strip them of their individuality, which had been their greatest asset in serving the army. Although the Indian enlistment program failed to meet expectations, it was a logical culmination of continued efforts to assimilate Indians into society as a whole through the military.[44]

43. Grant to Stanton, Aug. 1, 1866, LC, Grant Papers, ser. 5, 47, reel 21; Townsend to Sherman, Halleck, and Sheridan, Aug. 1, 1866, LS, AGO, 43, reel 30; Report of Sherman, Oct. 1, SW, AR, 1867, 37–38; Crook to AG, Sept. 4, 1871, Hayes Library, Crook Papers; Hayes, Annual Message, Dec. 2, 1878, in Richardson, comp., *Messages and Papers of the Presidents* 7:502–3.

For favorable reports, see Reports of Augur, Sept. 30, SW, AR, 1867, 59–60; Grant, Nov., ibid., 30; Ord, Sept. 27, ibid., 1869, 123; Hancock, Oct. 20, ibid., 66; Miles, Mar. 4, ibid., 1875, 84; Crook to Sheridan, Mar. 31, 1886, in Davis, *Truth about Geronimo*, 214–15. More critical accounts are in Swaine to Sherman, Aug. 24, 1881, LC, Sherman Papers, 56, reel 29; Sherman to Drum, Sept. 10, 1881, ibid., 95, reel 47; Roberts to Bradley, Dec. 27, 1885, National Archives, LS, Dept. of Arizona; Sheridan to Crook, Mar. 31, 1886, Box 44, LC, Sheridan Papers; Report of Sheridan, Oct. 10, SW, AR, 1886, 72.

44. Safford to Howard, Sept. 10, 1872, Bowdoin Library, Howard Papers; Report of Hoyt, Nov. 1, Secretary of the Interior, Annual Report, 1877, 398–99; Report of Price, Oct. 24, ibid., 1881, 13; Brooke to AAG, Nov. 21, 1890, National Archives, LS, Dept. of the Platte; Hagan, *Indian Police and Judges*; Proctor, Nov. 3, SW, AR, 1891, 14; Reports of Schofield, Sept. 24, ibid., 1891, 57–58; Sept. 30, ibid., 1892, 49; Oct. 4, ibid., 1893, 63–64; Oct. 1, ibid., 1894, 64–65; General Orders no. 28, Mar. 9, ibid., 1891, 81; Harrison to Proctor, Sept.

Recognizing the strengths and weaknesses of each service branch, experienced field leaders with full resources at their disposal organized mixed commands of regular cavalry, infantry, and Indian scouts. Small artillery detachments and volunteer units provided supplementary assistance.[45] Wiser officers learned to exploit the strengths of each particular service branch. These varied forces, restricted by poorly defined systems of command and policy-making and never able to devote all their energies to the western frontiers, confronted formidable Indian foes after 1865.

Most Indians enjoyed a number of strategic and logistical advantages when fighting the bluecoats. Their familiarity with the terrain was valuable throughout the post-Civil War years. The Indians' ability to live off the land further enhanced their mobility, particularly during the spring and summer months. Their capacity to operate without conventional lines of communication also freed warriors for combat duty who might otherwise have been tied down guarding tenuous supply lines.

Sioux, Cheyenne, Comanche, Arapaho, and Kiowa made up the majority of Plains Indians who took up arms against white expansion. Although each tribe possessed unique characteristics, some generalizations can be drawn. Speed, stealth, and ambush were fundamental elements of their tactical arsenals. Most combatants had several horses at their disposal, whereas regular army troopers had only one; shifting to fresh mounts thus enabled warriors to

---

5, 1891, LC, Harrison Papers, ser. 1, reel 33. Opponents included George Crook and Benjamin Grierson. See Crook to AG, Feb. 24, 1890, Hayes Library, Crook Papers; Report of Grierson, July 1, SW, AR, 1890, 172.

Good secondary accounts are by Bowie, "Redfield Proctor," 231–39; Tate, "Soldiers of the Line"; Dunlay, *Wolves for the Blue Soldiers*; and W. Bruce White, "American Indian as Soldier." A more detailed study has been compiled by Richard Upton, ed., *Indian as a Soldier at Fort Custer, Montana*. For Spanish antecedents, see Jones, *Pueblo Warriors and Spanish Conquest*.

45. Miles to Sherman, June 15, Oct. 2, 1876, LC, Sherman Papers, 44, reel 23; Testimony of Sherman, Jan. 7, 1874, House Rpt. No. 384, 43d Cong., 1st sess., ser. 1624, 15.

outdistance their bluecoat foes. In addition, warfare encouraged
initiative among braves, for military success ensured status and
wealth and allowed participants to add to their personal herds of
mustangs.[46]

Strategic moves are less clear. Once they had agreed on offensive
action, tribes gathered food and scouted for information regarding
the strength of local army opposition. Small, independent raiding
parties were discouraged, and decoys were sent out to draw army
attention from the site designated for attack. Frontal assaults were
rare; most efforts were designed to draw troops into terrain favorable
to ambushes and individual combat. Ironically, the inability of most
chiefs to establish effective control over all their warriors confused
their white enemies. Many army officers, incorrectly assuming that
complete authority rested with a few head men, were bewildered
by the unorthodox moves of a few undisciplined braves. Plains
Indians who managed to set aside tribal differences became particularly dangerous. The unusual strength of such alliances threatened
the small army detachments so common in the West. In such cases,
one officer warned that "total annihilation is the result of defeat."[47]
Nez Percés, Apaches, Modocs, and Paiutes were among the most
dangerous of the Indians living in other regions. While the smaller
size of these groups precluded major offensives on their part, they
nonetheless used terrain brilliantly and were virtually impossible to
dislodge from secure retreats. Anger at white encroachment and fear
of losing their cultural identity embittered these tribes, like the
Plains Indians, in their opposition to the army.[48]

46. Mishkin, *Rank and Warfare among the Plains Indians*, 61–63; Berthrong,
Southern Cheyennes, 12; Carter, *On the Border with Mackenzie*, 58, 290; Report of
Sherman, Nov. 7, SW, AR, 1877, 12; Secoy, *Changing Military Patterns on the
Great Plains*; Smith, "War Complex of the Plains Indians."

47. Grinnell, *Fighting Cheyennes*, 233; Berthrong, *Southern Cheyennes*, 225–28;
Utley, *Last Days of the Sioux Nation*, 10; Sheridan to Townsend, Nov. 19, 1878,
Box 20, LC, Sheridan Papers (quotation).

48. Crook, "Apache Problem," 259–60; Ball, *Indeh*, 78–81; Ogle, *Federal
Control of the Western Apaches*, 15.

Few military men in line or staff positions understood the unique problems these warriors presented. George Crook reported in 1873 that only two officers in the entire Department of Arizona "really grasped the situation"; six others "could carry out orders understandingly"; the remainder were brave and worked hard but were useless in fighting Apaches. A veteran of Apache warfare later observed that military officials in Washington were "hopelessly at sea . . . in [their] knowledge of these people, their mode of warfare, or the problem of catching them."[49]

Indians were not without weaknesses of their own, as the lack of discipline mentioned above demonstrates. Many of the factors that made government operations against Native Americans difficult also limited Indian military capabilities. Tribes seldom forgot traditional jealousies, even when confronted by an external menace. Premature attacks by overeager warriors often spoiled carefully laid plans. The lack of stored food and forage, along with a fierce spirit of independence, prevented large numbers of Indians from cooperating throughout long campaigns. In addition, few Indians understood the massive resources or the character of the United States and its citizens. Those Indians who visited large cities found it difficult to convince others of what they had seen. Most never understood the white man's determination to control the entire continent, and they deluded themselves into believing that minor tactical successes would deter expansion. Tradition and custom led many Indians to believe these victories sufficient; few recognized the need, and even fewer possessed the resources, to follow up such gains with more complete triumphs.[50]

49. Crook to Schofield, May 16, 1873, Box 39, LC, Schofield Papers (first two quotations); Davis, *Truth about Geronimo*, 74 (third quotation).

50. Josephy, *Nez Percé Indians*, 542–45; Betzinez, *I Fought with Geronimo*, 38, 47; Sherman to Augur, June 9, 1870, Ill. State Hist. Library, Augur Papers; Sheridan to Terry, May 16, 1876, Box 58, LC, Sheridan Papers; Whipple to Schofield, June 5, 1870, Box 42, LC, Schofield Papers.

A good example of Indian misunderstanding came during Gen. Alfred Terry's talks with Sioux councils in 1877. The Sioux believed that Terry, having failed

Serious problems thus faced both the army and the Indians as they grappled for military supremacy in the post–Civil War American West. Neither side could muster its full strength against the other. Intertribal rivalries, lack of discipline, and the inability or unwillingness to confront the very real specter of alien encroachment badly divided the Indians. Reconstruction, social unrest, and coastal defense responsibilities drew troops away from the inland frontiers. Confused administration and lines of command further weakened military efforts. The varied influences over Indian policy that usually prevented extremists from gaining complete control brought with them contradictions and inconsistencies. Controversies between staff and line officers, as well as between the secretary of war and the commanding general, caused still more disruptions.

Ideally, the army would have implemented clearly outlined War Department directives regarding Indian policy. These policies could have been outlined by the president and given to the secretary of war after detailed consultation with key advisors. Such discussions could have been held on a regular basis, incorporating input from reformers, ethnographers, western politicians, friendly Indian leaders, the Board of Indian Commissioners, and lower-level army officers, especially those directly involved in Indian conflicts.

In practice, strategic military policy regarding Indians was not made in such a fashion. Cabinet-level meetings on Indian affairs remained the exception rather than the rule throughout the period. Correspondence among army officers, the War Department, and members of Congress regarding Indians was also irregular and was undertaken largely in response to individual problems or in abbreviated spurts of feverish activity. On a lower level, Indian agents, department commanders, and field officers bombarded their superiors with letters about Indian problems. Both the War and Interior

---

to convince them to return to their reservations in the United States, would commit suicide (Anderson, "A Sioux Pictorial Account of General Terry's Council," 111). For a more general account of warfare by nonliterate populations, see Turney-High, *Primitive War*.

departments received reams of documents and routine correspondence. Most of this material, however, dealt with local details rather than with the broader context. Annual reports contained more substantive advice about Indians, but these recommendations were rarely followed by the higher civilian or military bureaucracy. Discussion of strategic military policy against Indians simply did not occur on a routine basis. Most planning was instead done in response to a particular problem. High-ranking officers within the army occasionally met with one another, but they relied on the formal annual reports for their planned communications about Indians. As a result, cooperation hinged on good personal relationships, which were often lacking.[51]

These difficulties notwithstanding, the vastly superior resources at the government's disposal, along with the many problems of resistance confronting hostile Indians, combined to give the army the strategic initiative. Millions of dollars in appropriations and virtually inexhaustible pools of supplies and manpower enabled the army to overcome the defects of its policy-making structure and eliminate the Indian military threat. The armed forces took the offensive from 1867 to 1869. Grant's Peace Policy halted army initiatives for the next three years, but aggressive doctrine again gained favor until 1880. With most Indians humbled in the wake of these renewed onslaughts, the military consolidated its earlier successes and annihilated minor Indian threats arising during the decades that followed. In implementing changing policies, the army used forts, railroads, telegraphs, converging columns, and mixed forces to pursue the Indians they labeled hostile. As events proved, administrative and organizational quagmires made the army inefficient but by no means impotent.

51. Suggestive are Prucha, "New Approaches to the Study of the Administration of Indian Policy," in his *Indian Policy in the United States*, 13–19, and Cosmas, *An Army for Empire*, 22–23, 33.

Chapter Two
The Characters and Their Culture

A number of factors influenced the army in its efforts to determine and effect strategy concerning the Indians. Although military operations did not always reflect white society's values, public perceptions of Indians and of western environment clearly affected army policies. The views of reformers and politicians had a similar effect. Senior officers, aware of the impact of such forces but anxious to achieve their own goals, tried to form plans that would appeal to the public without sacrificing personal or military integrity. Such shared experiences as West Point and the Civil War tended to have a harmonizing influence on these men, yet in an army plagued by feuds, pettiness, jealousy, and the general lack of attention to strategy against Indians, conditions rarely encouraged cooperation in regard to long-term design.

The general public viewed Indians with a mixture of admiration and hatred. Some Americans, influenced by writers such as James Fenimore Cooper, maintained romantic notions about the "noble savage" and his wilderness home.[1] More common was the image of the Indian as a bloodthirsty barbarian. According to this view, Indians were heathens who obstructed progress and could not be accepted into American society until they had been "civilized." But despite urgent pleas from the West for quick remedies to the so-called Indian problem, a significant portion of the American public still believed that patient training and education could save the Indians from savagery. These voters thus elected a sizable number of congressmen who displayed some sympathy for Indians.[2] The creek of compassion ran shallow, however, and neither the public nor Congress provided the time, money, or commitment that fundamental changes in Indian education or the reservation system would have required.[3]

That Indian questions received national attention at all should be credited to the efforts of reformers. Not surprisingly, many of these individuals had also been at the forefront of the earlier abolitionist movement. Confident that they were carrying out God's work, they believed that white injustices to Indians had caused most frontier violence. Although plagued by disputes concerning political tactics, they generally agreed on major goals. Indians were to become citizens and accept the laws of the United States. Civil service reform would eliminate corrupt government officials and Indian agents, and special Indian schools were to provide moral and vocational instruction. Most important, individual land grants, allotted to Indians in sev-

1. T. Garlick to Grierson, Feb. 4, 1869, Ill. State Hist. Library, Grierson Papers. Garlick had accepted the romantic views of Cooper's novels until he moved west. Actual contact with Indians altered his opinion, and he advocated sending them smallpox-infested blankets.

2. Dippie, *Vanishing American*, 82–94, 132–38; Berkhofer, *White Man's Indian*, 94–101; Priest, *Uncle Sam's Stepchildren*, 17–31, 57–65; Fritz, *Movement for Indian Assimilation*, 109–19; Trennert, "Popular Imagery and the American Indian."

3. Garfield, "Indian Question"; Hoxie, "End of the Savage," 160–62.

eralty, would allow Indians to become hard-working, responsible, Protestant farmers in the best tradition of the republic. Unfortunately, reformers' perceptions of Indians as misguided creatures needing the virtues of western civilization made it impossible for them to realize that their goals were often antithetical to firmly rooted Indian traditions and culture.[4]

Army officers had frequent opportunities to feel the effects of reformers. Neither socially nor physically isolated from their civilian counterparts, a high percentage of officers served in the East or in growing urban areas, where the concentration of reformers was high. Others secured periodic leaves of absence, during which they visited Washington to handle personal and military affairs.[5] In addition, a surprising number of persons involved in making Indian policy corresponded with reformers. While not always in agreement, generals William T. Sherman, Philip H. Sheridan, George Crook, Oliver Otis Howard, and Secretary of War Redfield Proctor maintained at least sporadic communication with reformers like Henry B. Whipple, Samuel F. Tappan, Herbert Welsh, and Henry L. Dawes.[6]

Ethnologists might be expected to have similarly influenced army policymakers, but there is little evidence that they did. In 1867, the Surgeon General's Office began collecting Indian skulls at the

---

4. Prucha, *American Indian Policy in Crisis*, 132–68; Berkhofer, *White Man's Indian*, 166–75; Mardock, *Reformers and the American Indian*, 1–18, 30–46; Burgess, *Lake Mohonk Conference*, 1–8; and Keller, *American Protestantism and United States Indian Policy*. Helen Hunt Jackson's *A Century of Dishonor* came to be a rallying point for reformers.

5. Gates, "Alleged Isolation of U.S. Army Officers."

6. Crook to Welsh, July 16, Nov. 24, Dec. 2, 1884, Hayes Library, Crook Papers; Crook to Whittlesey, Jan. 6, 1885, ibid.; Whipple to Sherman, Feb. 21, 1877, LC, Sherman Papers, 45, reel 23; Tappan to Sherman, May 9, 1873, ibid., 35, reel 19; Cree to Howard, Jan., 1873, Bowdoin Library, Howard Papers; Sheridan to Dawes, Sept. 6, 1879, July 14, 1886, General Correspondence, LC, Dawes Papers; Proctor to Welsh, July 19, Oct. 19, 1889, Proctor Library, Proctor Papers; Proctor to Dawes, June 25, 1890, ibid.; Proctor to Bullard, Feb. 16, 1891, ibid.

Army Medical museum. The following year it called upon medical officers in the field to send skulls or information "that may throw light on their ethnic character." Unfortunately, there is little record of similar correspondence between high-ranking military men and leading ethnologists. Such contacts might have helped soldiers to better understand Indian culture and might also have given scientists valuable new information about native tribes. Whereas Sheridan did assign officers William Philo Clark and John G. Bourke to study Indian cultures in 1881, these details were made only after the tribes under consideration had been defeated in battle. The small amount of earlier soldier-ethnographer correspondence that has been located usually concerns army efforts to secure buffalo skins and various wildlife species for the Smithsonian Institution.[7]

The lack of accurate data hampered politicians as well as soldiers. Although presidents and certain administrative officials contributed to military decision-making, their attitudes were based less on actual experience than on common misconceptions of Indians. President Andrew Johnson wanted to place Indians on reservations "remote from our highways and encroaching white settlements" and to aid in their "moral and intellectual improvement." Yet Reconstruction, civil rights for newly emancipated blacks, and impeachment proceedings occupied most of his and the nation's attention. Johnson left little record of his views on the major Indian conflicts during his administration, which included Winfield S. Hancock's 1867 Plains offensive; Sheridan's winter campaign of 1868–69; and George Crook's actions against the Paiutes from 1866 to 1868.[8]

Ulysses S. Grant's presidential victory in 1868 signalled a major change in the way presidents perceived Indians. Grant had admitted

7. "Memorandum for the Information of Medical Officers," Sept. 1, 1868, Fort Concho Res. Library; Fort Concho Post Returns (quotation); Hutton, *Phil Sheridan*, 341–42. Additional correspondence is in Endicott to Baird, May 7, 1886, LS, SW, reel 96; Endicott to Baird, Mar. 22, 1887, LC, Cleveland Papers, series 3, reel 110; Sheridan to Crook, July 7, 1884, Box 43, LC, Sheridan Papers.

8. Johnson, Annual Message, Dec. 3, 1867, in Richardson, comp., *Messages and Papers of the Presidents* 6:576 (quotation).

two years earlier that "I have never had any experience among hostile Indians myself and have never been in their country." Nonetheless, he expressed a degree of interest in them while serving as commanding general, suggesting to Sherman, who was then in charge of the critical Division of the Missouri, that all Indians should not be treated as hostile. As president, Grant stunned army men by implementing what has come to be known as his Quaker peace policy. Determined to prevent Indian extinction, he favored land severalty programs, a special territorial government for Indians, and reforms among their agents. He appointed an old army friend, Seneca Indian Ely S. Parker, as Commissioner of Indian Affairs. By 1870, Grant had turned control of many agencies over to religious denominations, including the Society of Friends. But he tended toward rhetoric rather than action and often yielded to political expediency. When charges of corruption forced Parker's resignation in 1871, Grant seemed to lose interest in the Indian question.[9] Although Grant's secretaries of the interior Columbus Delano and Zachariah Chandler still favored the peace policy, Commissioner of Indian Affairs Edward P. Smith (1873–75) admitted that the "wilder tribes" needed firm military chastisement. Despite a number of protests from Indian agents and reform groups, Grant refused to stop major army initiatives during his second term and decided not to halt blatant white instrusions onto Sioux reservations in the Black Hills in 1876.[10]

9. Grant to Sherman, Mar. 12, 1866, LC, Sherman Papers, 18, reel 10 (quotation); Grant, Annual Message, Dec. 6, 1869, in Richardson, comp., *Messages and Papers of the Presidents* 7:38–39; ibid., Dec. 4, 1871, 152; McFeely, *Grant*, 305–9, 317–18; Waltmann, "Circumstantial Reformer," 328–40.

For Parker's views, see his report of Dec. 23, Secretary of the Interior, Annual Report, 1869, pp. 445–51. See Long, ed., *Personal Memoirs of U. S. Grant*, 102–4, for Grant's pre–Civil War experiences in the Northwest.

10. Delano, Annual Report, Oct. 31, U.S. Secretary of the Interior, Annual Reports (hereafter cited as SI, AR), 1873, iii–v; Chandler, Annual Report, Oct. 31, ibid., 1876, v; George, *Zachariah Chandler*, 247; Report of Smith, Nov. 1, SI, AR, 1874, 314–16; Crawford, "Edward Parmalee Smith," in *Commissioners of*

Grant's characteristic inconsistencies proved critical. The peace policy was largely discredited in the final years of his administration. Contemporary observers believed the peace effort had resolved little; instead of bringing peace to the West, violence along the frontiers continued unabated. The stunning defeat of Lt. Col. George A. Custer's Seventh Cavalry at the Little Bighorn in June 1876 further outraged Americans, and the military was given free rein against the "barbarian inhabitants" of the northern plains.

Ironically, President Rutherford B. Hayes, Grant's successor, publicly supported reform principles during this period of heated Indian-white conflict. Recognizing that force sometimes proved necessary, Hayes wanted to put more emphasis "on humane and civilizing agencies." He added, "It may be impossible to raise them fully up to the level of the white population of the United States; but we should not forget that they are the aborigines of the country, and called the soil their own on which our people have grown rich, powerful, and happy. We owe it to them as a moral duty to help them in attaining at least that degree of civilization which they may be able to reach."[11]

Hayes' interior secretary, Carl Schurz, also favored humanitarian goals supporting Indian education, land in severalty, agriculture, and civil service reform.[12] Presidents Chester A. Arthur, Grover Cleveland, and Benjamin Harrison continued the trend. Yet all remained ignorant of the realities of Indian life. While advocating "civilization and citizenship," for example, Cleveland determined to crush Indian resistance. Proctor, Harrison's war secretary, supported assimilation through Indian enlistments in the regular army,

---

Indian Affairs, ed. Kvasnicka and Viola, 141–48; Keller, *American Protestantism and United States Indian Policy*.

11. Hayes, Annual Message, Dec. 2, 1878, in Richardson, comp., *Messages and Papers of the Presidents* 7:503 (quotation). See also ibid., Dec. 3, 1877, 7:475; ibid., Dec. 6, 1880, 7:624–25; and Williams, *Hayes*, 148–49.

12. Schurz, Annual Report, Nov. 1, SI, AR, 1878, iii; ibid., Nov. 1, 1880, 3–4; Schurz to Smith, May 25, 1877, LC, Schurz Papers, reel 85; Trefousse, *Carl Schurz*, 242–44; Schurz, "Present Aspects of the Indian Problem," 6.

as previously mentioned. It was clear, however, that despite such sympathetic pronouncements, the government and most Americans encouraged army aggressiveness when violence along the Indian frontiers threatened to stop white expansion.[13]

Late nineteenth-century presidents and key administrative officials thus agreed in principle with many of the paternalistic reforms advocated by humanitarians and Indian rights groups. But like many reformers of the day, they found little virtue in tribal culture or traditions. These views made acculturation imperative, and the presidents and their advisors found the army a convenient tool with which to convince reluctant Indians of white supremacy.

Army men often expressed similarly unsympathetic opinions about Indians and their place in American society. After the Civil War, William T. Sherman commanded the Division of the Missouri before replacing the newly elected president Grant as commanding general in 1869. For the next fourteen years Sherman dominated the army. Sherman claimed, in a letter to Indian reform leader Tappan, "You know that I have never advocated the killing of anybody, white or Indian, except as punishment for crime, or to save the lives and property of our own people."[14] His actions and statements, however, generally reflected a more belligerent stance. He believed that Indians had no right to prevent white expansion across the continent. According to him, they should be moved to reservations far from emigrant routes or lines of communication. Although friendly, peaceful tribes merited justice and government supplies, hostile groups should be chastised severely. After one particularly bitter defeat, Sherman advised Grant to "act with vindic-

---

13. Doenecke, *Presidencies of Garfield and Arthur*, 89–91; Arthur, Annual Message, Dec. 6, 1881, in Richardson, comp., *Messages and Papers of the Presidents* 8:55–56; ibid., Dec. 4, 1882, 9:143; Cleveland to Endicott, Dec. 22, 1885, LC, Cleveland Papers, ser. 2, reel 26; Harrison, Annual Message, Dec. 3, 1889, in Richardson, comp., *Messages and Papers of the Presidents* 9:45, 48; ibid., Dec. 9, 1881, 9:201–3; ibid., Dec. 6, 1892, 9:326; Bowie, "Redfield Proctor," 238.

14. Sherman to Tappan, July 21, 1876, LC, Sherman Papers, 90, reel 45; see also ibid., Sept. 24, 1868, and Sherman to Beecher, Mar. 6, 1879, ibid., 91.

tiveness earnestness against the Sioux, even to their extermination, men, women, and children." A narrow personal escape from Kiowa ambush near Fort Richardson, Texas, in 1871 particularly angered Sherman, who subsequently concluded that Indians "are of a mischievous nature; semi-hostile; and would be converted into hostile the very moment troops are withdrawn. Some people trust them. I do not." To combat the Indian threat, Sherman believed the military needed to launch vigorous offensives.[15]

Philip H. Sheridan, Sherman's personal friend and the nation's second most important military leader, also advocated the offensive. A New York native, he was graduated from West Point in 1853 at age twenty-two. Sheridan saw action against Indians along the Rio Grande and in the Pacific Northwest before the Civil War. "Little Phil" won Grant's favor in the West and showed even more promise commanding the Army of the Potomac's cavalry and leading the Army of the Shenandoah. The fiery Sheridan served four stormy years in the postwar South before being transferred into the Division of the Missouri in 1869. He maintained this post until 1883, when he took command of the entire regular army for the remaining five years of his military career.[16]

Sheridan's aggressiveness paid spectacular dividends during the Civil War. When confronting opponents who blocked white expansion into valuable new lands, he saw no reason to temper his actions: "The Indian is a lazy, idle vagabond; he never labors, and has no profession except that of arms, to which he is raised from a child, a scalp . . . constantly dangled before his eyes." Sheridan often expressed the hope that his Indian foes could be civilized and Chris-

15. Sherman to Grant, Dec. 28, 1866, Senate Executive Document, No. 15, 39th Congress, 2d session, II, 1867, serial 1277, 4 (first quotation); Testimony of Sherman, Jan. 6, 1874, House Rpt. No. 384, 43d Cong., 1st sess., ser. 1624, 4 (second quotation).

16. Sheridan to Sherman, Dec. 8, 1872, LC, Sherman Papers, 34, reel 18; on his early career, see Sheridan, *Personal Memoirs* 1:2–125. Rister, *Border Command*, discusses Sheridan's postwar career; Hutton, *Phil Sheridan*, is the new standard work.

tianized, but he believed that this was possible only after hostile tribes had been punished. Complaining of growing Cheyenne, Arapaho, and Sioux depredations, he declared that "these Indians require to be soundly whipped, and the ringleaders . . . hung, their ponies killed, and such destruction of their property as will make them very poor."[17]

Sheridan's views tempered in later years. In 1878, he reflected, "Alas for the poor savage! along came nineteenth century progress, or whatever it may be called, to disturb their happy condition. . . . We took away their country and their means of support, broke up their mode of living, their habits of life, introduced disease and decay among them, and it was for this and against this they made war. Could any one expect less?"[18]

John Pope also expressed views that were important in shaping the army's Indian policy. After graduating from West Point and serving in the Mexican War, Pope gained notoriety as an outspoken member of the Corps of Topographical Engineers during the 1850s. Pope's star shone brilliantly after the first year of the Civil War, only to be darkened by a disastrous defeat at Second Bull Run. A failure against the Confederates, he was transferred to the Department of the Northwest, where he conducted operations against the Sioux. In recognition of his long frontier service, fellow officers often sought out Pope's views on Indians. In 1862, he had advocated "exterminating or ruining" those who committed depredations, but he later realized that different treatments were required for the respective tribes. Although experience tempered his comments about most Indians, Pope continued to argue that the army's small size obliged the government to prevent trouble by disarming, dismounting, and feeding reservation tribes. He also advised that Indians be

17. Report of Sheridan, Nov. 1, SW, AR, 1869, 37 (first quotation); Report of Sheridan, Sept. 26, ibid., 1868, 12 (second quotation); ibid., Oct. 12, 1872, 35–36. See also his testimony of Jan. 26, 1874, in House Rpt. No. 384, 43d Cong., 1st sess., ser. 1624, 226.

18. Report of Sheridan, Oct. 25, SW, AR, 1878, 35–36.

moved to lands undesirable to whites, unconcerned that such land might also be of questionable value to an Indian agency.[19]

More sympathetic was George Crook, another hardened veteran of the antebellum army and the Civil War. Most Indians held the bewhiskered Crook in high esteem. As one Apache warrior remembered, "Crook was our enemy, but though we hated him, we respected him." Another recalled him as "a hard fighter . . . [who] played fair with us afterwards and did what he could to protect the Indians." Crook stressed honesty in dealing with his former foes at all times; they had to be accorded just treatment after having been defeated on the battlefield. He also insisted that opportunities for labor with adequate remuneration should be made available to Indians so that they would not be forced to steal for their very existence. Crook later reflected that "the Apache stands at the very head of the Indians on this continent for natural intelligence and discernment. He knows his rights and is not afraid to maintain them. If he were a white man, we would admire his virtues no less than we deprecate . . . his faults."[20]

Crook, unable to overcome his paternalistic conviction that Indians needed the white man's civilization, still maintained a greater respect for their culture than most of his colleagues. Because of this evenhanded view, he adopted many Indian methods in warfare.

19. Pope to Sibley, Sept. 17, 1862, in U.S. War Dept., *The War of the Rebellion: A Compilation of the Official Records of the Union and Confederate Armies* (hereafter cited as *OR*), ser. 1, 13:649 (quotation); Pope to Sherman, Aug. 11, SW, AR, 1866, 26–27; Reports of Pope, Sept. 26, ibid., 1876, 450; Sept. 15, ibid., 1871, 61; Oct. 3, ibid., 1879, 80–81, 86; Oct. 1, ibid., 1885, 166–67; Ellis, *General Pope and U.S. Indian Policy*, 232–36.

The Department of the Northwest (1862–65) included the states of Wisconsin, Iowa, Minnesota, and the territories of Nebraska and Dakota (Thian, *Military Geography*, 82).

20. Ball, *Indeh*, 111 (first quotation); Betzinez, *I Fought with Geronimo*, 120–21 (second quotation); Crook to AG, May 17, 1889, Hayes Library, Crook Papers (third quotation). Although overdependent on secondary sources, see Dunlay, "General Crook and the White Man Problem," 3–10. See also King, "George Crook," and "Needed: A Reevaluation of General George Crook."

Exceptional mobility and large numbers of friendly Indian auxiliaries characterized his commands and made him one of the army's leading Indian fighters. Whereas his less open-minded comrades continued to use more traditional methods, Crook was able to see at least a few benefits in the alien ways of his enemies.[21]

Perceptions of the environment also affected Indian policy. Although increasingly accurate scientific knowledge of the trans-Mississippi West was becoming available, most Americans continued to make sweeping generalizations about this huge region. Some, who still accepted the Great American Desert thesis, saw little value in white occupation of the Midwest. Increasing numbers of people, however, came to view western North America as a veritable Garden of Eden, whose rich farmlands and mineral deposits could support huge numbers of thrifty farmers and industrious miners. Growing realization of the land's bounty served to justify Indian removal, as Indians failed to use lands the way whites believed they should be used.[22]

Civilian views on the Black Hills region demonstrate how perceptions of the environment influenced military strategy. In the Treaty of Fort Laramie (1868), the government promised that the Sioux would retain the Black Hills in perpetuity. Subsequent Sioux raids into northern Nebraska and eastern Dakota and the routing of the Northern Pacific Railroad into the Yellowstone Valley put both Indians and whites on edge. Military expeditions through the heart of Indian hunting grounds in the Dakotas—notably the fifteen-hundred-man column commanded by

21. Crook discusses his views in "Apache Problem." See also Crook to Young Man Afraid of His Horses, Little Big Man, etc., Nov. 17, 1879, National Archives, LS, Dept. of the Platte; Crook to AG, Aug. 27, Nov. 22, 1883, Hayes Library, Crook Papers; Report of Crook, undated, SW, AR, 1884, 131. Three other officers discuss "Our Indian Question" in the *Journal of the Military Service Institution* 2, no. 6 (1881): 101–221.

22. Smith, *Virgin Land*, 123–32, 174–83, 201–10; Stegner, *Beyond the Hundredth Meridian*.

Col. David S. Stanley in 1873 and the one-thousand-strong force led by Lt. Col. George A. Custer the following year—further exacerbated the situation. Skirmishes between the bluecoats and the Sioux became increasingly common.[23]

Rumors of gold discoveries in the Black Hills spawned even greater interest in the region. In 1874, Interior Secretary Columbus Delano and Commissioner of Indian Affairs Edward Smith agreed that such rumors remained unfounded and maintained that the Black Hills were unsuitable for white settlement. But when the gold finds proved real, Smith underwent a dramatic reversal. His next annual report acknowledged the inevitability of white occupation and urged removal of the Indians. In the meantime, the trickle of trespassers grew into a torrent as the army was unable to stop gold-hungry miners. President Grant tacitly authorized the army to end its efforts to prevent white intrusions into the Black Hills, later claiming that "an effort to remove the miners would only result in the desertion of the bulk of the troops that might be sent there to remove them." Open warfare resulted involving whites and Indians.[24]

Army views of the West were also important. Ideally, Sherman would have moved Indians to lands that whites did not want. The western plains and rugged Southwest seemed for some years to

23. Utley, *Frontier Regulars*, 248–52. Army confusion on its proper response is seen in Terry to Custer, Sept. 3, 1874, National Archives, LS, Department of Dakota; Terry to AAG, Mar. 9, 1875, ibid.; Sheridan to Sherman, July 3, 10, 12, Box 58, LC, Sheridan Papers; Parker, "Majors and the Miners," 99–113.

24. Delano, Annual Report, Oct. 31, SI, AR, 1874, xiii; Report of Smith, Nov. 1, ibid., 317–18; Report of Smith, Nov. 1, ibid., 1875, 510–11; Report of Terry, Nov. 12, SW, AR, 1875, 64; Grant, Annual Message, Dec. 5, 1876, in Richardson, comp., *Messages and Papers of the Presidents* 7:401 (quotation). Note also the disagreement among members of the Special Sioux Commission on the value of the Black Hills. C. C. Cox believed it full of economic prospects and argued that whites would move in. Samuel Hinman, however, pointed out that Indians had been promised the land and maintained that no minerals had been found as of November 1874 (see SI, AR, 1874, 399–407). Vocal sparring between Custer and Hazen over the future potential of the northern plains added to the confusion (see Kroecker, *Great Plains Command*, 120–42).

provide a solution. In 1869, he advised Sheridan that "in truth the [Missouri River] country is not fit for white people at all." A year later, Sherman stated that

> The occupation of Arizona by the whites I am satisfied was premature and the cost of maintaining troops there is all out of proportion to the result. The best advise [sic] I can offer is to notify the settlers to withdraw, and then to withdraw the troops and leave the country to the aboriginal inhabitants. It seems to me a great waste of good material to banish soldiers to that desert, where it costs so much to maintain them.

He later urged Congress to force "Mexico to take Arizona back," promising to reduce his estimates of army needs by two cavalry regiments if this move was adopted.[25]

Sherman's perceptions of the southwestern environment helped shape his strategic actions against Indians in those areas. He assigned none of his best commanders to this desolate region, and few of the men assigned to the departments of Arizona or New Mexico enjoyed any success in controlling the local Indians. Major General James H. Carleton, who had earned some notoriety during the early 1860s, was unable to duplicate his Civil War successes. Major John S. Mason, colonels George W. Getty and George Stoneman, and generals E. O. C. Ord, Henry W. Halleck, and Irvin McDowell also failed to stem hostile Apache raids.[26] In 1871, the string of mediocre leaders was temporarily broken when Arizona's governor, Anson P. K. Safford, convinced President Grant to give command of the

25. Sherman to Sheridan, July 15, 1869, LS, AGO, 50, reel 37 (first quotation). See also his report of Nov. 5, SW, AR, 1866, 20. Sherman to Belknap, Jan. 7, 1870, LS, AGO, 51, reel 38 (second quotation); Testimony of Sherman, Jan. 6, 1874, House Rpt. No. 384, 43d Cong., 1st sess., ser. 1624, 5, 7 (third quotation). For similar views, see Sherman to Schofield, July 16, 1869, LS, AGO, 51, reel 37.

26. Utley, *Frontier Regulars*, 180. McDowell had been defeated at First Bull Run. E. O. C. Ord probably stood above the others, but he never achieved outstanding success. On Carleton's decline, see Trafzer, *Kit Carson Campaign*, 235.

Department of Arizona to George Crook, who was still a lowly lieutenant colonel. Aided by consistent support from division chief Schofield, Crook did a thorough job during four years in the Southwest as he doggedly pursued his Indian enemies. With Crook's departure, less capable commanders like August V. Kautz and Orlando B. Willcox again took control until 1881.[27]

While junior officers sparred with the Apaches, Sherman gradually recognized that large numbers of whites could find suitable habitation in the West. By 1878, he recognized the Plains as "the safety valve of the Nation," which "afford an outlet for the surplus population and add vastly to the wealth and property of all." The Southwest, with construction of the Southern Pacific Railroad now complete, also took on new value, albeit somewhat more slowly. Once "a minus quality in our National sum of wealth," it had become, even to the skeptical Sherman, "the permanent mine of silver to the United States" by 1882. Such a valuable region received the full attention of Sherman's army. As Indian depredations increased, he ordered the brutally effective Brig. Gen. Ranald Slidell Mackenzie and the proven Crook to the Southwest.[28]

27. Utley, *Frontier Regulars*, 200–5, 379–84; Schmitt, ed., *General George Crook*, 160; Schofield to Sherman, Sept. 14, 1871, LC, Schofield Papers; Crook to AG, Sept. 4, 1871, National Archives, LS, Dept. of Arizona; Crook to AG, Sept. 19, 1871, Hayes Library, Crook Papers; Gates, "General George Crook's First Apache Campaign," 310–20; Sherman to McCrary, Aug. 3, 1877, LS, AGO, 60; Schurz to Kautz, Mar. 2, 1878, LC, Schurz Papers, reel 86; Wallace, *Gen. August V. Kautz and the Southwestern Frontier*, 220–21; Sherman to AG, Sept. 10, 1881, LC, Sherman Papers, 95, reel 47; Sherman to Pope, Sept. 17, 1881, ibid. The talented Miles served briefly (1875–76) in northern New Mexico but was transferred to help defeat the Sioux after the Little Bighorn.

28. Sherman to Burnside, July 15, 1878, LC, Sherman Papers, 91, reel 45 (first quotation); Sherman to Willcox, Oct. 11, 1879, ibid. (second quotation); Sherman to Lincoln, Apr. 14, 1882, ibid., 95, reel 47 (third quotation); Utley, *Frontier Regulars*, 383–87. See also Schofield to Sherman, Sept. 16, 1872, Box 49, LC, Schofield Papers; Sherman to Sheridan, June 15, 1880, Sherman Papers, 91, reel 45; Sherman to McDowell, Apr. 28, 1882, ibid., 57, reel 30; Sherman to AG, Sept. 15, 1883, ibid., 61, reel 32.

Perceptions of Indians and the western environment thus strongly influenced army policy. Offensives designed to force the remaining Sioux and Northern Cheyenne out of the Black Hills followed the discovery of the region's economic value. This discovery correlated conveniently with popular opinion, which held that Indians needed the benefits of American civilization in order to become good citizens; until that happy time, lands once guaranteed to them in perpetuity could, if found economically productive, be taken from them in the interests of what whites called progress. The pervasiveness of these views had an important effect on military action against Indians. Reformers might halt army initiatives temporarily, but popular clamor for decisive action against Indian resistance demanded that the military maintain the overall offensive.

Such demands reinforced the military heritage of aggressiveness that officers carried into the Indian wars. The spirit of the offensive had been clearly evident in the American Revolution, as seen in the invasion of Canada and in George Washington's repeated attempts to gain the advantage in his Middle Atlantic campaigns. United States troops again took the offensive in the War of 1812, launching a series of ill-fated thrusts on Canada. The Mexican War offered yet another example of the country's offensive bent as Zachary Taylor, Stephen W. Kearny, and Winfield Scott all led invasion forces into Mexico.

The Civil War taught the effectiveness of aggressiveness as well. The Union defeated the Confederacy through relentless offensives led by vigorous generals like Grant and Sherman, not by the more cautious leadership of Henry Halleck or George B. McClellan. Attrition of enemy troops and aggressive maneuvers were the keys to northern victory. Recognizing the need for planning on a major scale, Grant and Sherman permanently seized the initiative and bested the stubborn rebels. Although both leaders suffered stinging defeats in the process—Grant at the Wilderness, Spotsylvania, and Cold Harbor, and Sherman at

Kennesaw Mountain—neither gave their weary opponents time to capitalize on tactical successes.[29]

Along with Sherman and Sheridan, those who were to play key roles in the army after 1865 had learned these lessons firsthand. Schofield, who succeeded Sheridan as commanding general in 1888, had performed brilliantly as a corps commander under Sherman and in a series of independent roles during the Civil War. Alfred H. Terry rose to military prominence with his successful siege of the Confederate stronghold of Fort Fisher, North Carolina. Ord, veteran of Indian action in Florida and the Pacific Northwest, likewise won his reputation in the civil conflict, serving under Grant until given control of the Army of the James. Irvin McDowell, Henry Halleck, Oliver Howard, and Winfield Hancock add to the seemingly innumerable examples of Indian-wars generals who won their spurs in the Civil War.[30]

Schofield, Ord, McDowell, Halleck, and Howard, along with Sherman, Sheridan, Crook, and Pope, were West Point graduates. Yet none had received adequate training in military strategy as part of their regular course work. Professor Dennis Hart Mahan, for many years responsible for the subject as part of his West Point engineering section, rarely found time for detailed discussions of strategic doctrine. The little strategic instruction that was offered tended to reinforce practical experience and youthful republican aggressiveness and applied largely to traditional, European-style warfare. Mahan did insist, however, that the army deal firmly with hostile Indians by driving into their lands and forcing them to fight or to make treaties. "We must either overawe by strong measures in anticipation," Mahan stated, "or else, when hostilities do commence, strike

29. Williams, *History of American Wars*, 248–53; Weigley, *American Way of War*, 128–52.

30. For Schofield, see Schofield, *Forty-six Years in the Army;* McDonough, *Schofield*; and Weigley, "Military Thought of John M. Schofield." For Ord, see Cresap, *Appomattox Commander*. For Halleck, see Ambrose, *Halleck*, 198–212, which is more favorable than the present account. For Howard, see Carpenter, *Sword and Olive Branch*, and Howard, *My Life and Experiences among Our Hostile Indians*.

such a blow that it should be handed down as memorable in the tradition of the tribe."[31]

Henry W. Halleck, having graduated third in his West Point class of 1839, published his *Elements of Military Art and Science* seven years later. Greatly influenced by the French strategist Baron Antoine Henri Jomini and by the Austrian general the Archduke Charles, Halleck emphasized concentration of forces, possession of key strategic points, and fortifications. Swayed by Jomini's distaste for guerrilla-type warfare, Halleck emphasized conventional military operations in his book, which was widely read. Halleck's controversial Civil War career led him from the West, where he had been a fine administrator but poor field general, to Washington, where he ultimately became chief of staff. From 1865 to 1869, he commanded the Division of the Pacific. His postwar reports reveal little interest in strategic thought applicable to his new foes.[32]

Younger officers educated after the Civil War benefitted from slightly better strategic training. Sir Edward Bruce Hamley's *Operations of War*, which stressed classic Napoleonic strategy, was adopted as a textbook at West Point in 1870. The legacy of offensive strategies also continued. General Schofield, West Point Commandant from 1876 to 1881, recommended "more extended instruction in the cavalry service required by our young officers on the frontier."[33] The Military Service Institution, a voluntary organization, was formed to stimulate military discussion in 1879. Articles like Col. John Gibbon's "Arms to Fight Indians" appeared in such military journals as the *United Service*. Although senior officers have left little record of intensive study of the subject, a few of their sub-

31. Ambrose, *Duty, Honor, Country*, 136–37; Morrison, "Educating the Civil War Generals," 109; Skelton, "Army Officers' Attitudes toward the Indians," 114; Griess, "Dennis Hart Mahan," 306–7 (quotations); Weigley, *Towards an American Army*, 45–53.

32. Connelly and Jones, *Politics of Command*, 27–29 and n. 12; Hattaway and Jones, *How the North Won*, 13 nn. 10–11.

33. Luvaas, *Education of an Army*, 149; Report of Schofield, Nov. 8, SW, AR, 1877, 150 (quotation).

ordinates expressed genuine interest in strategic thought. First Lt. C. A. L. Totten designed a war-gaming system called "Stratego, or the American game of War," which included "a series of textbooks and an elaborate apparatus for the more intelligent study of tactics, grand tactics, strategy, military history and the various operations of war." The War Department apparently made Totten's game available at West Point and the larger western posts by 1881.[34]

Interest in strategy grew slowly during the 1880s. In 1886, a board of officers rejected one proposed military textbook in part because it was unclear, limited, and poorly organized on the subjects of grand tactics and strategy. Capt. John Bigelow's *Principles of Strategy*, which briefly suggested strategic moves for use against Indians, was published in 1894. Three years later, the curriculum at the Infantry and Cavalry School at Fort Leavenworth included strategy as one of its five departments of curriculum, with subdivisions of military policy, geography, history, logistics, staff duties, the conduct of war, and map and wargame maneuvers.[35]

Americans were not unaware of the problems other nations faced in dealing with nomadic and seminomadic tribesmen on newly established frontiers. Sherman asked a subordinate in 1875 to "ascertain how a small force of British troops, aided by the native troops, govern two hundred millions of people" in India. John F. Finerty, special correspondent of the *Chicago Times* who accompanied Crook's 1876 Yellowstone expedition, speculated that "mounted,

---

34. Gibbon, "Arms to Fight Indians"; Spell to Ramsey, Apr. 20, 1880 , Minn. State Hist. Soc., Ramsey Papers, reel 24; Totten to Ramsey, Sept. 23, 1880, ibid., reel 25; Lincoln to Chairman, Senate Committee on Appropriations, Mar. 1, 1881, LS, SW, 91, reel 82; Ramsey, General Order, Apr. 24, 1880, ibid., 88, reel 80. For Totten's explanation, see his "Strategos."

35. J. C. Kelton to C. F. Manderson, Apr. 22, 1886, LS, AGO; Walton, *Sentinal of the Plains*, 166–68; Bigelow, *Principles of Strategy*, 149. See also Sherman to Sheridan, Nov. 22, 1881, LC, Sherman Papers, 95, reel 47. Important also was Emory Upton, often recognized as one of the army's foremost thinkers before committing suicide in 1881 (see Ambrose, *Upton and the Army*, 84–153). Nenninger, *Leavenworth Schools*, also addresses the subject.

. . . the Indian warrior could secure a retreat from the Chasseurs d'Afrique of [the president of France le comte Marie-Edmé-Patrice-Maurice de] Macmahon [sic], with all their Arab horses." President Hayes recalled that Sherman had discussed the English-Afghan war during an 1878 White House visit. In 1885, Crook complained that "things that may appear trivial at Washington, are frequently all important in the management of . . . dangerous Indians. The Sepoy Rebellion was supposed to have been caused by greased cartridges." The Division of Military Information, created in 1889, also published a pamphlet on "Colonial Army Systems of the Netherlands, Great Britain, France, Germany, Portugal, Italy, and Belgium" during the 1890s.[36]

Others sought to compare the Canadian western experience, which included much less Indian warfare, to that of the United States. General Hancock believed that the government should follow the British example and issue or sell only arms of inferior quality to Indians in Canada. In so recommending, Hancock hit upon a common complaint made by army men: why were Indians allowed to secure modern weapons from traders, many of whom had government authorization to distribute such arms? In following such a policy, Hancock charged, the government only made the army's tasks more difficult.[37]

Sheridan attributed the greater violence along the U.S. frontiers to illegal white encroachments. According to Miles, the Canadians had avoided bloodshed by refusing to force new customs on Indians and by emphasizing individual justice so that entire tribes did not suffer for the transgressions of certain individuals. There were also fewer whites migrating west in Canada and therefore fewer chances for confrontations.[38] Recognizing the more subtle differences be-

36. Michie, *Life and Letters of Emory Upton*, 302; Finerty, *War-Path and Bivouac*, 106; Williams, *Hayes*, p. 106; Crook to AAG, June 5, 1885, National Archives, LS, Dept. of Arizona; Bethel, "Military Information Division," 23.

37. Report of Hancock, Oct. 3, SW, AR, 1872, 42.

38. Report of Sheridan, Oct. 25, SW, AR, 1878, 34–35; Miles, "Indian Problem," 309–14.

tween the two countries' Indian policies proved even more difficult. The ten to twenty year lag between settlement in western Canada and that in the U.S. gave Canadians more time to adjust than their American counterparts. The Métis, a large population of half bloods, and the Canadian Shield, a rugged outcropping that inhibited direct overland communication between eastern and western Canada, provided human and geographic buffers not present in the United States. Finally, the Dominion government could not afford open Indian warfare. Its tiny mounted police force was the sole police power over both whites and Indians. Canadians sought to avoid a major Indian outbreak, whereas rapid expansion at virtually any cost dominated American thinking.[39]

American military leaders focused more attention on strategy as employed by and against traditional European powers than on policy against Indians. Sherman, Sheridan, and Schofield all conducted personal inspections of European military systems during their visits to the continent. Junior officers, including Emory Upton, Francis V. Greene, and William B. Hazen, also examined Europe's armies. Greene even compared Russian General Ivan Vladimirovich Gourko to Crook in physical appearance and mannerisms. Other direct comparisons between European and American situations, however, were rare. As Sherman explained, "I saw much abroad of interest, but their military & physical systems differ so widely from ours, that we can learn but little of them." Sheridan also seemed disappointed in the European armies.[40] Nonetheless, the importance that con-

39. Desmond Morton, "Comparison of U.S./Canadian Military Experience on the Frontier," in Tate, ed., *American Military on the Frontier*, 16–34; comments by Richard A. Preston, ibid., pp. 56–66; Stacey, "Military Aspect of Canada's Winning of the West"; Morton, "Cavalry or Police."

40. Sherman to Sheridan, Jan. 23, 1871, LC, Sherman Papers, 90, reel 45; Greene to Sherman, Oct. 10, 1877, ibid., 46, reel 24; Sherman to Hazen, Dec. 3, 1877, ibid., 90, reel 45; Special Orders No. 176, Aug. 3, 1881, Box 39, LC, Schofield Papers; Report of Drum, Nov., SW, AR, 1882, 23; Sherman to Augur, Oct. 4, 1872, Ill. State Hist. Library, Augur Papers (quotation); Hutton, *Phil Sheridan*, 201–6.

temporary military strategists of virtually every country placed on the offensive did not go unnoticed by Americans, who generally accepted the assertion that offensives provided the only sure means of decisively defeating an enemy.[41]

Individual personalities and feuds within the army also affected the coordination of Indian policy. Sherman was the most important force in molding postwar actions against the trans-Mississippi Indians. Born in Lancaster, Ohio, he was graduated from West Point in 1840 and served without distinction in Florida and California before resigning his commission in order to pursue unsuccessful careers in finance and law. He later became superintendant of a Louisiana military academy. Rejoining the army in 1861, Sherman was an innovative leader most noted for his Atlanta campaign and subsequent marches through Georgia and South Carolina, during which he cut loose from communications, avoided pitched battles, and brought the war home to the Southern people. "[They must] realize the truth that war is no child's play," argued Sherman "[We] must make old and young, rich and poor, feel the hard hand of war."[42]

In 1876, Senator Samuel B. Maxey [D–Tex.] described the general as "a brusque, quick spoken, quick moving, very plain, slender man, not at all handsome, but still with character strongly marked in his face." Fiercely loyal to those who had remained in the regular service, Sherman engaged in verbal duels with Congressman John A. Logan, champion of volunteer soldiers and, ironically, a former subordinate of Sherman's, Secretary of War Belknap, and Henry Van Ness Boynton, who had criticized Sherman's published memoirs. President Hayes also incurred the general's outspoken wrath

---

41. See essays by Crane Brinton, H. Rothfels, and Jean Gottmann, in Earle, ed., *Makers of Modern Strategy*, 85–92, 93–113, 234–59; McElwee, *Art of War*; Luvaas, "European Military Thought and Doctrine, 1870–1914," in Howard, ed., *Theory and Practice of War*, 71–88. Note also Callwell's *Small Wars*.

42. Sherman, *Memoirs* 2:266, 227 (quotations). Also valuable is Hart, *Sherman*. On Sherman's early career, see Clarke, *William Tecumseh Sherman*. On his later life, see Athearn, *William T. Sherman and the Settlement of the West*.

for making promotions and forcing retirements from the army against the general's wishes. Despite the controversies, Sherman's unwavering determination to base promotions solely on seniority, while angering many, seemed fairer to him than simply allowing ambitious officers to pull political strings.[43]

In an army troubled by low pay, infrequent promotions, and inadequate training, jealous officers often magnified petty quarrels into major controversies. Although Sherman handled such affairs as well as anyone on the scene, many of the army's prima donnas engaged in a series of behind-the-scenes duels that severely limited cooperation and smooth policy-making. Pope, egotistical, argumentative, and ambitious, became one of the more difficult senior officers in the postbellum army. His continuing feud with Fitz-John Porter over Porter's alleged failure to follow orders at Second Bull Run divided army loyalties for the remainder of the century. Pope also refused to serve under Halleck on the Pacific Coast in 1868, presumably because of Civil War disagreements, and battled with Sheridan over proper strategy, maintaining that only winter campaigns had a chance of success against poorly supplied natives. Pope concluded that summer offensives merely allowed Indian raiders to swoop behind troop columns to attack unprotected settlements.[44]

43. Maxey to his wife, June 17, 1876, Texas State Archives, Maxey Papers (quotation); Sherman to Augur, June 9, 1870, Ill. State Hist. Library, Augur Papers; Sherman to John Sherman, Nov. 17, 1875, LC, Sherman Papers, 41, reel 22; ibid., Dec. 6, 1875, 42, reel 22; John Sherman to Sherman, Dec. 10, 1875, ibid.; Sherman to Moulton, Mar. 9, 1876, ibid., 90, reel 45; Sherman to Boynton, Jan. 16, 1880, ibid., 91, reel 45; Williams, *Hayes*, 269, 307. Sherman and Logan eventually reconciled most of their differences. See Sherman to Logan, Feb. 11, 1883, LC, Logan Papers; and Sherman to Logan, Feb. 20, 1883, Sherman Papers, 96, reel 47.

44. On the Porter case, see Pope to Chandler, Mar. 1, 1870, LC, Chandler Papers, reel 3; Eisenschiaml, *Celebrated Case of Fitz John Porter*. Pope's poor relations with Halleck are cited in Pope to Grant, Dec. 30, 1867, LC, Grant Papers, ser. 5, 55, reel 24. The Sheridan-Pope controversy is in Sheridan to Sherman, July 18, 1874, Box 56, LC, Sheridan Papers; Sheridan to Sherman, Sept. 7, 1874, Box 11, ibid.; Pope to Sherman, Sept. 16, 1874, LC, Sherman Papers, 37, reel 20.

Pope's incessant quest for promotion further reduced his effectiveness. As columns from his Department of the Missouri and the Department of Texas readied for field operations during the Red River War of 1874–75, he sought to outshine rather than cooperate with his rivals in Texas. His field commander, the equally ambitious Miles, later complained that Pope failed to supply him properly during that campaign. Sheridan's remarks of 1872 summed up the difficulties: "Pope . . . is just in such a condition that he wants to fight something all the time."[45]

Pope and Sherman were not the only officers to bicker with their comrades. During the major southern plains offensives of 1868–69, Col. William B. Hazen was assigned to provide refuge at old Fort Cobb for those Indians who remained peaceful. Sheridan accompanied the main column as an observer. After an exhausting chase in the early winter, the bluecoats seemed ready to deal a devastating blow to the largest remaining body of recalcitrants when the latter suddenly presented the soldiers with Hazen's signed testimony declaring their innocence. In Hazen's defense, he had been handed an impossible task, as there was no way he could watch over Indians spread out over a hundred miles. Unfortunately, he and Sheridan had clashed during the Civil War, each claiming credit for first reaching the crest of Missionary Ridge at Chattanooga in 1863. Sheridan never forgave Hazen for either the Missionary Ridge dispute or the failure to catch the Indians, asserting that his subordinate had been duped by the Indians.[46]

Sheridan's inability to pardon subordinates for disagreeing with

45. Pope to Miles, Aug. 5, 1874, National Archives, LS, Dept. of the Missouri; Miles to Sherman, Sept. 27, 1874, LC, Sherman Papers, 37, reel 20; Sheridan to Sherman, 1872, ibid., 34, reel 18 (quotation).

46. Hazen to Sherman, May 5, 1877, LC, Sherman Papers, 46, reel 24; Utley, *Frontier Regulars*, 149–58, 301 n. 16. Hazen had in fact often expressed his desire to punish depredating Indians. See his report of Oct. 16, 1866, House Ex. Doc. No. 45, 39th Cong., 2nd sess., VII, ser. 1289, 5; and Hazen to Sherman, Jan. 2, 1869, Senate Ex. Doc. No. 40, 40th Cong., 3rd sess., ser. 1360, 17. On Hazen, see Kroecker, *Great Plains Command.*

him added to the army's internal rivalries. In addition to the spats with Hazen and Pope, Sheridan broke ranks with Crook, once a close personal friend. Crook began to turn against his fellow Ohioan and West Point graduate after he decided that Sheridan, then his superior, took too much credit for Civil War victories at Fisher's Hill and Cedar Creek during the Shenandoah Valley campaign of 1864. Later, Crook's sympathies with Indians, which earned the support of reformers like Herbert Welsh, led to opposition from some of his fellow officers, most notably Sheridan, who had recommended Crook for promotion as late as 1866.[47]

The Sheridan-Crook alliance was doomed from the beginning, as it brought together two stubborn, fiercely independent men. Crook routinely failed to inform superiors of his actions in the field; Sheridan expected his subordinates to remain in close contact with him. Crook's poor handling of the campaigns against Sitting Bull and Crazy Horse in 1876 and 1877 further disgruntled the impatient Sheridan, as did leaks to the press that Sheridan attributed to Crook. Although Crook denied the charges, Sheridan later stated that he "has given me a good deal of disappointment."[48]

Their relationship soured completely during Crook's last tour of southwestern duty. Age and increased sympathy for the Indians' plight made Crook reluctant to engage in the grueling pursuits that had once characterized his military service. Sheridan also opposed Crook's increasing reliance on Indian scouts and readily accepted his

47. Crook to Herbert Welsh, Jan. 3, 1888, Hayes Library, Crook Papers; Smith to Howard, Jan. 12, 1872, Bowdoin Library, Howard Papers; Sheridan to Stanton, May 2, 1866, LC, Johnson Papers, series 1, reel 22. Hutton, *Phil Sheridan*, 123–25, has a good account of the Crook-Sheridan relationship.

48. Sheridan to Sherman, Jan. 22, 1879, LC, Sherman Papers, 49, reel 25 (quotation). Complaints about Crook are in Sheridan to Sherman, July 27, 1876, Box 58, LC, Sheridan Papers; Sheridan to Crook, July 16, Oct. 30, 1876, ibid.; Sheridan to Crook, Jan. 29, 1877, Sherman Papers, 45, reel 23; Crook to Drum, Feb. 11, 1877, ibid.; Sherman to Sheridan, Feb. 17, 1877, ibid., 90, reel 45; Sherman to Sheridan, Feb. 21, 1877, LS, AGO, 60, reel 47; Schofield to Sheridan, June 11, 1885, Box 52, LC, Schofield Papers.

request for transfer back to the northern plains in 1886. Thus clashes of personalities were crucial in preventing the two from reconciling differences in military theory and practice.[49]

The inordinately ambitious Miles was another of the army's most controversial leaders. Only twenty-two when the Civil War erupted, he participated in every major battle on the eastern front except Gettysburg. Although he was not trained at West Point, Miles led troops in the Red River War of 1874–75, in the Sioux and Nez Percé campaigns of 1877, and in action against the Bannock Indians in 1878. Awarded his general's star in 1880, Miles headed the departments of Arizona, the Columbia, and the Missouri until taking over the Pacific division eight years later. He returned to the Department of the Missouri from 1890 to 1894, moved to the East from 1894 to 1895, and gained the coveted position of commanding general, which he held from 1895 to 1903.[50]

Miles's brilliant military record hides some of the more unpleasant sides of his personality. His skillful use of combined arms columns and determined pursuits have earned him a place ahead of all other Indian fighters. Yet his unquenchable thirst for national prominence and promotion left a bittersweet taste with contemporaries. He married Mary Hoyt Sherman, the niece of Gen. William Sherman and influential senator John Sherman [R–Ohio]. Miles then shot off a stream of letters to his uncle William, unabashedly revealing both his desire to become secretary of war and his high opinion of his

49. Crook to Bradley, Sept. 7, 1885, U.S. Army Hist. Res. Coll., Bradley Papers; Roberts to Lockett, Nov. 26, 1885, National Archives, LS, Dept. of Arizona; Roberts to Pierce, Nov. 27, 1885, ibid.; Report of Sheridan, Oct. 24, SW, AR, 1885, 61–62; Sheridan to Crook, Dec. 29, 1885, Box 36, LC, Sheridan Papers; Report of Sheridan, Oct. 10, SW, AR, 1886, 72; Endicott to Parkman, Feb. 4, 1886, LC, Cleveland Papers, ser. 3, reel 102. Almost ten years earlier, Sherman had criticized Crook's overdependence on Indian scouts in combat (Sherman to Sheridan, July 17, 1876, LS, AGO, 69, reel 46).

50. Johnson, *Unregimented General*, and Tolman, *Search for General Miles*, badly need to be superseded by full- length scholarly works. DeMontravel's "Career of Lieutenant General Nelson A. Miles" is too uncritical. Utley's chapter on Miles in Hutton, *Soldiers West*, is excellent.

own abilities. Miles recognized the value of a good public image in aiding promotions, and he compiled two lengthy autobiographies that advanced his military attributes and reformist sympathies for defeated Indian foes. These sympathies, not always evident in his official correspondence, could well have been aimed at gaining humanitarian support for a projected presidential campaign.[51]

Personal ambition rather than genuine concern for Indian welfare often guided Miles's actions in the West. One Indian foe regarded him as "a coward, a liar, and a poor officer." Sherman accused him of being "too apt to mistake the dictates of his personal ambition for wisdom" and "not just and fair to his comrades and superiors." Brig. Gen. David S. Stanley believed "Miles . . . made a business of looking after the advancement of himself." Others maintained that he claimed undue credit for the capture of Chief Joseph in 1877 and Geronimo in 1886.[52] Miles's ruthless quest for power and promotion overcame any personal or moral scruples in his determination to succeed. Sheridan commented, "Miles has no idea of money; but very little for the regulations, also ambitious . . . as to have but little delicacy for the rights of juniors or superiors; but he is a good pushing officer. . . . [whom] I would like to have when there is a necessity for an action near."[53]

51. Utley, Introduction to *Personal Recollections* by Miles; Ranson, "Nelson A. Miles as Commanding General"; S. B. Maxey to Maxey, Jan. 21, 1879, Texas State Archives, Maxey Papers; Miles, *Personal Recollections* and *Serving the Republic*.

52. Ball, *Indeh*, 111 (first quotation). For a contrasting view, see Sherman to Sheridan, July 19, 1879, LC, Sherman Papers, 91, reel 45 (second quotation); Stanley to Schofield, Apr. 14, 1889, Box 42, LC, Schofield Papers (third quotation); Miles to Howard, Jan. 8, Jan. 31, 1877, Bowdoin Library, Howard Papers.

Other disputes with Pope, Capt. George F. Price, and Col. James W. Forsyth may be seen in Pope to Miles, Sept. 24, 1874, National Archives, LS, Dept. of Missouri; Dunn to Miles, Nov. 3, 1874, ibid.; and Alger to Dickinson, Nov. 21, 1895, LC, Lamont Papers. For yet another example, see Alger to Spooner, May 2, 1902, LC, Spooner Papers (courtesy Dr. Lewis L. Gould, University of Texas).

53. Sheridan to Sherman, July 21, 1879, LC, Sherman Papers, 50, reel 26. For other support for Miles, see Proctor to Harrison, Sept. 16, 1889, LC, Harrison Papers, ser. 1, reel 22; John Sherman to Harrison, Apr. 4, 1890, ibid., reel 26.

Other army men were unable to equal Miles's military achievements due to early deaths or personal problems. Ranald Mackenzie established a reputation as an Indian fighter which, had he not died at age forty-eight, might have rivaled those of Crook or Miles. After graduating at the top of his West Point class in 1862, Mackenzie fought with the Army of the Potomac before commanding a cavalry division in the Army of the James. Despite his youth, he was appointed Colonel of the Fourth Cavalry Regiment soon after the war. He gained a reputation as an effective field leader in action against Indians in Texas, Mexico, the Indian Territory, and the northern plains throughout the 1870s. The Indians dubbed him "Bad Hand," a nickname derived from the Civil War wound which cost him two fingers. The ruthless Mackenzie once ordered the slaughter of over one thousand captured horses and mules rather than risk having the Indians retake them. He believed the military should "go where they [hostile tribes] live and hurt them as much as possible." His intense rivalry with Miles for promotion, however, combined with arduous frontier service, lingering war wounds, and syphilis-induced insanity caused Mackenzie's premature demise.[54]

The flamboyant Lt. Col. George A. Custer, compiling a spectacular if somewhat inconsistent record during the Civil War, won Sheridan's favor by his aggressiveness. Although Custer performed well during the southern plains offensives of 1868–69, his repeated flaunting of higher authority put him in President Grant's bad graces

54. Wallace, *Ranald S. Mackenzie on the Texas Frontier*, 5–15, 145, 190–94, 195 n. 8. Lincoln to Sherman, Apr. 29, Sherman Papers, 58, reel 30; Sherman to Lincoln, Apr. 29, 1882, ibid., 95, reel 47; Mackenzie to AAG, Oct. 1, 1874, in Wallace, ed., *Ranald S. Mackenzie's Official Correspondence*, 124; Mackenzie to Augur, July 17, 1873, U.S. Army Hist. Res. Coll., Mackenzie Papers (quotation); Carter, *Old Sergeant's Story*, 18; Crane, *Experiences of a Colonel of Infantry*, 113, 139–40; Sheridan to Sherman, Dec. 28, 1883, Box 43, LC, Sherman Papers.

Some fellow officers were jealous of Mackenzie's spectacular success. In the wake of Mackenzie's first raid into Mexico, Edward Hatch wrote, "It will answer his purpose. At Washington they are determined to promote him to a Brigadier as surely as they made him a Colonel" (Hatch to Grierson, Aug. 13, 1873, Ill. State Hist. Library, Grierson Papers).

by 1876. Custer hoped for a dramatic victory against the Sioux, yet he was fearful lest the Indians escape unscathed as they had so often. In the face of what proved to be overwhelming enemy strength, he divided his Seventh Cavalry; the resulting annihilation of his troops at the Little Bighorn was the army's most shocking defeat of the nineteenth-century Indian wars.[55]

Illness and alcoholism prevented Eugene A. Carr from achieving great success. A West Point graduate in 1850, Carr distinguished himself in prewar Indian conflicts and won the Congressional Medal of Honor for gallantry at Pea Ridge in 1862. Following the Civil War, he performed with only mixed success in Kansas, Colorado, and Arizona; his abilities diminished as his health deteriorated. As former war secretary Proctor recalled, "He was a good fighting officer during the War and has done good service against the Indians, but . . . he is not what he has been."[56]

Equally ineffective were tentative, unaggressive field leaders. Commanding Fort Phil Kearny in 1866 was Col. Henry B. Carrington, a veteran of five years' desk duty. He became overly cautious in the face of Sioux threats, and restless subordinates chafed at the resulting inactivity. Disregarding Carrington's order to remain close to camp, Capt. William J. Fetterman led some eighty men into a fatal trap laid by Oglala and Miniconjou Sioux. Carrington's incapacity for decisive action in the wake of the Fetterman debacle led his superiors to move him to a safer, less important command.

---

55. Books on Custer include Monaghan, *Custer*; Ambrose, *Crazy Horse and Custer*; and Utley, *Custer and the Great Controversy*. Distinctive is Hofling, *Custer and the Little Big Horn: A Psychobiographical Inquiry*.

56. Proctor to the President, June 29, 1892, LC, Harrison Papers, ser. 1, reel 26. For a different view, see King, *War Eagle*.

Carr admitted that he had drinking problems. "I find that I cannot manage King Alcohol, and have entered into an irrevocable obligation never again to use alcoholic stimulants of any kind whatever: it will be a great deprivation, on account of my health, but it had to be done, & is done" (Carr to Sherman, Nov. 3, 1880, LC, Sherman Papers, 53, reel 27). Unfortunately, a subsequent letter from Sherman to Willcox, Dec. 29, 1881, ibid., 95, reel 47, indicates Carr's efforts proved futile.

Similarly, Phil Sheridan castigated Lt. Col. Alfred Sully because of Sully's unwillingness to accept casualties or to keep up a vigorous pursuit during the southern plains offensives of 1868–69.[57]

Age also took its toll. Oliver Otis Howard, who had lost an arm at the Battle of Seven Pines, served a tumultuous term as head of the Freedman's Bureau after the Civil War. A genuine humanitarian and deeply religious, he became President Grant's peace emissary in Arizona in 1872 before gaining command of the Department of the Columbia two years later. Howard's lethargic performance against the Nez Percé in 1877 embarrassed the army. In the midst of the campaign Sherman suggested, "If you are tired, give the command to some young energetic officer." Howard replied, "I never flag. . . . Neither you nor General McDowell can doubt my pluck and energy." Sherman's response a day later noted the age problem clearly: "Glad to find you so plucky. Have every possible faith in your intense energy, but thought it probable you were worn out, and sometimes I think men of less age and rank are best for Indian warfare. They have more to make."[58]

John M. Schofield, who graduated in Sheridan's West Point class of 1853, managed to avoid the intense political infighting that beset many of his peers. A reliable division, corps, and army commander during the Civil War, Schofield represented the army in a secret mission to France concerning Emperor Maximilian's ill-fated foray into Mexico. He served briefly as secretary of war in 1868 and 1869 and then held down a series of responsibilities until he was appointed commanding general in 1888. By acting as a chief of staff in which

57. Carrington to Litchfield, Oct. 4, Nov. 25, 1866, Jan. 3, 1867, Senate Ex. Doc. No. 33, 50th Cong., 1st sess., 1887, I, ser. 2504, 31–32, 36, 39; Testimony of Carrington, 1867, ibid., 47; Augur to Nichols, Feb. 19, 1867, National Archives, LS, Dept. of the Platte; Sherman to Augur, Feb. 28, 1867, Ill. State Hist. Library, Augur Papers. On Sully, see Sheridan to Sherman, Nov. 29, 1868, LC, Sherman Papers, 24, reel 13.

58. Sherman to Howard, Aug. 24, SW, AR, 1877, 13 (first quotation); Howard to Sherman, Aug. 27, ibid. (second quotation); Sherman to Howard, Aug. 28, ibid. (third quotation). For Howard's account, see his *Nez Percé Joseph*.

he served as advisor rather than rival, Schofield got along with civilian superiors in Washington. Keenly interested in military administration, he made few strategic innovations useful against Indians but was a dependable officer.[59]

Christopher C. Augur also managed to retain the respect of his colleagues. Augur attended the U.S. Military Academy with Grant from 1839 to 1843 and later participated in the Mexican and Rogue River conflicts. He returned briefly to West Point as commandant of cadets before proving his abilities as a thoughtful, responsible leader during the Civil War. Augur subsequently earned high praise from Grant, Sherman, and Sheridan for his capable management of several departments. His quiet efficiency, long experience against hostile tribes, and discreet handling of complex affairs made him a rarity among officers of the period.[60] Much the same could be said about Alfred H. Terry. For many years the ranking general officer without West Point training, he compiled a competent if not brilliant post–Civil War military record. Like Augur, Terry proved more cooperative than many of his peers. Superiors found his lack of open ambition especially endearing.[61]

Numerous problems beset the army's officer corps after 1865. Overcaution and age prevented some from successfully combatting elusive Indians. Abrasive personalities, petty animosities, and personal ambition precluded cooperation even at the departmental level. "Cordial support among commanders" of divided columns was frequently impossible to achieve.[62] Even the most renowned Indian

59. Schofield, *Forty-six Years*; Weigley, "Military Thought of Schofield."

60. Praise for Augur is in Sherman to Tappan, Sept. 24, 1868, LC, Sherman Papers, 90, reel 45; Sheridan to Sherman, Nov. 18, 1872, ibid., 18, reel 18; Sheridan to Belknap, Feb. 24, Box 12, LC, Sheridan Papers; Sherman to Augur, Feb. 11, 1884, June 27, 1884, Feb. 9, 1885, and July 4, 1885, Ill. State Hist. Library, Augur Papers.

61. Bailey, *Pacifying the Plains*.

62. Merritt, "Important Improvements in the Art of War," 186–87.

fighters—Crook, Miles, and Mackenzie—sometimes found success to be fleeting. Others never achieved the greatness expected of them by their peers. The difficulties that beset Custer, Carr, Carrington, Fetterman, and Sully exemplified the pitfalls that plagued officers on western duty. Anxious for success, bored with the dull routine of military life, many among even the most promising could not cope with the problems of Indian service.

In the absence of regular strategic policy-making, individual personalities played a fundamental role in determining army policy after the Civil War. Although Sheridan and Sherman remained friends, cliques of junior officers grouped around each leader. Sheridan's favorites included Custer and Wesley Merritt; Sherman continued to support old comrades Hazen, Benjamin H. Grierson, Ord, and Howard. Crook distrusted Sheridan; Pope refused to serve under Halleck. A few gained alliances with presidents—Hazen with Garfield, Crook with Hayes, and Sheridan with Grant. Almost everyone feared the ambitious Miles and Mackenzie, who grappled with each other for promotion.[63]

No single factor dominated the thinking of those who attempted to formulate military strategy against Indians. The frontier experiences of other countries, for example, had little apparent effect on United States military policy. Most key officers viewed all Indians suspiciously, which allowed the officers to brush aside the moral misgivings that might have tempered some of their more brutal actions. Subhuman obstacles to civilized expansion could be dealt with ruthlessly, they reasoned. Perceptions of the environment affected strategic thought: those who regarded western lands in favorable terms stressed the need to open them up for white settlement and to push Indians into less desirable areas with all deliberate speed. Sherman initially viewed much of the trans-Mississippi region as a useless wasteland and was content to give this land to the Indians

63. Hutton, *Phil Sheridan*, 43, 107, 123–40, has an excellent account of these struggles.

in order to end the western struggles. He later changed his opinion and came to believe that all of the West should be opened to white settlers. He and Sheridan thus determined to crush Indian resistance.

The American military entered the second half of the nineteenth century with little strategic heritage outside of a vague appreciation of the value of offensives. Lessons learned at West Point, during the Civil War, and on the frontiers reinforced this tradition of aggression, but many officers differed in opinion about the timing of attacks against Indians and what type of soldiers to use in such strikes. The isolated nature of many commands combined with the independent spirit fostered by aggressive training to hamper most cooperative efforts. Indian campaigns were incredibly demanding, requiring patient yet determined pursuit and a good deal of luck. Because overcautious officers achieved little success and overaggressive leaders invited annihilation, the army took no resolute stand regarding Indian policy, even on matters purely military. Practical politics rather than cultural or educational influences thus dominated high-level military planning. After all, the vast majority of Americans demanded immediate, decisive results. Unwilling to wait for the implementation of lengthy Indian reform programs advocated by humanitarians, the country turned to a divided, unsure, yet powerful military to overcome the Indian threat.

Chapter Three
Problems of Politics and Policy

In 1872, Representative Henry W. Slocum [D–N.Y.], a Civil War veteran wounded at First Bull Run, decried the army's increasing role in postbellum politics: "We draw on the Army for our stump orators, we call on them to preside at the polls. . . . If we desire to negotiate for the purchase of an island in the sea, the negotiations must be carried on by a brigadier general. If the merchants of New York wish storage for their goods they must go to a colonel of the staff. We can hardly pass a bill through Congress without the aid of a field officer."[1]

1. U.S. Congress, House, *Cong. Globe*, 42nd Cong., 2nd sess., 1875, pt. 3, 1875.

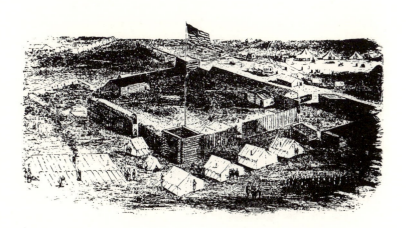

The Civil War had indeed expanded the army's size and importance in the United States. In 1860, the maximum allowable strength of the army was 12,698; in 1870, despite repeated cuts, the figure stood at 35,353. In addition, some two million men had served for the North in the Civil War; another nine hundred thousand were veterans of Confederate service.[2] Yet the army's involvement in American political life was even more pronounced than numbers alone might indicate, because the confused nature of the country's Indian programs precluded a clear delineation between military and political affairs regarding Indians. The size and composition of the regular army, the appropriations and powers given the War and Interior Departments, and the international considerations often associated with Indian matters were of vital interest to politicians as well as to military officials.

Like Representative Slocum, many Americans distrusted the army and its postwar strength. Traditionally, the public favored a small standing army, believing that larger forces threatened liberty, democracy, and peace. Pacifism evident in the late nineteenth century amplified the antimilitary sentiment. Theorists such as Herbert Spencer and capitalists led by Andrew Carnegie labeled the military wasteful, nonproductive, and unnecessary. Labor leaders too remained critical, charging that regular officers served as the pawns of industrialists. The army's role in putting down strikes in 1877 and 1894 heightened working class fears. Political leaders often joined the derisive chorus. Congressman Fernando Wood [D–N.Y.] called officers "idle vagabonds who are so well paid and do nothing." Fellow representative John A. Logan [R–Ill.] claimed that "many of our officers have very little else to do than wear their uniforms and attend receptions."[3]

2. Heitman, *Historical Register* 2:597, 611; Matloff, ed., *American Military History*, 192; Williams, *History of American Wars*, 225.

3. Huntington, *Soldier and the State*, 153–58, 222–25; Mardock, *Reformers and the American Indian*, 61–62, 71; Cooper, *Army and Civil Disorder*, 218–20; *Cong. Globe*, 40th Cong., 3rd sess., 1869, pt. 2, 925–27 (quotations).

Yet Americans after 1865 did not have a "complete, unrelenting hostility . . . toward virtually all things military." Significant numbers of educators and ministers portrayed soldiers as loyal servants of the republic. In contrast to labor leaders, the press gave the army good marks in strikebreaking activities. Westerners often pulled political strings to acquire army bases, desiring the protection and economic benefits afforded by the military presence. Even many Indian agents agreed that military force was sometimes necessary against hostile tribes. A military background, furthermore, did not prevent officers from achieving political prominence. Ulysses S. Grant had been a professional soldier, as was Winfield S. Hancock, Democratic candidate for president in 1880. Presidents Rutherford B. Hayes, James A. Garfield, Benjamin Harrison, William McKinley, and Theodore Roosevelt also won varying degrees of acclaim for their military service. While most Americans still preferred the amateur soldier who had returned to civilian life to the straitlaced professional army man, postbellum society did not always oppose the military.[4]

In this mixed political climate the army sought to maintain the support it needed to guarantee favorable legislation. Influenced by Sherman's opposition to overt political involvement except in cases of absolute necessity, most officers avoided public pronouncements regarding the presidency. A few, however, could not resist. Grant's election pleased many, though he proved less favorable to the army than expected. Hayes's victory meant that George Crook, already on his mercurial rise through the ranks, had a powerful ally in the White House. Both were Ohio natives; further, Hayes had served under Crook's command during the Civil War and hung Crook's portrait in his library. Hancock's unsuccessful 1880 campaign gained the behind-the-scenes support of fellow officers such as Schofield and Ord. Sherman claimed later that in the final days of Hayes's admin-

4. Huntington, *Soldier and the State*, 226–27 (quotation), see also 158. Kemble, *Image of the Army Officer*, 107–53; Langley, "Democratic Tradition and Military Reform," 192–200.

istration, the Republican president retaliated against Schofield and Ord by refusing both of them for promotion; instead Hayes was "determined to create a vacancy for General Miles on the openly expressed theory that the army was not gratified enough to the Republican Party."[5]

The army's limited political influence continued to be felt during the 1880s. After Apache raids in the Southwest, President Cleveland's reputation depended on the army's ability to retaliate effectively against the tribe, and he pressed for decisive military action. As senator, Benjamin Harrison had supported Colonel Grierson's quest for promotion; Grierson and Major General Howard sent congratulatory notes to Harrison on his Republican nomination for the presidency in 1888. Miles penned a more extensive missive in the wake of Harrison's election, recommending that the president-elect recognize the importance of western affairs to the nation as a whole. Thus despite Sherman's dictum against political involvement, individual officers maintained some direct correspondence with the nation's political chiefs. Such connections, however, remained limited both in scope and in number.[6]

Military officers and congressmen were more often in contact for official business. Whether a result of a keen understanding of America's political system or simply because officers testified so frequently before congressional committees, this aspect of civil-military relations drew more attention from army officers. Key military issues

5. Crook to Hayes, Oct. 31, 1869, Hayes Library, Crook Papers; Hayes to Crook, Dec. 15, 1869, ibid.; Hayes to Mrs. Crook, Sept. 25, 1871, ibid.; Crook to Webb C. Hayes, Dec. 11, 1881, ibid.; Crook to Hayes, Dec. 18, 1881, ibid.; Sherman to Pope, Oct. 24, 1881, LC, Sherman Papers, 95, reel 47 (quotation); Schofield to Flood, Sept. 29, 1880, Box 13, LC, Schofield Papers; Flood to Schofield, Oct. 8, 1880, ibid., Box 11.

6. Faulk, *Geronimo Campaign*, 94; Sheridan to Crook, Dec. 29, 1885, Box 36, LC, Sheridan Papers; Harrison to Grierson, Endicott, June 22, 1885, LC, Harrison Papers, ser. 2, reel 47; Howard to Harrison, June 25, 1888, ibid., ser. 1, reel 8; Grierson to Harrison, ibid.; Miles to Harrison, Nov. 10, 1888, ibid., ser. 1, reel 12.

were appropriations for Indian supplies, the proper departmental location for the Bureau of Indian Affairs, and the maximum size and composition of the regular army.[7]

The funding and distribution of Indian supplies has little apparent connection with military strategy. As officers often pointed out, however, growing numbers of reservation Indians were in fact (if perhaps not in theory) becoming increasingly dependent on government aid. Treaty obligations required the government to provide varying degrees of support to Indians who accepted reservation life, in the form of rations, clothing, agricultural implements, and weapons. According to reformers, reservation tribes were to give up nomadic hunting and become farmers. The government was expected to provide certain necessities during the interim. In reality, Congress usually failed to appropriate enough money to fund such programs. Army officers and Indian agents alike knew that broken promises led peaceful Indians to mistrust them while encouraging nonreservation tribes in their armed opposition. Officials, complaining that starving Indians did not understand red tape or the "failure of an appropriation," recognized the direct correlation between the lack of food and Indian difficulties. "We are going to have trouble with these Indians . . . ," warned Sherman. "The Indian appropriations always fall short, and the army is in no condition to help."[8]

Both War and Interior Departments agreed that short supplies cause dissatisfaction among Native Americans and threatened the efficacy of government policy. No consensus existed, however, when discussion turned to the Bureau of Indian Affairs. Originally set up under the jurisdiction of the War Department, the bureau was moved to the newly created Interior Department in 1849. The bureau became a source of heated debate during the 1850s and again

7. Thomas, *American War and Peace*, 185–210.

8. Report of Crook, Sept. 23, SW, AR, 1878, 91 (first quotation); Sherman to Sheridan, May 12, 1877, LS, AGO, 60, reel 47 (second quotation). See also Sherman to Sheridan, Apr. 30, 1870, LC, Sherman Papers, 90, reel 45; Report of Sheridan, Oct. 25, SW, AR, 1878, 36–37.

sparked controversy after the Civil War. Promilitary sentiment held that its return to the War Department would reduce corruption in the administration of Indian affairs and would streamline federal policy-making. Those opposing such a transfer held that the peaceful duties of the Indian bureau were incompatible with the military goals of the army.

Objective observers recognized that the government's Indian policy was fostering neither peace along the frontiers nor the "civilization" of Indians. Attention thus focused on proposals to return the Bureau of Indian Affairs to the War Department as a possible improvement. Army officers eagerly joined the fray. On June 7, 1866, Grant noted that "every act of busy Indian agents demonstrates the importance of transferring [the] Indian Bureau to [the] War Department." In 1867, he advised Secretary of War Edwin Stanton, "If the present practice is to be continued, I do not see that any course is left open to us, but to withdraw our troops to the settlements or call upon Congress to provide means and troops to carry on formidable hostilities against the Indians until all the Indians or all the whites . . . are exterminated."[9]

Others also sprang to the attack. Reformer Welsh admitted that "I have known the Governor of a great State laughingly admit that for political hacks who were unfit for anything else he found places in the Indian service." Brigadier General Pope assailed the bureau's inefficiency and the divided jurisdiction that resulted from its position outside the War Department. Inspector General Nelson H. Davis cited the commonly held theory that Indians preferred to deal with the army. Sherman added that "the Army is more kindly disposed toward the Indians than the citizens generally." Schofield, commanding the Pacific division, had reversed his earlier opposition

9. Grant to Rawlins, June 7, 1866, LC, Grant Papers, ser. 5, 54, reel 24 (first quotation); Grant to Stanton, Feb. 1, 1867, ibid., ser. 5, 47, reel 21 (second quotation). See also Grant to Sherman, Jan. 15, 1867, ibid.; Grant to Sherman, Mar. 12, 1866, LC, Sherman Papers, 18, reel 10; Report of Grant, Nov. 21, SW, AR, 1866, 17–18; Report of Grant, Nov. 24, ibid., 1868, ix–x.

to transfer by 1875. "No class of citizens is more desirous of peace with the Indians than are officers of the Army," wrote Schofield. "There is no glory to be won in savage warfare." Army efforts culminated the following year when no less than sixty officers submitted reports to the House Military Affairs Committee supporting army control of the Indian bureau. Only two officers, General Howard and Surgeon Gen. J. K. Barnes, opposed its projected transfer to the War Department.[10]

Army officers criticized Indian agents almost gleefully. Some soldiers attributed the failure of civilian agents to their short terms of office and lack of power. Others, including Col. John Gibbon, believed the agents were too concerned with "elevating his [the Indian's] *soul*" and were too ignorant of his *"bodily"* wants." Most criticism centered around charges of corruption. The veteran Crook declared that there was "too much money in this Indian business" and hoped "that the honest & good people of the Country should understand what a gigantic fraud this Indian ring is."[11] Although

10. Welsh, "Meaning of the Dakota Outbreak," 448 (first quotation); Pope to Grant, Jan. 25, 1867, Senate Ex. Doc. No. 13, 40th Cong., 1st sess., 1867, ser. 1308, 49–52. Pope later reversed his position on transfer, arguing that much of the corruption in the Indian Bureau had ended. Testimony of Pope, Jan. 22, 1874, House Rpt. No. 384, 43d Cong., 1st sess., 1874, ser. 1624, 7–8. Testimony of Davis, Jan. 17, 1874, ibid., 167–69; Testimony of Sherman, Jan. 31, 1874, House Rpt. 384 (second quotation); Sherman to Saunders, Nov. 27, 1878, LC, Sherman Papers, 91, reel 45; Report of Schofield, Sept. 20, SW, AR, 1875, 122 (third and fourth quotations); Report of House Military Affairs Committee, Mar. 9, 1876, House Rpt. No. 354, 44th Cong., 1st sess., II, 1876, ser. 1709, 4–6; Howard to Banning, Feb. 25, 1876, ibid., 40; Barnes to Banning, Feb. 3, 1876, ibid., 168.

Although a public supporter of transfer, Sheridan wrote confidentially, "I care nothing about the transfer of the Indian Bureau to the War Dept. I don't want it. The transfer would be better for the Indian, . . . & it would be better for the Government, but I doubt if it would be better for the Army" (Sheridan to Sherman, Nov. 17, 1878, Sherman Papers, 48, reel 25).

11. Hazen to Sherman, Nov. 10, 1868, Senate Ex. Doc. No. 18, 40th Cong., 3rd sess., 1869, ser. 1360, 15–16; Report of Gibbon, Oct. 4, SW, AR, 1878, 69 (first quotation); Crook to Hayes, Nov. 28, 1871, Hayes Library, Crook Papers

Pope testified that most of the dishonest agents had been cleared from government rolls by 1874, Sheridan launched a vigorous campaign against alleged Interior Department corruption several years later. Challenged by Secretary of the Interior Schurz to document his claims, Sheridan called upon department commanders for evidence and presented a supplementary report listing specific charges in December 1878.[12]

Such interdepartmental resentment made cooperative efforts to administer Indian affairs extremely unlikely. Agent John P. Clum was "energetic and particularly desirous of demonstrating that the Indian Dept. has no need of the Army," wrote Colonel Kautz. "I shall give him every chance if he wants to risk his scalp in that sort of way." Sheridan forbade subordinates to correspond directly with the Interior Department, requiring them to communicate through slower army channels instead. The Interior Department responded in kind. Sherman found it almost impossible to get copies of Indian treaties from that agency. In addition, Indian agents commonly refused to divulge the locations of their wards.[13]

Although these problems hindered collaboration, some officers

---

(second quotation). Unrau, "Civilian as Indian Agent," argues that reports of agent dishonesty were exaggerated greatly. Keller, *American Protestantism and United States Indian Policy*, 235, notes that "the average Peace Policy agent remained at his post for 2.3 years."

12. Testimony of Pope, Jan. 22, 1874, House Rpt. No. 384, 43d Cong., 1st sess., ser. 1624, 7–8; Sheridan to Dept. Commanders, Nov. 25, 1878, Box 20, LC, Sheridan Papers; Sheridan to Sherman, Nov. 26, 1878, ibid.; Report of Sheridan, Dec. 22, 1878, Box 92, ibid.; Schurz to Miles, Dec. 26, 1878, LC, Schurz Papers, reel 86. Sheridan later gloated, "Old Schurz, just as you and I expected played the adroit in the correspondence but he has not made much by it. I made no attack on him, but on his system, and the evidence furnished will have its effect" (Sheridan to Pope, Jan. 11, 1879, Box 21, Sheridan Papers).

13. Sheridan to Ord, Feb. 18, 1874, Box 10, LC, Sheridan Papers; Kautz to Schofield, June 11, 1875, Box 5, LC, Schofield Papers (quotation); Sherman to Grant, Nov. 6, 1865, LC, Sherman Papers, 17, reel 10; Sherman to Brunot, Feb. 17, 1874, ibid., 90, reel 45; Sherman to Augur, Nov. 23, 1868, Ill. State Hist. Library, Augur Papers.

strove to improve relations with the civilian agents. Grierson joked and competed in friendly horseraces with Agent Lawrie Tatum in Indian Territory. Even the crusty Sheridan praised Commissioner of Indian Affairs Ely S. Parker. When convinced of their sincerity and competence, Crook cooperated with civilian agents. In addition to his frequent correspondence with reformers, Crook tried to establish working relationships with agents in Idaho, the Dakotas, and Arizona.[14]

In spite of such friendly overtures, these officers still maintained that the army should have ultimate control over Indian affairs. They and other officers proposed that the army, and not the Interior Department, should distribute supplies to Indians, reasoning that one branch of the government should not be feeding Indians while another was fighting them. An efficient, sensible policy administered by the army would replace the uncoordinated actions formerly undertaken by two distinct agencies, argued army critics. Military veterans also pointed out that the division of authority tarnished the all-important government image in Indian eyes. "They must believe that the power in charge of them has absolute power, and this belief cannot be weakened without danger," warned Crook in 1885. Instead of bewildering Indians with a divided front of civil agents, army officers, and special envoys, the army believed that one all-powerful department would ease relations between Indians and whites.[15]

Interior Department officials and reformers rejected these proposals. Exploiting the nation's traditional suspicions of the military,

14. Grierson to Alice Grierson, Feb. 14, 1872, Ill. State Hist. Library, Grierson Papers; Report of Sheridan, Nov. 1, SW, AR, 1869, 38; Crook to Floyd-Jones, Aug. 2, 1869, National Archives, LS, Dept. of the Columbia; Crook to Mc-Gillycuddy, Sept. 29, 1880, Hayes Library, Crook Papers; Crook to Teller, Mar. 27, 1883, ibid. On Tatum, see Cutler, "Lawrie Tatum and the Kiowa Agency." Henry J. Waltmann, "Ely Samuel Parker," in *Commissioners of Indian Affairs*, ed. Kvasnicka and Viola, 123–33.

15. Grant to Sherman, May 29, 1867, LC, Grant Papers, ser. 5, 47, reel 21; Report of Crook, Sept. 9, SW, AR, 1885, 175 (quotation).

they pointed out the evils of increasing the army's power. Transferring the Bureau of Indian Affairs would help legitimize a large standing military establishment, which in turn threatened democratic institutions. While civil agents went forth with peace and Christian love in their hearts, army officers had been trained for war. Reformer Welsh's testimony before the House Military Affairs Committee in 1876 typified the sentiments of many concerned Americans. He admitted that "I have seen enough of Generals Augur, Stanley, Ord, and others, to satisfy me that there are in the Army men who are eminently fitted for that work [distributing supplies]." Yet Welsh added that "General Sherman has no belief in the civilization of the Indians; and there is the difficulty." Welsh acknowledged that transferring the Indian bureau to the War Department might save money, but he deemed civilizing functions more important. "If the Indians are transferred to those who have no belief in their civilization, of course we could not expect much co-operation."[16]

Others criticized the army's methods of handling Indians. Agent John B. Sanborn stressed the futility of fighting Indians. "Pursuing them with a command sufficiently large, only one or two can occasionally be seen," he argued, "while with a small command, they are wont to mass and destroy it." He further charged that army officers "seem to be ruled and controlled by the ranchmen and contractors." Indian agents also asserted that Christian teaching and generous gifts, rather than the use of force, would lead the Indians onto the path of civilization. The agents believed their military counterparts to be guilty of rash, overaggressive actions. Extremists charged that the army covered up massacres. "I find it to be a secret

16. Testimony of Welsh, Feb. 26, 1876, House Rpt. No. 354, 44th Cong., 1st sess., II, 1876, ser. 1709, 218 (quotations). See also Report of the Indian Peace Commission, Jan. 7, 1868, House Ex. Doc. No. 97, 40th Cong., 2nd sess., XI, 1867, ser. 1337; Report of Browning, Nov. 30, SI, AR, 1868, iv; Report of Taylor, Nov. 23, ibid., 467–75; Report of Smith, Nov. 1, ibid., 1875, 521–23; Report of Schurz, Nov. 1, ibid., 1880, 17–18; D'Elia, "Argument over Civilian or Military Indian Control," 224.

order," claimed one correspondent, "that officers in the field are instructed not to report to their chief officially the full amount of killings, so that the public cannot find out their actions."[17]

As in the army, a few Indian agents and Interior Department officials cooperated with their rivals. Secretary of the Interior Jacob D. Cox, himself a Civil War veteran, found his former military associations helpful, and he noted in 1869 that "army officers . . . have co-operated with the greatest zeal in carrying out a peaceful policy." His commissioner of Indian affairs and fellow veteran, Parker, agreed that a "harmony of action" existed between the two departments. In 1872, Commissioner Edward Smith responded to army complaints by attempting to set up a superintendency in the Arizona Territory that would allow military commanders to speak with one person in authority instead of a confusing multitude of minor agents.[18]

More eager to smooth civil-military relations was Commissioner of Indian Affairs John Q. Smith. Particularly popular with the army was his January 1876 decision to permit offensives against nonreservation Sioux. Despite pleas from an agent at Standing Rock, Smith stressed the need "to execute threats of military operations so clearly made," and recommended that the army be cut loose from Interior Department controls and allowed to enter the field. Interior Secretary Zachariah Chandler agreed, thus clearing the way for the Sioux War of 1876.[19]

17. Sanborn to Browning, May 18, 1867, Senate Ex. Doc. No. 13, 40th Cong., 1st sess., ser. 1308, 113 (first and second quotations); Sanborn to Sherman, June 26, 1867, LC, Sherman Papers, 26, reel 14; Morrill to Whipple, Mar. 29, 1874, U.S. Army Hist. Res. Coll., Crook-Kennan Papers (third quotation); Doolittle, "Condition of the Indian Tribes," Senate Ex. Doc. No. 156,, 39th Cong., 2nd sess., 1867, ser. 1279, 6–7; Report of Mix, Nov. 15, SI, AR, 1867, 18; Wynkoop to Murphy, Sept. 14, ibid., 310–14; Report of Robinson, Nov. 16, ibid., 1868, 737–38; Schurz, "Present Aspects of the Indian Problem," 2.

18. Reports of Cox, Nov. 15, SI, AR, 1869, ix (first quotation), and Parker, Dec. 23, ibid., 448 (second quotation); Smith to Howard, June 12, 1872, Howard Papers.

19. Smith to Secretary of the Interior, Jan. 21, 1876, Box 91, LC, Sheridan

Above the bureaucratic struggles and mutual denouncements loomed Congress, especially powerful in the wake of the 1867–68 investigations, impeachment and trial of Andrew Johnson. Congress was the final arbiter not of Indian policy but of key questions concerning it, including the proposed transfer of the Indian bureau and the size of the regular army. Unfortunately, congressmen rarely considered these topics—so vital to Indian affairs—on their own merits. Instead, these issues became associated in almost every Capitol Hill debate with the equally controversial subjects of Reconstruction and the limits of federal authority.

Congress had dealt with several aspects of military conduct in the Civil War. The powerful Committee on the Conduct of the War, dominated by Republicans like Senator Benjamin F. Wade [Ohio], its chairman, had harrassed Union generals that it classified as Confederate sympathizers.[20] Congress continued to influence postbellum military policy through its control of appropriations and jobs. Reducing military expenditures remained a major item on the congressional agenda after the war. Grant, displaying surprising political acumen, warned Pope in 1865, "The cost of keeping the amount of cavalry called for on the prairies is so enormous. I wish you would cut down the expeditions all you can, and direct the animals be grazed." Grant's sense of the legislative mood was correct. An act of July 28, 1868, set the regular army at ten cavalry, five artillery, and forty-five infantry regiments, an aggregate of just over fifty-four-thousand men. This was a far cry from the volunteer army of the Civil War, which had been over one million strong.[21]

Papers (quotation); Smith to Chandler, Jan. 31, 1876, ibid.; Chandler to Secretary of War, Feb. 1, 1876, ibid.; Sherman to Smith, Jan. 23, 1878, LC, Sherman Papers, 90, reel 45; Sherman to Schurz, Jan. 25, ibid.

20. Williams, *Lincoln and the Radicals*, 65–76.

21. Grant to Pope, June 19, 1865, LC, Grant Papers, ser. 5, 46, reel 20 (quotation); Grant to Sherman, Aug. 21, ibid.; Grant to Stanton, Dec. 11, 1866, ibid., 47, reel 21; Report of Stanton, Nov. 14, SW, AR, 1866, 3; Report of Townsend, Oct. 20, SW, AR, Appendix, 1–3. Although the act reduced the

Later attacks on military funding grew more severe. Critics pointed out that even the 1868 reductions left the army 300 percent larger than it had been a decade earlier. Congressman William Lawrence [R–Ohio], a Union veteran, argued that "if there is one thing upon which the people of all political parties in this country are united in opinion it is that there ought to be a reduction in the expenditures for the Army and for the Navy." Most of his colleagues agreed. Congressman Fernando Wood [D–N.Y.] demanded that the army be cut to prewar levels. Others criticized James A. Garfield [R–Ohio], chairman of the House Military Affairs Committee and an army supporter, for spending too much time attacking the Indian bureau and not enough working out a viable army reduction plan. Despite Garfield's stalling tactics, the law of March 3, 1869, cut twenty infantry regiments from army rolls, thereby reducing the legal maximum to 37,313 men.[22]

The Democratic resurgence during the 1870s further weakened the army's position. Although attacks on the regular force were by no means limited to the House of Representatives or to the Democratic party, the Senate and Republicans in general were more sympathetic to army interests, despite the influence of militia advocate John Logan. Democratic attacks against Republican-dominated Reconstruction and against a powerful federal government carried over to the army, which had been a vital tool in the Republican arsenal. Military efforts against Indians were affected accordingly. A smaller regular army without complete authority to implement Indian policy could conduct only a limited number of strategic moves. Most troops had to be doled out in small, company-

number of troops available for duty, the regular army was still considerably larger than its 1861 strength of 39,273 (Heitman, *Historical Register* 2:601, 605).

22. For examples of debate, see *Cong. Globe*, 40th Cong., 3rd sess., 1869, pt. 2, 925–26 (quotation), 927, 950, 1328–29, 1334; Doolittle to President, May 9, 1867, LC, Johnson Papers, ser. 1, reel 27; Townsend to Sherman, Sept. 29, 1868, LS, AGO, 48, reel 35; Report of Sherman, Nov. 20, SW, AR, 1869, 23–24.

sized parcels along the long frontiers. Large-scale, simultaneous assaults against all tribes that the government believed dangerous were, as a result, impossible.[23]

The 1870s were a difficult time for army bills in Congress. An act of July 15, 1870, cut the maximum legal number of enlisted men to thirty-thousand.[24] Officers decried accompanying reductions in appropriations for housing and cavalry mounts. One complained privately that "members of Congress are most ignorant and in their legislation in regards to the army, the lack of knowledge on their part affects us most severely." Beginning in 1874, appropriations provided for a maximum of only twenty-five-thousand enlisted men.[25] However, a House-supported measure that would have reduced the army to 22,000 troops was stillborn in joint conference two years later as a result of Custer's disaster at the Little Bighorn. Pro-army legislators seized the opportunity to reverse the recent trend; Sherman advised Sheridan in July 1876 that "Congress is now in Session willing to give us all we want." New legislation allowed the president to increase the number of men per cavalry company from sixty-four to one hundred during the emergency resulting from Custer's defeat. Congress also approved funding for two new forts in the Yellowstone River country.[26]

Yet as the initial outrage over the Custer defeat wore off, Henry B. Banning [Ohio] and Edward S. Bragg [Wisc.] led House Dem-

23. Logan, *Volunteer Soldier of America*. Valuable are Rothman, *Politics and Power*; Morgan, *From Hayes to McKinley*; and Langley, "Democratic Tradition and Military Reform," 192–200.

24. U.S. Statutes at Large 16 (July 15, 1870): 315–21.

25. Kautz Diary, Dec. 31, 1873, LC, Kautz Papers (quotation); Belknap to Senate Appropriations Committee, Feb. 28, 1871, LS, SW, 65, reel 61; Heitman, *Historical Register* 2:613.

26. Sherman to Sheridan, July 22, 1876, LS, AGO, 59, reel 46 (quotation); *Cong. Rec.*, 44th Cong., 1st sess., 1876, pt. 4, 3356–57, 3463–64, 3468, 3780, 3839, 3845–49, pt. 5, p. 4743; Cameron to the President, Aug. 11, 1876, LS, SW, 80, reel 73; Report of Sherman, Nov. 10, SW, AR, 1876, 24; Report of Sheridan, Nov. 25, ibid., 445–47. Maxey to his wife, July 15, 1876, Texas State Archives, Maxey Papers.

ocrats in introducing new reduction measures. When the Senate failed to slash the army to seventeen-thousand or to prohibit the use of troops to support Republican state governments in Louisiana and South Carolina, the House of Representatives refused to pass an army appropriations bill. Soldiers were without pay from July to November 1877, when a special session of Congress finally approved a stopgap measure. Congressman Gustav Schleicher [D–Tex.] warned Sherman that, although most of the Texas delegation supported the army, "We feel the dilemma which makes us powerless and even makes our own support almost impossible. The only thing which would help us would be the removal of troops from those States [South Carolina and Louisiana]." Sherman admitted that the army owed the Texans "a debt of gratitude," and predicted that the army would be "slaughtered" in the next session without their support.[27]

As expected, Banning, Bragg, and their associates resumed the offensive in 1878. House Democrats lambasted the army's alleged interference in the disputed presidential elections of 1876, in which Republican Rutherford B. Hayes was awarded a controversial victory over Samuel J. Tilden, and in the labor strikes of 1877, during which angry workers blocked rail traffic over much of the nation. "During the last ten years not one-half of our Army has been employed for legitimate purposes," argued Milton I. Southard [D–Ohio]. "Its use has consisted mainly of running elections and keeping the dominant party in power." Former Confederate officials, such as John H. Reagan [D–Tex.] (Postmaster General) and Washington C. Whitthorne [D–Tenn.] (State Adjutant General), demanded cuts in military salaries and in the number of enlisted men. Several Republicans like John Logan championed the militia at the expense of the regular army. Benjamin F. Butler [R–Mass.], recalling the

27. *Cong. Rec.*, 44th Cong., 2nd sess., 1877, pt. 3, 2111–12, 2178, 2246–49, 2251–52; Schleicher to Sherman, Apr. 2, 1877, LC, Sherman Papers, 46, reel 24 (first quotation); Sherman to Sheridan, Nov. 29, 1877, ibid., 90, reel 45 (second quotation).

exploits of volunteers and militia throughout the country's history, believed the frontier could be defended by giving arms to families "with strong, stalwart workingmen at their heads." The House passed another measure reducing the number of enlisted men to twenty-thousand, but with such western senators as Aaron A. Sargent [R–Cal.], Samuel Maxey [D–Tex.], Henry M. Teller [R–Colo.], and John James [R–Kan.] leading the vocal opposition, the Senate again refused to accept the House bill.[28]

Congress organized a joint committee to resolve the impasse. Chaired by former Union general Ambrose E. Burnside [R–R.I.], the committee drew up plans for a comprehensive reorganization of the regular army. The Burnside committee recommended a twenty-five-thousand-strong force, with eighteen infantry, five artillery, and eight cavalry regiments. The adjutant general's and inspector general's departments were to be combined into a general staff. Sherman and Sheridan gave their approval, as did Congressman Banning. But staff officers, militia advocates, and die-hard regular-army opponents, anxious to avoid the loss of influence such a move would have entailed, joined those demanding restrictions in the president's use of the military against civilians in lobbying to defeat the Burnside measure.[29]

Debate concerning the proposed transfer of the Bureau of Indian Affairs to the War Department was no less heated. The House agreed with army claims that such action would improve efficiency and streamline jurisdiction in Indian administration and, guided by Military Affairs Committee Chairman Garfield, it passed transfer bills in 1867 and 1868. The Senate, more sympathetic to the views of Indian reformers, refused to support such legislation. Military men believed that they had circumvented Senate opposition when President Grant began using army officers as superintendents and

28. *Cong. Rec.*, 45th Cong., 2 sess., 1878, pt. 1, 963–69, pt. 4, 3615–17, 3677 (first quotation); 3631–35 (second quotation), 3798–99, pt. 5, 4180, 4183; Boylan, "Forty-Fifth Congress and Army Reform," 173–86.

29. Thomas, "Ambrose E. Burnside and Army Reform," 3–13.

agents in the Indian service. Grant's decision to give the military full authority over Indians outside reservations also satisfied officers. Congress, smarting at Grant's interference in its patronage and shocked by Maj. Eugene M. Baker's slaughter of 173 Piegan Indians (including 53 women and children) in the Department of Dakota, retaliated in 1870. It refused to support transfer of the bureau and made regular officers ineligible for civil positions, thus dashing army hopes on several counts.[30]

Subsequent congresses acted along similar lines; as a result, the Bureau of Indian Affairs was never transferred to the War Department. In 1876, the House Military Affairs Committee again recommended that the Indian office be shifted to the War Department. Two years later, the House Committee on Indian Affairs made similar proposals despite minority claims that "to talk of any civilizing influence in the Army, seems to us, preposterous." Army officials recognized that, as the perceived Indian threat diminished, congressional interest in the transfer issue also waned. As Secretary of War Redfield Proctor advised Secretary of the Interior John W. Noble in 1890, "If it [transfer of the bureau] was an open question twenty-five or fifty years ago, it is not now."[31]

The failure of the Burnside proposal and the transfer bills marked the end of significant congressional interest in the army until the Spanish-American War. Sectional rivalries cooled, and Congress easily passed an army appropriations bill in 1879. Naval theorists seized the opportunity to push their own interests. Naval officers and

30. Garfield, "Indian Question in Congress and in Kansas," 33; Sherman to Sheridan, May 8 and June 11, 1869, LS, AGO, 50, reel 37; Utley, *Frontier Regulars*, 197–98; Grant, Annual Message, Dec. 5, 1870, in Richardson, comp., *Messages and Papers of the Presidents* 7:109.

31. House Rpt. No. 240, 44th Cong., 1st sess., I, 1876, ser. 1708, 1–12; House Rpt. No. 354, 44th Cong., 1st sess., II, 1876, ser. 1709, 1–6; Maxey to his wife, Mar. 7, June 21, 1876, Texas State Archives, Maxey Papers; House Rpt. No. 241, 45th Cong., 2nd sess., I, 1878, ser. 1822, 1–12, 19 (first quotation); Proctor to Noble, Dec. 27, 1890, Proctor Library, Proctor Papers (second quotation).

dynamic leaders like senators Joseph R. Hawley [R–Conn.] and John T. Morgan [D–Ala.] and representatives Henry Cabot Lodge [R–Mass.] and William McAdoo [D–N.J.] convinced Congress to launch massive naval modernization programs. European involvement in the Pacific, threats to the Monroe Doctrine, and dreams of an international marketplace protected by majestic new battleships were more politically viable than the bluecoats' enforcement of an uncertain Indian policy. In addition, army leaders never mounted a congressional lobbying campaign as effective as that of their naval counterparts, although Sheridan did mount a strong effort to expand Yellowstone Park's boundaries and have that area policed by the army.[32] This failure at lobbying was at least in part attributable to Sherman's dominance within the army. His adamant refusal to become immersed in the legislative process was a legacy that Sheridan and Schofield for the most part accepted.

Army relations with Mexico, Canada, and the State Department also affected the military's handling of Indian affairs. Fiercely independent tribes living along the nation's northern and southwestern borders had neither the need nor the inclination to respect international boundaries. Army officials charged that these Indians committed depradations in the United States and then crossed the border into Mexico or Canada. Military men wanted permission to pursue guilty tribesmen into foreign lands; they also sought international cooperation in their efforts to defeat hostile borderland tribes.

Disputes with Mexico were the most controversial. Emperor Maximilian's abortive foray into Mexico in the mid–1860s caused special concern in the United States, with many afraid that French support

---

32. *Cong. Rec.*, 46th Cong., 1st sess., IX, pt. 2, 1928–42, 2062–83, 2103–55, 2199–243; Sexton, "Forging the Sword," 280, 288–91; Karsten, "Armed Progressives," in *Military in America*, 238–39; Hutton, *Phil Sheridan*, 355–60. Langley, "Democratic Tradition and Military Reform," 192–200, emphasizes the efforts of those who sought to apply business reforms to the military.

for the short-lived regime was indicative of renewed European involvement in the Americas. While Grant refused a State Department request that he go to Mexico and handle the situation personally, Sheridan did assemble some fifty-thousand men along the Rio Grande as an indication of U.S. concern. As Mexicans ousted Maximilian and regained control of the central government, increased Kickapoo and Apache raids from Mexico into Texas and New Mexico led the State Department to propose in 1870 that the United States Army be allowed to pursue Indians across the border. Mexican authorities, afraid of damaging their domestic political reputations, refused the request. United States policymakers then resorted to attempts to lure troublesome Mexican-based tribes onto reservations in the United States. Impatient American civil and military officers found these efforts unsatisfactory, but political unrest and opposition to Yankee incursions in Mexico made effective cooperation difficult. In February 1873, after Sherman had ordered Christopher C. Augur to consult with Mexican authorities, Augur, commanding the Department of Texas, complained that "the trouble, at present, is to find such authority."[33]

Lightning struck three months later. Mackenzie, transferred with his Fourth Cavalry to Texas to deal with the border problem, crossed the Rio Grande during the night of May 17, destroyed three Indian villages the next morning near Remolino, forty miles west of Piedras Negras, and returned to the United States on May 19. In secret meetings held a month earlier, Sheridan had given Mackenzie permission to make this extralegal strike with the implicit consent of

33. Memo, "General Grant and the Mexican Mission," Oct. 27, 1866, LC, Johnson Papers, ser. 1, reel 25; Schofield, *Forty-six Years in the Army*, 378–93; Clendenen, *Blood on the Border*, 56–57, 62–63; Augur to Sherman, Feb. 19, 1873, National Archives, LS, Dept. of Texas (quotation); Sheridan, endorsement of May 20, 1873, U.S. Army Hist. Res. Coll., Mackenzie Papers. Augur later expressed hope that some Mexican officials could be helpful. Augur to Fuero, Jan. 5, 1875, LS, Dept. of Texas; Augur to Sherman, Jan. 11, ibid.; Augur to Ochoa, Mar. 10, ibid.

Grant and Secretary of War Belknap.[34] Sheridan later acknowledged that "Mackenzie has done a good thing. I told Blank [probably Belknap or Sherman] when here a short time ago that Mackenzie was going over and he said all right." Mackenzie knew that both Sheridan and Augur would vigorously support his aggressiveness. The move was not totally unexpected by State Department officials, whose protests, along with those of Mexican officials, were surprisingly mild.[35]

The action at Remolino was more akin to a massacre than a battle, as Indian warriors were away hunting when the attack occurred. Mackenzie's swift thrust nonetheless slowed border depredations for two years and convinced about four-hundred Kickapoos to move north to the Indian Territory. But as memories of the strike dimmed, Indian raids again reached intolerable levels. In 1874, the state of Texas created a special Ranger force to deal with Indian and Mexican raiders along the lower Rio Grande. The regular military also stepped up its efforts in Texas; new department chief Ord requested naval support on the Rio Grande. The navy's response came in the form of USS *Rio Bravo*, a sidewheel steamboat that patrolled the area from 1875 to 1879. The naval presence apparently did little to deter cattle rustlers; nonetheless, it indicated a degree of federal interest in south Texas.[36]

34. Carter, *On the Border*, 422–23; Testimony of McCrary, Dec. 10, 1877, House Misc. Doc. No. 64, 45th Cong., 2nd sess., VI, ser. 820, 7.

35. Sheridan to Augur, May 27, 1873, U.S. Army Hist. Res. Coll., Mackenzie Papers (quotation); Sheridan to Belknap, May 22, 28, 1873, Box 58, LC, Sheridan Papers: Sheridan to Mackenzie, June 2, 1873, Mackenzie Papers; Augur to Sheridan, June 4, 1873, National Archives, LS, Dept. of Texas; Sheridan, endorsement of June 5, 1873, Box 9, LC, Sheridan Papers; Mackenzie to Augur, June 6, 1873, Mackenzie Papers; Augur to Sheridan, July 22, 1874, LS, Dept. of Texas. See also "Private Letter Book of Col. R. S. Mackenzie 4 Cavalry, 1873–74," Mackenzie Papers; Rippy, *U.S. and Mexico*, 288–89.

36. Utley, *Frontier Regulars*, 358–59; Wallace and Anderson, "R. S. Mackenzie and the Kickapoos," 116, 124–26; Robinson, "U.S. Navy vs. Cattle Rustlers," 43–52. Primary accounts are in Carter, *On the Border*, 429–55; and Beaumont, "Over the Border with Mackenzie."

Ord sought to combine the army's efforts with those of Texas
Rangers, the small U.S. naval presence in the lower Rio Grande
valley, and Mexican forces. An army detachment supported Texas
Ranger Capt. Leander H. McNelly's cross-border raid on Las Cuevas
in late 1875. Such schemes proving ineffective, Ord contacted Senator Maxey [D–Tex.], who in turn spoke with the Mexican minister
in Washington. Temperamental, active, and impatient, Ord sent
Lt. Col. William R. Shafter into Mexico in the early summer of
1876. Although Ord assured Sherman that "Sheridan gave me a
quasi permission when I was in Washington, by saying why the
devil dont [sic] you do it," Ord worried that Secretary of State
Hamilton Fish "may present my name to the president for removal
on charges of violating neutrality." Responding to criticism from
Sherman, who apparently had not given approval for the raid, Ord
later asserted, "I talked the matter over with him [Sheridan] and
the president. Sheridan said 'Why the devil dont [sic] you go over
after them'—the President said—'I would have given orders to do
so long ago, but for the news papers which would have raised the
cry that I was making war against Mexico.' "[37]

Ord's initiative made him a hero to Texans. His contempt for
Indians was clear: Apaches in particular were "robbers and murderers" who should be hunted by troops "as they would wild animals." Determined to stop the border raids, he proposed invading
northern Mexico in order to set up authorities who would cooperate
with the United States. Such a move, he maintained, would help
the Texas Pacific Railroad and guarantee southern Democratic support for the army. Ord also established close contact with John W.
Foster and John Weber, members of the United States legation in

37. Ord to Sherman, July 6, 1875, LC, Sherman Papers, 39, reel 21; Ord to
Governor of Texas, May 13, 1875, National Archives, LS, Dept. of Texas; Ord
to Ammen, Aug. 19, 1875, ibid.; Ord to AAG, Nov. 18, 1875, ibid.; Ord to
Potter, Nov. 19, 1875, ibid.; Maxey to Ord, Dec. 17, 24, 1875, Bancroft Library,
Ord Papers; Davis to Belknap, June 29, 1875, ibid.; Ord to Sherman, June 27,
1876, LC, Sherman Papers, 43, reel 23 (first two quotations); Ord to Sherman,
Nov. 13, 1876, Ord Papers (third quotation).

Mexico, discussing with them that country's attitudes and efforts to solve the border problem. The irrepressible Ord also met with Hayes, Sherman, Secretary of War George W. McCrary, and Secretary of State William M. Evarts, convincing his superiors to give him the authority to pursue marauders across the Rio Grande "when his troops are either in sight of them or upon a fresh trail."[38] Evarts advised his minister to Mexico that Mexican consent for such a crossing was preferable but not essential.[39] Still not satisfied, Ord informed Congressman Schleicher [D–Tex.] that "The army people are all much obliged to you especially and the Texas Delegation generally for your successful efforts in our favor. . . . If the Texas Delegation, will in a body call on the President to let Texas have that part of the Army, 5,000 men, for her protection, which that delegation secured to it by their votes, they can I am quite sure get it."[40]

With mounting congressional attacks threatening its very existence, the army was dependent on Texan support by 1877. Increasingly suspicious of Ord's handling of the delicate border situation, Sherman was torn by conflicting emotions. He and Ord, whom he characterized as "a rough diamond, always at work," had enjoyed a thirty-year friendship. Yet his trusted subordinate, Sheridan, believed that Ord was incapable of handling the department and called for Ord's removal. Pulling the popular Ord from Texas risked angering that state's delegation and invited disastrous congressional

38. Report of Ord, Sept. 27, SW, AR, 1869, 121 (first and second quotations); Ord to Sherman, Nov. 13, 1876, Bancroft Library, Ord Papers; Ord to Shafter, Apr. 1, 1877, ibid.; Ord to Schleicher, Nov. 24, 1877, ibid.; Foster to Ord, July 16 and Aug. 26, 1878, ibid.; see numerous letters from Weber to Ord, Nov. 17, 1877–Apr. 18, 1880, ibid.; Sherman to Foster, June 9, 1876, LC, Sherman Papers, 90, reel 45; McCrary to Sherman, June 1, 1877, LS, SW, 82, reel 75 (third quotation).

39. McCrary to Sherman, June 1, 1877, LS, SW, 82, reel 75; Evarts to Foster, Mar. 31, 1877, Stanford Univ. Library, Shafter Papers, reel 1; Cresap, *Appomattox Commander*, 309–13.

40. Ord to Schleicher, Nov. 24, 1877, Bancroft Library, Ord Papers.

defeats. Mexico, under the new Porfirio Díaz regime, demanded that United States Army intrusions be halted. Tension grew when Lieutenant Colonel Shafter and Lieutenant John L. Bullis encountered Mexican troops during another border incursion in September 1877. The Hayes administration, while extending recognition to the Díaz government the following year, refused to withdraw permission for Ord to give hot pursuit across the border.[41]

At this point Mackenzie and his Fourth Cavalry, fresh from service in the Black Hills and the Indian Territory, returned to the fray. In July 1878, Ord sent Mackenzie and over one thousand men into Mexico. Mackenzie twice bullied a smaller Mexican force into retreat; Mexican protests reached new extremes. But as the Díaz government gained stability, Mexican Gen. Geronimo Treviño stepped up efforts to crush Indian offenders in his country. Strong congressional criticism of Hayes's brinkmanship and the increased evidence of Mexico's willingness and ability to deal with the problem, which Ord acknowledged in 1879, led the president to revoke the "Ord Order" the following February. Within a year, Hayes shocked the army by forcing Ord, a Democrat, into retirement, allowing fellow Republican Miles to secure his general's star.[42]

Officials of all concerned agencies were determined to prevent a similar crisis along the southern borders of New Mexico and Arizona. Here the situation was reversed, as Indians from the Fort Stanton and Chiricahua reservations under the elusive leadership of Victorio and Geronimo plundered Chihuahua and Sonora. In response, colonels George P. Buell and Eugene A. Carr led a strong force into Mexico in September 1880 in an abortive attempt to join forces

41. Sherman to Terry, Dec. 5, 1880, LC, Sherman Papers, 91, reel 45 (quotation); Sheridan to Sherman, ibid., 46, reel 24; Sheridan to Sherman, Dec. 12, 1879, ibid., 51, reel 26; Pope to Sherman, Feb. 18, 1880, ibid.; Hackett, "Recognition of the Diaz Government," 41–55; Rippy, *U.S. and Mexico*, 296–309.

42. Utley, *Frontier Regulars*, 362–65; Rippy, *U.S. and Mexico*, 309–10; Wallace, ed., *Ranald S. Mackenzie's Official Correspondence* 2:201–10; Moffitt to Bullis, Nov. 16, 1878, Bancroft Library, Ord Papers; Ord to Sherman, Jan. 30, 1879, LC, Sherman Papers, 49, reel 25; Report of Ord, Oct. 1, SW, AR, 1879, 93.

with Col. Joaquin Terrazas. A year and a half later, Lt. Col. George
A. Forsyth crossed the border in pursuit of hostile Apaches. Crook
led a more effective expedition in 1883, and captains Emmet Crawford, Wirt Davis, and Henry W. Lawton followed Crook's example
in 1885–86.[43]

While not without incident, American forays into Mexico in the
Far Southwest were less controversial than those from Texas across
the Rio Grande. Mexican troops shot Captain Crawford in one particularly violent episode, but several precautionary measures prevented even greater furor.[44] Having experienced near disaster in
Texas and Coahuila, both sides seemed cognizant of the explosive
potential of U.S. forays into Mexico. Hayes's recognition of the Díaz
regime and revocation of the Ord Order made it easier for the
Mexican president to sign reciprocal crossing agreements. Secretary
of War Robert Lincoln kept the State Department well informed of
army actions.[45] Crook also deserves much credit. He corresponded
directly with Mexican officials, including generals Bernardo Reyes
and B. Topete, Sonoran Governor Luis Torres, and Consul A. V.
Lomelo, seeking cooperation in handling guilty Indians. Risking
War Department censure, Crook also visited authorities in Sonora
and Chihuahua in the spring of 1883, paving the way for his expeditions into Mexico. Crook's successor, Miles, also spoke with
Torres in August 1886, easing Mexican fears of a United States
invasion.[46]

43. Utley, *Frontier Regulars*, 365–74, 379–400; Clendenen, *Blood on the Border*,
92–112; Greene, "Crawford Affair," 143–53.

44. Utley, *Frontier Regulars*, 387–95.

45. Crosby to Secretary of State (hereafter SS), Sept. 11, 1880, LS, SW, 88,
reel 80; Lincoln to SS, Sept. 28, 1881, ibid., 93, reel 83; Lincoln to SS, Jan. 17,
1882, ibid., 95, reel 84; Lincoln to SS, Mar. 6, 1882, ibid., 96, reel 84; Lincoln
to SS, May 1, 1882, ibid., 97, reel 85; Sherman to AG, May 2, 1882, LC, Sherman
Papers, 95, reel 47; Lincoln to SS, Apr. 9, 1883, LS, SW, 102, reel 87.

46. Crook to Reyes, Nov. 14, 1882, National Archives, LS, Dept. of Ariz.;
Crook to Lomelo, Mar. 28, 1883, ibid.; Crook to AG, Apr. 30, 1883, ibid.;
Crook to Major Gen. Commanding Mexican Troops, Mar. 28, June 13, 1883,
Hayes Library, Crook Papers; Crook to Topete, Nov. 22, 1883, ibid.; Crook to

The cooperative efforts of the War and State Departments which characterized the method of handling problems in the Far Southwest also typified affairs regarding Canada. As in the Southwest, however, domestic political unrest threatened to disrupt international relations. Many Canadians, seizing upon expansionist statements by Grant, Secretary of State Fish, and Senator (later Secretary of War) Alexander Ramsey [R–Minn.], feared American takeover. The 1867 purchase of Alaska by the United States was often perceived as an attempt to isolate British Columbia from the newly created Dominion. While calmer heads recognized that the American public lacked interest in northern expansion, the threat of annexation never fully disappeared.[47]

Later events further threatened the international harmony necessary for a judicious solution to Indian affairs in the north. Many Americans of Irish heritage, for example, sympathized with the Fenian movement of the late 1860s and early 1870s, which threatened to disrupt the new Dominion. However, the U.S. military remained neutral, and Secretary of War Belknap assured the State Department that Fenians from the United States would not be allowed to invade Canada. Led by Louis Riel, the Métis of the Red River area, anxious to retain cultural distinctiveness and political rights, rebelled against Canadian authorities in 1869. Previous assurances of American neutrality notwithstanding, Belknap's refusal to allow British ships carrying supplies for the Dominion's counterthrust through the American canal at Sault Ste. Marie lent credence to Canadian fears. Faced by a sizable British-Canadian force, Riel fled and his rebellion collapsed; nonetheless, the incident posed a further obstacle to international harmony.[48]

Torres, Apr. 14, 1884, and June 12, 1885, ibid.; Miles to Ruiz, Apr. 28, 1886, LS, Dept. of Ariz.; Drum to Endicott, Aug. 20, 1886, LC, Cleveland Papers, ser. 2, reel 38.

47. Warner, *Idea of Continental Union*, 95–98, 105, 131, 251–54; Hitsman, *Safeguarding Canada*, 224–28.

48. Neidhardt, *Fenianism in North America*, 131–33; Stacey, "Fenianism and the Rise of National Feeling in Canada," 238–59; Belknap to SS, Oct. 3, 1867,

The two nations patched up most of their problems before Sitting Bull's flight into Canada brought their respective military forces into direct contact. The North West Mounted Police opposed American military pursuit across the border but feared that the new influx of Indians would endanger the already diminished buffalo herds and lead to violence between the Sioux, Blackfeet, and Cree. In an attempt to avoid violence, Commissioner James McLeod of the North West Mounted Police arranged for Sitting Bull and General Terry to meet at Fort Walsh in October 1877.[49]

Although army officers trusted that Canadian officials acted in good faith, the officers recognized that the Fort Walsh talks had failed and they feared that the Sioux would reenter the United States and rally all the disaffected tribes. Eager to avoid this possibility, Miles requested permission to lead a strike across the border. General Sherman ordered Miles to do nothing of the sort without the president's direct authorization. In July 1879, Sherman advised Sheridan to keep a close watch over Miles and to maintain amicable relations with Canada. A meeting between Secretary of War McCrary and Secretary of the Interior Schurz yielded similar conclusions—that caution was more desirable than a controversial cross-border raid.[50]

Officials in the War, State, and even Interior departments continued to monitor the tense situation, maintaining close communications with Dominion authorities as well. Sitting Bull's surrender at Fort Buford in July 1881 seemed a melodramatic denouement to the struggle. Miles, however, believed that the army should be

---

LS, SW, 67, reel 62; Warner, *Idea of Continental Union*, 109–12; Preston, *Defence of the Undefended Border*, 46–50.

49. Turner, *North West Mounted Police* 1:passim.; Report of Schurz, Nov. 1, SI, AR, 1877, iv–v; McLeod to Terry and Lawrence, Oct. 17, 1877, House Exec. Doc. No. 1, pt. 1, 44 Cong., 2nd sess., ser. 1741, 345; McCrary to Terry, Sept. 6, 1877, LS, SW, 81, reel 74.

50. Miles to Sherman, Jan. 8, 1878, LC, Sherman Papers, 46, reel 24; Sherman to Miles, Feb. 9, 1878, ibid., 90, reel 45; Sheridan to Sherman, Oct. 19, 1878, Box 20, LC, Sheridan Papers; Sherman to Sheridan, Apr. 13, July 19, 25, 1879, LC, Sherman Papers, 90, reel 45; *New York Times*, July 23, 24, and 25, 1879.

ready to push farther north. "I think it too soon to occupy the Boundary line now, when we are ready for that the North Pole may be the boundary," he predicted. A general respect for the institutions of Britain and the Dominion prevented such sentiment from destroying relations; moreover, Sherman clearly reiterated his unqualified opposition to crossings into Canada. War secretaries Lincoln and Endicott remained interested in the situation along the nation's northern boundary and corresponded regularly with their peers in the State Department. Potentially explosive events, such as the Riel Rebellion in the western interior of Canada in 1885, were resolved without damage to political relations.[51]

The United States military had to contend with regional and local politics and practicalities as well as international problems. The army, as an active, visible agent of Washington's power and authority, provided much more than just security. Cities west of the Mississippi looked to the military for many services. A fort meant jobs and patronage. A successful military post needed food, building materials, clothing, mules, horses, household items, and recreational facilities. Supply contracts for hungry men and animals could make or break a western trader. Army troops patronized saloons, stores, and brothels, and officers mixed with their wealthier, better-educated civilian neighbors. The military thus influenced the economic, social, and political structure of the states, territories, and communities it protected.[52]

51. McCrary to SS, Sept. 3, 1879, LS, SW, 85, reel 78; Ramsey to SI, Jan. 15, 21, 24, 1881, ibid., 91, reel 82; *New York Times*, July 21, 1881; Miles to Sherman, Dec. 12, 1881, LC, Sherman Papers, 57, reel 30 (quotation); Tweedale to SS, Apr. 12, 1882, LS, SW, 95, reel 84; Lincoln to SS, Apr. 12, 1883, ibid., 102, reel 87; Endicott to SS, Apr. 22, 1885, ibid., 110, reel 87; Endicott to SS, Apr. 22, 1885, ibid., 110, reel 94; Endicott to SI, SS, June 21, 1887, LS, AGO, 117, reel 100.

52. Maginnis to Lamont, Feb. 15, 1893, LC, Lamont Papers; Mattison, "Army Post on the Northern Plains," 41–42. On western politics, see Lamar, *Dakota Territory* and *Far Southwest*; and Gould, *Wyoming*. The army's role in facilitating settlement is seen in Guentzel, "Department of the Platte and Western Settlement."

Forts, the backbone of the army's western presence, also provided a key element in nineteenth-century military efforts against Indians. Offensive expeditions could be organized and scouting parties based at these secure positions. Ideally, military posts were located according to rational plans agreed upon by political as well as military leaders, according to regional rather than local needs. This was seldom the case. No one could predict where or when new settlements would spring up. In addition, the frontiers did not move in the strictly linear fashion that would have facilitated the army's tasks. Settlers tended to move in sporadic bursts to isolated pockets of territory rather than according to predictable patterns, thus precluding the army's construction of a neat line of equidistant forts in advance of settlement.

Special conditions in Texas caused further difficulties. During Reconstruction, troops often protected federal authority in the state's interior rather than fighting Indians on the frontiers. Army officials believed Texans deliberately exaggerated Indian outrages so as "to have all the troops removed from the interior." Sheridan's infamous remark "If I owned hell and Texas, I would rent out Texas and live in hell!" added to the animosity at the military and the federal government of many Texans. State ownership of public lands created additional problems, as the army's limited budget seldom included funds for outright land purchases in Texas. Instead, the army leased the land on which it built forts. Cagey speculators, smelling the scent of potential profits, often discovered where posts were to be constructed, bought the land themselves, and then charged the military exhorbitant rates. The War Department's heavy-handed threats to withdraw the army from Texas altogether proved to be impolitic, but the uneasy tenancy worried officials for the remainder of the century.[53]

53. Sheridan to Grant, Oct. 12, 1866, LC, Grant Papers, ser. 5, 54, reel 24 (first quotation); Belknap to the Gov. of Texas, Aug. 14, 1871, LS, SW, 67, reel 62; Highland, "Sheridan's 'Hell and Texas' Remark," 197–98 (second quotation). See also Sheridan to Grant, Oct. 3, 1866, Senate Ex. Doc. No. 19, 45th Cong., 2nd sess., I, 1878, ser. 1780, 7.

To further complicate the military's problems on the frontiers, some westerners became particularly adept at securing an army presence. A delegate, congressman, or governor who obtained or increased military garrisons in his area gained important leverage with constituents. Francis E. Warren of Wyoming realized better than most the political and economic advantages of having military forts. In defending Fort McKinney's continued existence, he wrote in 1894,

> From every point of view [Fort] McKinney ought to be retained. . . . It is a great pity that our member of Congress, [Henry A.] Coffeen, should have stirred up the subject of removing this post to another point, because, for a Senator or member of Congress to even intimate that a post should or could be removed, is to admit its lack of usefulness. It has long been known by men of sense that to intimate to the War Department a desire to change the location of a post, or to cut down a reservation, is to invite its destruction.[54]

Two years later, Warren pointed out the benefits of Indian outbreaks for justifying continued military presence. "The Indian scare seems to have blown in some good," Warren explained, "in the way of increasing the force at the Post."[55] Warren's boosterism continued long after any serious Indian threat had passed. In a 1902 letter he again pled Wyoming's case:

> I know of no post in the United States which is better fitted for artillery than is Russell. There are several thousand acres of beautifully situated land—all the room necessary for drilling artillery,

54. Warren to C. H. Parmelee, Sept. 22, 1894, West. Hist. Res. Center, Warren Papers (courtesy of Dr. Lewis L. Gould, University of Texas). Gould has labeled Warren "a pork-barrel virtuoso and bureaucratic in-fighter unmatched in the history of the West" (Gould, "Francis E. Warren and the Johnson County War," 142). See also Hansen, "Congressional Career of Senator Francis E. Warren."

55. Warren to Moore, Oct. 29, 1895, West. Hist. Res. Center, Warren Papers. Paschal to Lamont, Mar. 19, 1894, Box 35, LC, Lamont Papers, is also instructive.

cavalry, or infantry, or all together, in regiment, brigade, or division. There is any amount of grass and water for the support of animals throughout the year, if it is thought best to pasture. And, in fact, every facility which I can think of is present and applicable.[56]

Military leaders recognized that political considerations often influenced the determination of sites for posts. It was obvious that civilian recommendations for military sites depended far too frequently on the dollar. Consequently, officers stressed that forts be built according to regional rather than local needs. But the army's dependence on Congress for appropriations made it absolutely essential to include legislators in the selection process, a practice that senior officers used to woo prospective allies or to reward loyal supporters. The Texas delegation won special consideration for its promilitary stance despite its lack of cooperation in securing public lands for the army. Texan support, essentially from Senator Maxey, was crucial to prevent the reduction of the regular army below twenty-five-thousand. Senator John Sherman introduced his brother William to Maxey on a West Point–bound train in June 1876. Maxey related that the general "was very sociable and wholly without airs." The two recognized that cooperation was in their mutual interest. As Maxey recalled, "Seeing that he wanted to be friendly I met him halfway, not only because it was right, but because it is to the interest of Texas with her immense frontier to be protected, that I should be on good terms with the General of the Army." And when Sheridan considered building a new post between either

56. Warren to Corbin, Apr. 30, 1902, ibid. For other examples of Warren's boosterism, see Warren to Breckons, Mar. 20, 1898, ibid.; Warren to Gillette, Nov. 24, 1911, ibid.; Warren to Boehme, Mar. 22, 1912, ibid. Sheridan to Sherman, Apr. 10, 1880, Box 59, LC, Sheridan Papers; Sheridan to Pope, Apr. 15, ibid.; Singisen to Sheridan, May 5, 1884, ibid., Box 34; Sheridan to Dolph, Nov. 8, 1887, ibid., Box 44; Ruger to Gov. of Montana, Aug. 30, 1890, National Archives, LS, Dept. of Dakota; Maxey to his wife, Feb. 17, 1876, Texas State Archives, Maxey Papers; Maxey to Maxey, Feb. 5, 1879, ibid.

forts Sill and Griffin or forts Concho and Elliott, he asked the "Texas delegation to fix the most suitable point of the two."[57]

Perhaps the most comprehensive effort to rationalize the location of forts came when Sherman filed extensive reports on the value of existing forts during an extended tour of the Southwest and the Pacific Coast. The thrust of his argument was that the railroads, by easing troop movements and encouraging new settlement, had fundamentally changed the defensive needs of the West. His recommendations, however, were followed only sporadically. Politics, new Indian outbreaks, and a general shortage of barracks throughout the West prevented the army from implementing Sherman's plans on a major scale.[58]

Traders, contractors, and merchants were among the chief benefactors of the army's western presence. These men also stood to make a profit from nearby Indian agencies. Although many businessmen carried on their affairs honestly, some were notoriously corrupt. Army and Interior Department officials complained that western merchants provoked violence with Indians in order to attract more soldiers, government supply contracts, and money. Colonel Stewart Van Vliet, quartermaster of the Department of the Missouri, discounted reports of Indian depredations in 1873. "They are the same old stories gotten up by scoundrels who want to involve us into an

57. Grant to Sherman, Mar. 2, 1868, LC, Grant Papers, ser. 5, 47, reel 21; Crosby to Van Gise, Apr. 6, 1878, LS, SW, 88, reel 76; Belknap to SI, Jan. 23, 1876, ibid., 79, reel 72; Testimony of Davis, Jan. 17, 1874, House Rpt. No. 384, 43d Cong., 1st sess., 1874, ser. 1624, 161; Maxey to Maxey, June 16, 1876, Texas State Archives, Maxey Papers (first quotation); Maxey to his wife, June 17, ibid. (second quotation); Cresap, *Appomattox Commander*, 313–16; Horton, *Samuel Bell Maxey*, 78; Sheridan to Sherman, Mar. 19, 1878, Box 19, LC, Sheridan Papers (third quotation); McCrary to Speaker of the House, Apr. 3, 1878, LS, SW, 88, reel 76.

58. Sherman to Ramsey, Apr. 3, 1880, LC, Sherman Papers, 91, reel 45; Sherman to Terry, July 20, 1880, ibid.; Sherman to Lincoln, Mar. 13, 30, Apr. 14, ibid., 95, reel 47; Sherman to Lincoln, Oct. 16, 1882, ibid., 96, reel 47; Sherman to Huntington, Nov. 16, 1882, ibid.; Sherman to Sheridan, Mar. 7, 1883, ibid.; Sherman to Lincoln, July 2, 29, Aug. 30, 1883, ibid.

Indian war in order to get their hands in the Treasury," he wrote.[59] In Arizona, merchants, businessmen, and thieves within the infamous "Tucson ring" promoted Indian troubles and cooperated with dishonest Indian agents in providing substandard rations to reservation tribes, hoping to bring in the army with its lucrative government contracts.[60]

The frequency of such practices led many officers to place the blame for continuing difficulties with Indians squarely on civilian contractors and traders. The army was particularly critical of those who legally or illegally traded arms, alcohol, government goods, and stolen cattle with Indians. So serious did the problem become in western Texas and eastern New Mexico that in 1871 Sherman wanted to place the entire region under martial law in order to apply "a rightful remedy."[61] Legislators did not take effective action. Any general laws regulating merchants would have met with insurmountable opposition from business interests in Congress.[62] Cheating the federal government, it seemed, was accepted practice, providing that the right people cheated.

Westerners also found the use of volunteers against Indians fi-

59. Van Vliet to Sherman, May 4, 1873, LC, Sherman Papers, 35, reel 19 (quotation); Report of Sheridan, Nov. 14, SW, AR, 1866, 48; Dunn to Osborn, July 8, 1874, National Archives, LS, Dept. of Mo.; La Flesche to Dawes, Mar. 22, 1882, LC, Dawes Papers; Sherman to Sheridan, May 18, 1870, LS, AGO, 52, reel 39; Burlingame, "Military-Indian Frontier in Montana," 63, 65.

60. Faulk, *Geronimo Campaign*, 13; Betzinez, *I Fought with Geronimo*, 43–46; Ord to Logan, Dec. 29, 1869, LC, Logan Papers; Report of Crook, Sept. 9, SW, AR, 1885, 178.

61. Sherman to Belknap, June 30, 1871, LS, AGO, 54, reel 41 (quotation); Belknap to SI, July 22, 1871, LS, SW, 66, reel 62; Report of Augur, Sept. 28, SW, AR, 1872, 55. For the trader-army controversy, see also "Official Correspondence Relating to Fort Sill, 1869–1876," in LC, Belknap Papers.

62. For examples of business influence in Congress and its effect on the army, see Thayer to Stanton, Apr. 7, 1868, LC, Stanton Papers; Stanton to Rucker, Apr. 9, ibid.; Manderson to Schofield, Nov. 15, Dec. 6, 1883, Box 16, LC, Schofield Papers.

nancially enticing. The reliance upon massive numbers of citizen soldiers to respond to emergencies was firmly embedded in American military tradition. Not surprisingly, many westerners believed that local residents, armed with their own weapons and riding their own horses, could deal with Indians more effectively than could regulars. A few army officers agreed. In addition, federally funded volunteer units provided an excellent means of reducing unemployment and of infusing money into depressed regions.[63]

Most regular officers, skeptical of militia efficiency and effectiveness and aware of the army's uncertain place in American society, opposed the use of such units except in cases of extreme need. Undisciplined volunteers were known to attack Indians without discriminating between the guilty and the innocent. The most blatant example of such an incident came in 1864, when Col. John M. Chivington and seven hundred Colorado volunteers slaughtered the Indian inhabitants of some one hundred lodges at Sand Creek, Colorado. Chivington's thirst for political advancement apparently allowed him to overlook the fact that the overwhelming majority of the Indians were women and children. Three separate government investigations criticized the massacre sharply but could not reverse the loss of confidence among Indians regarding white motives. In 1867, Sherman advised Augur to assure the Sioux that regulars would not act so irresponsibly. Ord's comments summed up the general feeling. "If the President wants war [with Mexico], he can get it by calling out Texas Volunteers. . . . These Texas frontiersmen would to make money plunge the country into a war with all Europe."[64]

63. Report of Mason, Apr. 21, SW, AR, 1867, 98; Reynolds to Oakes, July 30, 1870, National Archives, LS, Dept. of Texas; Report of McDowell, Oct. 16, SW, AR, 1866, 34; Hancock to Sherman, May 24, National Archives, LS, Dept. of Mo.; Report of Sherman, Oct. 1, SW, AR, 1867, 35; Stanton to Halleck, Sept. 27, 1866, LS, AGO, 43, reel 30.

64. Sherman to Augur, Mar. 12, 1867, Ill. State Hist. Library, Augur Papers; Ord to Sherman, Oct. 25, 1877, Bancroft Library, Ord Papers (quotation). See

Although a decided majority of westerners sought federal military assistance, a few believed that the resulting difficulties outweighed the benefits. Reform-minded individuals charged the troops with fomenting racial tensions along the frontiers. Interior Department agents stressed the need to keep Indian agencies and schools away from what they believed to be the demoralizing effects of large army posts. Governor Lyman E. Knapp of the District of Alaska sought to oust the company of marines stationed there in the late 1880s and early 1890s, accusing them of giving liquor to the natives and corrupting women. Lyman believed an armed revenue cutter could patrol the long Alaskan coastline more effectively than a land-based force.[65]

Even more controversial were the army's attempts to prevent whites from trespassing on Indian reservations. In letters and reports throughout the post–Civil War period, officers frequently cited illegal transgressions onto Indian lands and their fruitless attempts to stop them. White intruders poured into areas rumored to have gold. The rangelands of the Indian Territory were attractive to cattlemen of the 1880s. Officers who caught such trespassers had little authority to punish them; the penalties for intrusions of this nature were fines levied by sympathetic civil courts rather than imprisonment. Some officers, having carried out their orders, found themselves victims of suits pressed by the very citizens they had apprehended.[66]

---

also Report of Sherman, Oct. 1, SW, AR, 1867, 35; *Army and Navy Journal*, Aug. 12, 1876, 10; and Testimony of Sherman, Nov. 21, 1877, House Misc. Doc. No. 64, 45th Cong., 2nd sess., VI, ser. 1820, 24–25.

65. Whitman to Howard, June 16, 1872, Bowdoin Library, Howard Papers; Knapp to Noble, Feb. 23, 1892, LC, Harrison Papers, series 1, reel 34; Noble to the President, Mar. 16, ibid.; Proctor to Noble, Dec. 21, 1889, Proctor Library, Proctor Papers.

66. Augur to Hartsuff, Jan. 27, Mar. 12, 1870, Box 6, LC, Sheridan Papers; Belknap to SI, Jan. 15, 1873, LS, SW, 72, reel 65; Belknap to SI, June 22, 1874, ibid., 75, reel 68; Report of Hayt, Nov. 1, SI, AR, 1879, 104–6; Arthur, Annual Message, Dec. 6, 1881, in Richardson, *Messages and Papers of the Presidents* 8:50;

Pope, having witnessed many futile efforts to clear the Indian Territory of unauthorized whites, concluded that, "As matters stand, the whole affair is simply a serious [sic] of processions to and from the Kansas line, for the general amusement of the people of this region." Despite presidential orders, complaints from Indians and their agents, and continuous army efforts, the problem was never settled satisfactorily. As was all too common on the frontiers of the American West, the army was unable to fulfill the government's treaty obligations regarding trespasses on Indian land.[67]

Indeed, special problems threatened the military-political collaboration essential to carrying out effective Indian policy. A notable example occurred in the cases of Kiowa chiefs Satanta and Big Tree. A civil court found the two guilty of murder, and sentenced them to death. Governor Edmund J. Davis hoping to gain favor with the Grant administration by his show of support for the peace policy, promptly commuted their sentence. Vigorous protests by Sherman and Sheridan were ineffectual, and the two Indians returned to their tribes. In another incident, Col. Joseph Reynolds, commander of the Department of Texas from 1869 to 1872, made an unsuccessful bid to become one of the state's senators in Washington. With growing numbers of Texans flocking to rival Democratic banners, Reynolds's controversial attempt further split the state's faction-ridden Republican party. Perceived by many contemporary observers as an extralegal quest by a power-hungry soldier for control of the state government, the Reynolds campaign gained no laurels for the army.[68]

Lincoln to Attorney General, May 26, 1882, LS, SW, 97, reel 85; Lincoln to the President, Feb. 2, 1883, ibid., 102, reel 87; Lincoln to Attorney General, Feb. 19, 1883, ibid.; Lincoln to the President, July 30, 1884, ibid., 108, reel 91; Endicott to SI, Nov. 6, 1885, ibid., 112, reel 95; Report of Miles, Aug. 25, SW, AR, 1893, 122.

67. Report of Pope, Oct. 2, SW, AR, 1883, 130. See also his earlier reports of Sept. 22, ibid., 1881, 114–15.

68. Davis to Sherman, Feb. 7, 1874, LC, Sherman Papers, 36, reel 19; Casdorph, *History of the Republican Party in Texas*, 19.

Another bitter political dispute split Colonel Kautz, commander of the Department of Arizona, and Arizona Governor John Philo Hoyt. According to Kautz, Governor Hoyt wanted to have him replaced with someone who would transfer departmental headquarters from Prescott to Tucson, a move that would give Hoyt and his cronies greater influence over military supplies and contracts. With western governors and legislators bombarding the War Department with complaints about the army's failure to protect citizens from Indian attack, the trust and cooperation between civil and military authorities that was vital to frontier defense thus proved to be tenuous indeed.[69]

Political disputes, repeated white intrusions onto Indian reservations, the controversial role of volunteers, and insatiable requests for military patronage embittered many officers. As Maj. Alfred L. Hough raged in 1879, "These frontier people are wholly unscrupulous. It is an outrage that we of the Army who have all the hardships to encounter should be made such catspaws of, mere tools of ambitious men who care only for their own interests, and cater to the public for popularity." Brigadier General John R. Brooke reported that an 1890 Indian scare "was occasioned by a couple of settlers . . . who . . . saw the Indians in war paint chasing and shooting beef that had been issued. Concluding that this meant an uprising they returned to Beaver and spread an alarm and considerably excited some of the settlers." Sherman admitted that his refusal to launch offensives in response to each complaint angered many frontier settlers but added that "as I don't ask [for] their votes I can stand their personal abuse."[70]

---

69. Kautz to Sherman, Apr. 9, May 12, 1877, LC, Sherman Papers, 46, reel 24; Sherman to McCrary, Aug. 3, 1877, LS, AGO, 60, reel 47; Report of Kautz, Aug. 15, SW, AR, 1877, 138–40; Kautz Diary, Dec. 31, 1877, LC, Kautz Papers; Stanton to Grant, Oct. 11, 1866, LC, Johnson Papers, ser. 1, reel 24.

70. Hough to wife, Nov. 1, 1879, in Athearn, ed., "Major Hough's March into Southern Ute Country," 109 n. 16 (first quotation); Brooke to Ruger, June 19, 1890, National Archives, LS, Dept. of the Platte (second quotation); Sherman

Almost all army men shared Sherman's view. The army, despite denunciations by politicians, civil officials, and even some westerners, saw itself as playing a noble role in the Western drama. The Indian menace had to be dealt with in order for America's grand experiment in pushing democracy across the continent, they believed, to proceed. Although impatient officers complained about the delays and trials of the American political system, the army worked by its own choice within that framework and was as a result subjected to a variety of checks and examinations. Its relations with Congress, the president, and most other government departments were stormy. Like the government's handling of other issues—notably that of the Pacific railroads—sectionalism, particularism, federalism, mismanagement, and sheer avarice clouded questions that were vital to Indian policy and military strategy. Issues such as the size of the army and the possible transfer of the Indian bureau from the Interior to the War Department never received sufficient debate on their own merit.[71]

The army's halfhearted attempt to remain free of the political arena was best expressed by Sherman: "The army has no 'policy' about Indians or anything else. It has no voice in Congress, but accepts the laws as enacted . . . and executes them with as much intelligence, fidelity, and humanity as any other body of citizens."[72] Though the goal was admirable, the army could not remain apolitical in the late nineteenth century; its efforts to discourage officers from taking an interest in politics eliminated whatever advantages it might have had in the wake of its Civil War exploits and was contrary to human nature. Sherman's petulant move of army headquarters to St. Louis during his dispute with Secretary Belknap clearly exemplified his involvement in politics, his own pronouncements to the

---

to John Sherman, June 17, 1868, LC, Sherman Papers, 23, reel 13 (third quotation).

71. Farnham, "'Weakened Spring of Government'" 662–80.

72. Sherman to Preston, Apr. 17, 1873, LC, Sherman Papers, 90, reel 45.

contrary. The military's bitter fights with Congress over the size of the army and the transfer of the Indian bureau, along with the widely publicized disputes concerning Reconstruction and between the commanding generals and the secretaries of war, clearly associated the military with politics in the public eye.[73] This lack of political sagacity combined with unfavorable public opinion and structural flaws in the War Department's command hierarchy to limit the strategies available to military leaders. These problems exacerbated the country's failure to decide on a clear Indian policy and nearly destroyed an entire people.

73. Hutton, *Phil Sheridan*, 327.

Chapter Four
The Regulars Move West, 1865–1869

The collapse of the Confederacy found United States Indian policy in its customary state of disarray. Seven decades of intermittent warfare, Indian removals, and treaties had solved few of the conflicts between whites and Indians. Furthermore, the army had failed to construct a clear strategic policy to resolve the problem. Some of the nation's greatest military heroes—Grant, Sherman, Sheridan, and Schofield, for example—now held key positions in the army. Having defeated the Confederates, they turned their attention to the western Indians. Would these men consciously apply Civil War strategic doctrine against their new foes? Although they indeed stressed the offensive (albeit in a general manner), detailed examination of the years after 1865 indicates that Civil War veterans did not deliberately use Civil War strategies against hostile tribes. In-

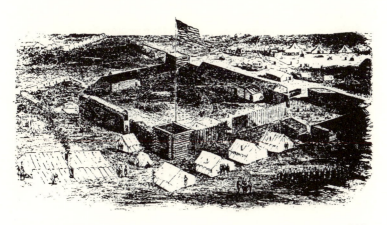

stead, the strategy and tactics of the Indian wars were formulated in the same manner as the government's overall Indian affairs were— as a haphazard, inconclusive response to the distinctive conditions of the western frontiers.

As men like Sherman and Grant completed their tasks in the closing days of the Civil War, western military leaders faced the prospect of combatting larger numbers of Indians still defiant of government authority. In the West, the army had achieved few decisive results except for Christopher "Kit" Carson's subjugation of the Navajo. Even worse, regular officers now had to deal with tribes infuriated by Col. John M. Chivington's massacre of Black Kettle's Cheyenne at Sand Creek, Colorado. Realizing the dangerous situation, western commanders determined in the spring of 1865 to take the offensive. Some spoke of fielding twelve thousand troops against Indians. General Pope advised General Grant that "I think the Government will find it true economy to finish this Indian war this season, so that it will stay finished. We have troops enough now on the plains to do it and can do it now better than hereafter."[1]

In command of the sprawling, newly created Division of the Missouri, which included the departments of the Northwest, Missouri, and Kansas, Pope finally settled on a strike involving five-thousand soldiers, less than half the strength projected by earlier plans. Supply mix-ups, contract squabbles, and opposition from Senator James R. Doolittle's [R–Wisc.] newly created joint congressional committee on Indian relations delayed Pope's grand offensive, originally scheduled for April 1865, until the summer. Military demobilization then hampered efforts to gather troops for the campaign, and excessive costs caught the attention of President Andrew Johnson, Secretary of War Edwin Stanton, and Secretary of the Treasury Hugh McCulloch. In June, Grant labeled the expenses of maintaining cavalry on the Great Plains "enormous;" by August, Stanton advised Grant that "the subject [of expenses] still occupies

---

1. Pope to Grant, June 19, 1865, Grant Papers, series 5, 54, reel 24 (quotation); Utley, *Frontiersmen in Blue*, 231–336.

individual labor. Reflecting the common belief that such a process needed time to take hold among the various tribes, he also argued that Indians should be moved where they "can never again be brought into contact with white emigration, nor obstruct the settlement and development of the new territories." Corse found Pope's reports "very able." Sherman recommended them to Grant as "worthy [of] your study"; Grant in turn labeled them "very admirable."[5]

Pope believed that, with these recommendations, he could prevent the annihilation of the Plains tribes. Removing Indians from emigrant trails would reduce bloodshed and save the tribal remnants. Pope recognized that implementing his proposals would take many years, and in the meantime, military action was necessary. He thus urged that the scattered frontier forts be consolidated at key strategic points; by concentrating the tiny garrisons at larger posts, officers could undertake active operations. These offensives, he maintained, should consist of small parties striking deep into the enemy's homeland; it had been discovered that only small columns could escape detection and maintain the element of surprise essential for military success. Pope also warned that, since the army's limited size prevented it from guarding every point of danger, emigrants and settlers should be prepared to defend themselves.[6]

P. St. G. Cooke's reports received less attention. Although commander of the Department of the Platte and another longtime veteran of frontier service, his recommendations apparently went no further than the offices of the Division of the Missouri. In January 1866, he requested more Indian scouts and army regulars, larger posts to

5. Pope to Sherman, Aug. 11, SW, AR, 1866, 26–27 (first quotation); Corse to Sherman, Dec. 12, 1865, LC, Sherman Papers, 17, reel 10 (second quotation); Sherman to Grant, Nov. 6, 1865, ibid. (third quotation); Grant to Sherman, Mar. 14, 1866, LC, Grant Papers, ser. 5, 47, reel 21 (fourth quotation).

Pope was gratified that Sherman had found his "opinions & suggestions on Indian policy . . . interesting & useful" (Pope to Sherman, Oct. 25, 1866, Sherman Papers, 19, reel 11).

6. Pope to Sherman, Aug. 11, SW, AR, 1866, 23–30; earlier reports include a letter of Feb. 6, 1864, US. War Dept., OR, ser. 1, 34, pt. 2, 259–64.

overawe potential troublemakers, and expeditions into Indian lands during the early spring, when poor grass still limited enemy mobility. Cooke's military talents had diminished with age, however, and his influence with fellow officers waned because of his mediocre Civil War record. His recommendation that a proposed column include two cavalry companies armed with "sharpened sabres, omitting the carbines in their cases," won no additional plaudits in 1867.[7]

Sherman, desperate for information and bored with life at divisional headquarters, decided to observe his command firsthand. After suffering through a restless winter at St. Louis, he made two tours through the Division of the Missouri in the summer of 1866. He recognized that "it is very important that I & other generals of departments should come out to extreme parts, for otherwise every little drunken quarrel or horsethieving is exaggerated into a big bug-bear."[8] Others concurred with Sherman's judgment. Corse toured his Minnesota district in early spring, predicting that the troop dispositions he made en route would "close the Indian troubles." Sheridan went to Texas to investigate complaints about Indian depredations; he concluded that the calls were in reality exaggerated attempts to get the army transferred from its Reconstruction duties in the interior of the state.[9]

Armed with Pope's reports and a new knowledge of the West, Sherman mapped out more comprehensive military plans during the closing months of 1866. Sherman's annual report, based on his belief

7. Cooke to Nichols, Jan. 3, 1866, National Archives, LS, Dept. of the Platte; Cooke to Palmer, Jan. 8, 1867, ibid. (quotation).

8. Sherman to Rawlins, Sept. 21, 1866, House Ex. Doc. No. 23, 39th Cong., 2nd sess., VI, ser. 1288, 16. See also Sherman to Grant, Aug. 29, 1866, LC, Grant Papers, ser. 5, 54, reel 24. On Sherman's tour, see Athearn, *William Tecumseh Sherman*, 45–97.

9. Corse to Sherman, Mar. 29, 1866, LC, Sherman Papers, 18, reel 10; Sheridan to Grant, Oct. 3, 1866, Senate Ex. Doc. No. 19, 45th Cong., 2nd sess., I, 1878, ser. 1780, 7; Sheridan to Rawlins, Nov. 8, 1866, LC, Grant Papers, ser. 5, 54, reel 24; Report of Sheridan, Nov. 14, SW, AR, 1866, 48.

that the Plains consisted of grasslands unsuited for farming, proposed an Indian-free "railroad belt" across the region. He wanted to restrict the Sioux to an area north of the Platte, west of the Missouri, and east of the Bozeman Trail. Similarly, the Arapaho, Cheyenne, Comanche, Kiowa, Apache, and Navajo would be kept south of the Arkansas and east of Fort Union, New Mexico. "This would leave for our people exclusively the use of a wide belt, east and west," he reasoned, ". . . in which lie the two great roads, and over which passes the bulk of travel to the mountain Territories." Although moving the Plains Indians would be difficult, Sherman assumed that traditional spring-summer offensives would be effective. He hoped to secure reinforcements sufficient to accomplish the task by spring 1867. In the meantime, he noted, "all I ask is comparative quiet."[10]

Sherman's 1866 report reflected views similar to those of traditional makers of Indian policy. He did not recognize Indians as equals but as a parent might regard wayward children. They could be moved from their traditional homelands, he believed, because to allow them to remain would discourage western migration by whites. Removal, argued Sherman, would enable them to live on huge reservations in Indian Territory or southern Dakota on lands undesirable to whites. These beliefs reflected and continued the long American tradition of Indian removal. Sherman offered few new ideas for the military aspect of relations between Indians and whites in 1866. He avoided the issue of concentration of forts and assumed that traditional offensive columns led by professional officers could defeat enemy tribes.

In December 1866, news from Fort Kearny shattered the comparative quiet Sherman sought. The Sioux had protested the continued use of the Bozeman Trail and harassed the fort's garrison throughout the fall and early winter of 1866. Determined to whip

10. Report of Sherman, Nov. 5, SW, AR, 1866, 20–21 (first quotation); Sherman to Rawlins, Aug. 21, 1866, House Ex. Doc. No. 23, 39th Cong., 2nd sess., 1867, ser. 1288, 6 (second quotation). Grant approved of Sherman's plans (Grant to Stanton, Jan. 15, 1867, LC, Grant Papers, ser. 5, 47, reel 21).

The Campaigns of 1867

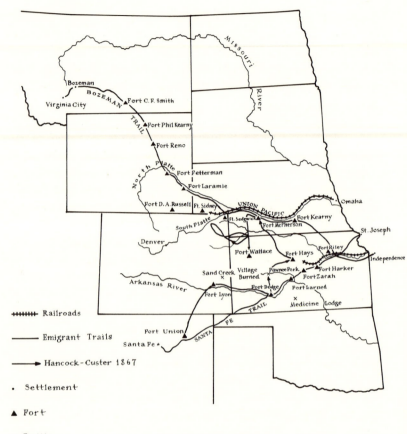

Railroads

Emigrant Trails

Hancock-Custer 1867

• **Settlement**

▲ **Fort**

× **Battle**

Sources: Adapted from Utley, *Indian Frontiers*, pp. 62, 121; *Frontiersmen in Blue*, p. 321; *Frontier Regulars*, p. 121

Red Cloud's warriors single-handedly, Capt. William Fetterman's eighty men were themselves annihilated outside the fort.[11] While advising Grant that "we must act with vindictive earnestness against the Sioux, even to their extermination, men, women, & children,"

11. On the Fetterman defeat, see Cooke to Carrington, Sept. 27, 1866, National

Sherman offered few specific plans against the tribe he singled out for such punishment. As noted earlier, the post's commander, Col. Henry Carrington, was unable to handle the crisis, and was quietly moved to a less demanding position in Colorado. "Unprecedented" snowfall delayed a retaliatory strike by Col. John Gibbon in early 1867.[12]

By the time the snows had melted, a new peace commission, sponsored by the Interior Department and appointed by President Johnson to deal with the Sioux reservation, had made Sherman's threats obsolete. Sherman still maintained that the Sioux needed to be "taken down a good many notches," but he agreed with Augur's suggestion to postpone the offensive until the peace commission completed its tasks. Although chaired by a general, Alfred Sully, the commission recommended a peaceful approach to the West and brought a halt to army aggressions on the northern plains.[13]

No such interference prevented Major General Hancock from conducting operations as he saw fit in the Department of the Missouri that spring. Accumulating evidence of what he believed were Chey-

---

Archives, LS, Dept. of the Platte; Carrington to Litchfield, Oct. 4, 1866, Senate Ex. Doc. No. 33, 50th Cong., 1st sess., 1887, I, ser. 2504, 31–32; Litchfield to Carrington, Senate Ex. Doc. No. 15, 39th Cong., 2nd sess., II, ser. 1277, 14; Carrington to AAG, Jan. 3, 1867, Senate Ex. Doc. No. 33, 50th Cong., 1st sess., I, ser. 2504, 39; Utley, *Frontier Regulars*, 102–11.

12. Sherman to Grant, Dec. 28, 1866, Senate Ex. Doc. No. 15, 39th Cong., 2nd sess., II, ser. 1277, 4 (first quotation); Augur to Nichols, Jan. 30, Feb. 8, 13, 1867, National Archives, LS, Dept. of the Platte (second quotation); Augur to Wessells, Feb. 16, 1867, ibid.

13. Augur to Nichols, Mar. 6, 1867, ibid.; Sherman to Augur, Mar. 12, 1867, Ill. State Hist. Library, Augur Papers (quotation); Augur to Sherman, May 18, 1867, National Archives, LS, Dept. of the Platte; Sherman to Grant, May 19, 1867, LC, Stanton Papers, reel 11. In reality, Ely S. Parker reported that the commission told Interior Secretary Orville Browning "that we did not want military operations for the coming season delayed on our account," as "a state of war exists" in the Tongue and Powder River country (Parker to Rawlins, Apr. 1, 1867, LC, Johnson Papers, ser. 1, reel 26).

enne outrages, Hancock informed Sherman that "it would be to our advantage to have these Indians refuse the demands I intend to make, [as] a war with the Cheyennes would answer our purposes. . . . This matter, I wish to dispose of in March or April, before the grass comes up." Sherman vigorously supported Hancock's proposals. If interviews with key chiefs were unsatisfactory, Sherman believed that Hancock, "a just and fair man," should force the Indians to terms. After first warning agents Edward W. Wynkoop and Jesse H. Leavenworth of his intentions, Hancock moved out from Fort Riley in April 1867 at the head of a mixed column of cavalry, infantry, and artillery that eventually totalled some fourteen hundred troops. With a professional military officer leading regular soldiers, the Hancock expedition was expected to be more effective against the southern plains tribes than had been the earlier efforts of volunteers. Assisting Hancock was the dashing Lieutenant Colonel Custer.[14]

Cursory talks with a variety of tribal leaders failed to satisfy Hancock of the Indians' pacific intentions. Believing the use of force to be justified, Hancock burned Indian villages near Pawnee Fork, Kansas, and dispatched Custer with a flying column after Sioux and Cheyenne warriors. Despite these efforts, the vaunted spring offensive of 1867 was an expensive failure. Hancock's powerful force could not compel hostile tribes to fight.[15] Reformers rejected Sher-

14. Hancock to Wynkoop, Dec. 17, 1866, National Archives, LS, Dept. of the Mo.; Hancock to Sherman, Jan. 14, 1867, ibid. (first quotation); Sherman to Grant, Feb. 18 (second quotation) and 19, 1867, LC, Grant Papers, ser. 5, 55, reel 24; Hancock to Sherman, Feb. 23, Mar. 2, 1867, LS, Dept. of Mo.; Sherman to Augur, Mar. 12, 1867, Ill. State Hist. Library, Augur Papers; Hancock to Wynkoop, Mar. 11, 1867, Senate Ex. Doc. No. 13, 40th Cong., 1st sess., 1867, ser. 1308, 78; Hancock to Leavenworth, Mar. 11, ibid., p. 99; Sherman to Hancock, Mar. 14, 1867, House Ex. Doc. No. 240, 41st Cong., 2nd sess., VII, 1870, ser. 1425, 99; Hancock to Nichols, May 22, 1867, ibid., 78–79.

Wounds received at Gettysburg still troubled Hancock. See Schofield to Hancock, Sept. 19, 1868, U.S. Army Hist. Res. Coll., Hancock Papers.

15. Millbrook, "West Breaks in General Custer"; Utley, *Frontier Regulars*, 120–

man's assertion that the expedition had prevented the development of a massive Indian coalition, and they charged Hancock with inciting a war on the Plains. Indeed, angry warriors struck isolated settlements throughout the summer, forcing Sherman, ordinarily opposed to such measures, to stiffen defenses with volunteers.[16]

Congress reacted to the Hancock debacle by forming yet another peace commission, composed of noted reformers Samuel Tappan and John Sanborn, Commissioner of Indian Affairs Nathaniel G. Taylor, and Chairman of the Senate Committee on Indian Affairs John B. Henderson [D–Mo.]. President Johnson selected the other members—General Sherman, Brigadier General Terry, and retired Brigadier General William S. Harney, veteran of many pre–Civil War Indian fights. Following extensive meetings with a number of chiefs, the commission recommended that the federal government adopt a new pacific policy toward its Indian wards. Despite conflicting testimony by army officers, the report further stated that Sherman's railroad belt violated agreements with the Cheyenne, Arapaho, and Apache. Because of the lack of communication between government agencies, no one had informed Sherman of the treaty provisions. Hancock, too, had been misled: "He had just come to the department, and circumstances were ingeniously woven to deceive him," noted the report. "His distinguished services in another field of patriotic duty had left him but little time to become acquainted with the remote or immediate causes producing these troubles."[17]

24; House Ex. Doc. No. 240, 41st Cong., 2nd sess., VII, 1870, ser. 1425, 50–128.

16. Sherman to Grant, May 19, 1867, LC, Stanton Papers, reel 11; Hancock to Sherman, May 24, 1867, National Archives, LS, Dept. of Mo.; Sherman to Grant, June 8, 1867, LC, Grant Papers, ser. 5, 55, reel 24; Sherman to Leet, July 1, SW, AR, 1867, 66; Wynkoop to Murphy, Sept. 14, SI, AR, 1867, 310–14; Report of Mix, Nov. 15, ibid., 18.

17. "Report of the Indian Peace Commission," Jan. 7, 1868, House Ex. Doc. No. 97, 40th Cong., 2nd sess., XI, ser. 1337, 1, 13 (quotation), 14, 16, 21–22. Christopher Augur served on the commission in Sherman's stead while the latter conferred with President Johnson (Johnson to Grant, Oct. 4, 1867, LC,

The peace commission's demand that kindness replace military might as the government's chief means of implementing Indian policy limited the army to the defensive on the Great Plains. According to new plans, Indians would be gathered in two huge territories. The first, encompassing the lands between Kansas and Texas, was to include southern plains tribes and the Five Civilized Tribes; the second, including the country between the forty-sixth parallel and Nebraska, would be reserved for the northern tribes. Renewed efforts to "civilize" the Indians were also recommended. Army officials, unhappy with their loss, complained of their lack of influence in the government and scoffed at the idealistic reformers who seemed to hold all the political strings.[18]

In the meantime, military men assessed their mistakes and prepared for the day when they would be freed from their civilian fetters. Clearly, handling the Indians demanded fundamental changes in military operations. Hancock's 1867 column, having every reason for success in army eyes, had produced results no better than those of the volunteers of 1865. The failure to force the Plains warriors to battle could no longer simply be attributed to the poor leadership of political generals or to the undisciplined actions of volunteers. Wounds received at Gettysburg still hampered Hancock, but he was nonetheless a West Point–educated professional. And in the aggressive Custer, Hancock had one of the army's brightest young stars. More significant, the political muscle displayed by the reformers indicated that the army's power could be severely limited. Still thirsting to revenge the Fetterman disaster, the army knew it could not waste its next opportunity, should such an opening arise.

Discussion during the period of enforced dormancy on the Great Plains concerned the long-espoused theory that small posts cost too

Johnson Papers, series 3A, IV, reel 42; Grant to Augur, Oct. 5, 1867, LC, Grant Papers, series 5, 56, reel 25).

18. Bailey, *Pacifying the Plains*, 30–50.

much money, depleted manpower otherwise available for field operations, and failed to stop Indian depredations. During the early 1850s, Indian agent Thomas Fitzpatrick, Col. Thomas T. Fauntleroy, and Gen. Winfield Scott had all suggested that small, isolated posts merely showed the army's weakness. Pope had renewed discussion of the topic; in July 1867, Inspector General of the Division of the Pacific Maj. Roger Jones also deemphasized small posts in a confidential report on the military situation in Arizona. In addition to reiterating the traditional arguments, Jones believed that too many small forts forced the army to appoint incompetent officers as post commanders. [19]

Irvin McDowell, commanding the California department, refuted the Jones report one month later. McDowell acknowledged the logic of Jones's theory but argued that concentration of manpower had in practice been unsuccessful. Reducing the number of small forts hinged on the effectiveness of expeditions sent out from the larger establishments but such efforts had produced only indifferent results. Division commander Halleck sided with McDowell, pointing out that concentration would strip many flourishing frontier settlements of protection. No immediate action was taken, and concentration remained a much-disputed issue for the next decade, advocates seeing it as a strategic panacea, opponents as a catastrophic mistake. [20]

By contrast, all agreed that railroads would be a key element in any new plans. Although Secretary of War Stanton had seemed unsure of the railroads' military advantages, Grant supported government aid to the lines and warned Sherman that their completion would drastically alter frontier defensive needs. Sherman, although not the first to recognize the

19. Fitzpatrick to Lea, Nov. 24, 1851, House Doc. No. 1, 32nd Cong., 1st sess., ser. 613, 335–36; Fitzpatrick to Alfred Cumming, Nov. 19, 1853, House Doc. No. 1, 33rd Cong., 1st sess., ser. 690, 362; Fauntleroy to Jesup, July 31, SW, AR, 1852, 127–28; Report of Scott, Nov. 21, SW, AR, 1851, 161; Report of Jones, July 15, ibid., 1867, 84–85.

20. Report of McDowell, Aug. 14, SW, AR, 1867, 86–91; and Halleck, Sept. 18, ibid., 72–73. For other reports favoring concentration, see Steele to AAG, Mar. 20, 1866, National Archives, LS, Dept. of the Columbia.

significance of railroads to western development, became one of the most vocal advocates of transcontinental building. Troops were required to check Indian threats to construction teams at all costs. From a military standpoint, the iron horse would ease the movement of troops and supplies across vast western regions. More important, the railroads would encourage settlers, who could overcome Indian resistance by sheer numbers and stubborn persistence in their belief that they, as farmers and stockraisers, had more right to the land than roving bands of hunters.[21] Convenient also were the military ties of many key railroad men. Grenville M. Dodge, chief engineer for the Union Pacific; William J. Palmer, president of the Kansas Pacific; and W. W. Wright, superintendent of the Kansas Pacific—all had served under Sherman or Sheridan in the Civil War. Old military acquaintance made cooperation and reciprocal favors, such as military escorts or complimentary railroad passes, common between army officers and railroad bosses.[22]

Similar agreement among officers was evident regarding the need for offensives. Accomplished European theorists and generals such as Napoleon Bonaparte, Antoine Henri Jomini, and Karl von Clausewitz all advocated offensive thrusts, although their respective emphases were very differently conceived. Officers stationed throughout the American West concurred; like their European counterparts, however, they often differed on the types of offensives to use. Having made the trip from San Antonio to Las Cruces, Nelson Davis contended that "active field operations" provided the only means of preventing Indian depredations. Halleck, chief of the Pacific division, maintained that small, secret expeditions should be directed

21. Stanton to Sherman, Sept. 2, 1865, LC, Stanton Papers, reel 10; Grant to Sherman, Oct. 31, 1865, Jan. 26, 1867, LC, Grant Papers, ser. 5, 46, reel 21; Sherman to John Sherman, Apr. 27, 1866, LC, Johnson Papers, ser. 1, reel 22; Sherman to Grant, May 27, 1867, Grant Papers, ser. 5, 55, reel 24; Sherman to Stanton, June 17, 1867, Senate Ex. Doc. No. 13, 40th Cong., 1st sess., ser. 1308, 121; Report of Sherman, Oct. 1, SW, AR, 1867, 36; Sherman to Augur, Feb. 28, Nov. 23, 1868, June 9, 1870, Ill. State Hist. Library, Augur Papers.

22. Hutton, *Phil Sheridan*, 39.

at "known Indian haunts." In the Department of the Platte, Hazen suggested that three-fourths of his troops engage in field operations. From St. Paul, Corse hoped to organize small cavalry columns to crush would-be Indian raiders.[23]

Although all officers stressed the need for mobility, few specified the means of achieving quick movement. Details of the proposed operations thus remained uncertain. Traditionally, offensives commenced in the spring or summer, when mild weather allowed horses to forage in the field. A growing number of officers, noting that the timing of these offensives was not working, suggested alternatives. In March 1866, commander of the Department of the Columbia Frederick Steele suggested that infantry might surprise the Indians of southern Oregon in their winter camps. In September of the same year, Platte department commander Cooke advised Colonel Carrington at Fort Kearny that he might "manage to surprise Red Cloud's bands in winter camps by Infantry. Two or three hundred Infantry with much suffering, perhaps, might thus accomplish more than two thousand troops in the summer." Major James Van Voast "informed himself as much as possible on the subject" and scraped together a few companies. But unusually bad weather, overwhelming Indian strength, and the timorous attitude of Carrington at Fort Kearny forced the indefinite postponement of the winter attack in the North.[24]

23. Davis to Sherman, Mar. 24, 1866, LC, Sherman Papers, 18, reel 10 (first quotation); Report of Halleck, Sept. 18, SW, AR, 1867, 72–73 (second quotation); Report of Hazen, Oct. 16, 1866, House Ex. Doc. No. 45, 39th Cong., 2nd sess., VII, ser. 1289, 5; Corse to Sherman, Mar. 2, 1866, Sherman Papers, 18, reel 10.

24. Steele to AAG, Mar. 20, 1866, National Archives, LS, Dept. of the Columbia; Cooke to Carrington, Sept. 27, 1866, Senate Ex. Doc. No. 15, 39th Cong., 2nd sess., II, Ser. 1277, 8 (first quotation); Litchfield to Carrington, Nov. 12, 1866, ibid., 14; Litchfield to Van Voast, Oct. 13, Nov. 29, 1866, LS, Dept. of the Platte; Cooke to Van Voast, Nov. 6, ibid.; Cooke to Nichols, Nov. 10, ibid.; Cooke to Wessells, Dec. 27, ibid. (second quotation); Cooke to Sherman, Dec. 28, ibid. Carrington had given every indication that he would launch a winter move: "I will operate all winter, whatever, the season if supported, but to redeem

On the southern plains, Hancock had also contemplated action during the winter season of 1867–68. Insufficient supplies, the potentially devastating effects on horses of a winter campaign, and the watchful eye of the peace commission led him to decide against such a move. Sherman had previously speculated about the success of a winter campaign. "Now is the time for action," the division chief had argued in February 1867, "for if we wait for grass their ponies will get fat and an indian [sic] with a fat pony is very different from him with a starved one." Sherman thus displayed a new willingness to use different, if not novel, means to defeat his Indian foes.[25]

As commander of the key Division of the Missouri, Sherman chafed at the peace commission's moratorium. During the Civil War he had been free to invade the South according to his own military judgment. He enjoyed no such independence during the postbellum years. Throughout 1867, the general sought authority to punish all Indians found outside reservations, and he predicted that renewed violence would show the folly of the peace commissions. Counseling patience, trusted subordinate Augur suggested that the temporary peace could be beneficial. Warfare, he asserted, was inevitable; he believed that in "another year we will be ready for them" with well-prepared offensive columns.[26]

Although the peace initiative halted army offensives on the Plains, violence continued to mark Indian-white relations in southern Oregon. Here, Crook exhibited the aggressive spirit that had brought

---

my pledge to open and guarantee this line" (Carrington to Grant, Dec. 21, 1866, LC, Grant Papers, ser. 5, 54, reel 24). See also Carrington to Litchfield, Nov. 25, 1866, Senate Ex. Doc. No. 33, 50th Cong., 1st sess., I, 1887, ser. 2504, 36.

25. Hancock to Hunt, Aug. 10, 1867, National Archives, LS, Dept. of Mo.; Hancock to Sherman, ibid.; Hancock to Hoffman, Jan. 26, 1867, ibid.; Sherman to Grant, Feb. 18, 1867, LC, Grant Papers, ser. 5, 55, reel 24 (quotations). See also his report of Oct. 1, SW, AR, 1867, 32.

26. Sherman to Grant, June 18, 1867, LC, Grant Papers, ser. 5, 55, reel 24; Augur to Sherman, June 24, 1867, National Archives, LS, Dept. of the Platte (quotation); Sherman to Leet, July 1, SW, AR, 1867, 67.

him to the forefront of his country's Indian fighters. Crook's feats of endurance amazed fellow officers and enlisted personnel alike. His tireless pursuits, utilizing swarms of Indian auxiliaries and mules to provide added mobility, set important precedents. Continuing offensives into the winter, Crook's forces delivered devastating psychological and economic blows to even the most secure Indian haunts. By 1868, the Paiutes sued for peace. In recognition of his prowess, the bewhiskered Crook was given command of the Department of the Columbia.[27]

Experience had by now convinced some officers that attacks had to threaten the homes and villages of hostile Indians and if necessary kill all those who resisted, be they men, women, or children. Repeated efforts to bring mounted warriors to battle had for the most part been complete failures. Army men theorized that offensives directed at noncombatants, forcing Indian men to protect their families, would reduce mobility and allow the army's slower columns to catch and chastise Indians considered hostile. Sherman explained that, as pursuit of mobile Cheyenne and Sioux warriors was almost impossible, "the only mode of restraining them is by making them feel that we can reach their families and property." Grant believed that, with Apaches, "There is no alternative but active and vigorous war till they are completely destroyed, or forced to surrender as prisoners of war." Pacific division chief Halleck spoke in similar terms. Crook's superior in Oregon, Frederick Steele, noted that "Crooks [sic] command takes no prisoners. The scouts dispose of all enemies before the troops get up."[28]

Along with the growing determination to strike against all members of hostile tribes existed a broadening consensus regarding friendly Indian scouts, to whom Steele had referred. In July 1866,

27. Utley, *Frontier Regulars*, 185–87.

28. Report of Sherman, Oct. 1, SW, AR, 1867, 34 (first quotation); Report of Grant, Nov., ibid., 30 (second quotation); Report of Halleck, Sept. 18, ibid., 72–74; Report of Steele to Fry, Oct. 15, 1867, National Archives, LS, Dept. of the Columbia (third quotation).

Congress authorized the recruitment of one thousand such allies. The following year General Halleck asked for a thousand for his Pacific division alone, as "they would save the more valuable lives of many white men." Augur, heading the Department of the Platte, also demanded twelve hundred such recruits for his own area. The two hundred Pawnees he had already enlisted knew the country, rarely deserted, and saved the army money by using their own ponies. The high marks given these scouts convinced Sherman to call for two thousand Indian troops in his own report. "If we can convert the wild Indians into a species of organized cavalry," theorized Sherman, " . . . it accomplishes a double purpose, in taking them out of the temptation of stealing and murdering, and will accustom them to regular habits and discipline, from which they will not likely depart when discharged."[29]

The speculation concerning optimal strategy continued while the peace commission completed its study of the problems between Indians and whites on the Plains. Sherman, Terry, and Augur juggled military responsibilities with their duties on the commission as talks continued through 1868. In the meantime, controversies concerning federal occupation of the South had an unexpected effect on western military operations. Sheridan, commanding the Fifth Military District (Texas and Louisiana), had drawn bitter criticism from conservative whites for his heavy-handed rule. While implying that Sheridan be moved from his command, Sherman suggested to Grant in July 1867 that the fiery Sheridan could "help us very much if he were to have a cavalry command." Hoping to end Indian resistance quickly, Sherman wanted Sheridan to strike into Indian territory from Texas with a strong command.[30]

Unwittingly, President Johnson made Sherman's plan possible.

29. Grant to Stanton, Aug. 1, 1866, LC, Grant Papers, ser. 5, 47, reel 21; Townsend to Sherman, Halleck, and Sheridan, Aug. 1, 1866, LS, AGO, 42, reel 30; Report of Townsend, Oct. 20, SW, AR, 1866, appendix, 2; Reports of Halleck, Sept. 18, ibid., 1867, 74 (first quotation); Augur, Sept. 30, ibid., 59–60; and Sherman, Oct. 1, ibid., 37–38 (second quotation).

30. Sherman to Grant, July 4, 1867, LC, Grant Papers, ser. 5, 55, reel 24.

Overruling Grant's strong protests, Johnson relieved Sheridan of his Gulf command. The president viewed Sheridan as a failure and saw the transfer to the Department of the Missouri as a way to remove a troublesome officer from the more politically sensitive duties of Reconstruction. Johnson conjectured that Indian troubles would give Sheridan the opportunity to display "the energy, enterprise, and daring which gave him so enviable a reputation during our recent civil struggle." Little did the president realize the importance that this step would have in shaping Indian affairs. Sheridan's tendentious and insensitive views of Indians and his cold determination to protect white settlers on the Plains meant, in effect, that Sherman now had a subordinate eager and qualified to crush all Indian resistance.[31]

As Sheridan settled into his new command in mid-1868, the peace commission was completing its tasks. Six months earlier (October, 1867), Kiowa, Comanche, Kiowa-Apache, Cheyenne, and Arapaho chiefs had signed treaties with the commission at Medicine Lodge Creek, Kansas. The Medicine Lodge agreements concentrated the Kiowas, Comanches, and Kiowa-Apaches on one large reservation in Indian Territory; the Cheyennes and Arapahoes gathered at another. After the army abandoned its Bozeman Trail forts (Phil Kearny and C. F. Smith), the peace commissioners also secured concessions from northern tribes at Fort Laramie. The Sioux and other northern tribes agreed to live on reservations west of the Missouri River in present-day South Dakota, with hunting rights along the Republican and north of the Platte rivers. The government was to provide certain supplies and annuities while the tribes adjusted to the new boundaries.[32]

Unfortunately, the treaties failed to halt Indian-white violence on the Plains. Full-scale warfare did not shatter the uneasy truce

31. Johnson to Grant, Aug. 19, 1867, LC, Johnson Papers, ser. 1, reel 28.

32. Perry, ed., *Consolidated Treaty Series* 133:414–26; for the Fort Laramie agreements, see ibid., 136:92–109.

established in the North by the Fort Laramie talks until 1876; the Medicine Lodge agreements, by contrast, lasted less than a year. Indian raids and depredations off the southern reservations continued as chiefs were unable to control warriors who had little inclination to adopt the white man's ways or to respect his artificial boundaries. The federal government had also been slow in providing Indians with the annuities, arms, and ammunition promised in the Medicine Lodge treaties. In response to the mounting crisis in the lower plains, the peace commission reassembled at Chicago in October 1868. Senator John Henderson's absence gave Sherman and the army a majority of votes. The military men, seizing this rare opportunity to determine federal Indian policy, pushed through several resolutions that increased the army's authority. Their own backgrounds, views of Indians, personal experiences in the West, and reports from subordinates in the field all pointed to their aggressive bent. War on the southern plains was imminent.[33]

Sherman and Sheridan, anticipating more freedom to conduct offensives, agreed on tentative plans a month before the commission even met. Sheridan hoped to clear the area north of the new transcontinental railroad in preparation for a winter attack on the tribes south of the Arkansas River; to that end, he sent Lt. Col. Luther P. Bradley to scout the area around the forks of the Republican River on the central plains. In Bradley's words, his command was "to kill all the buffalo we find, & drive the Arappahoes [sic] & Cheyennes south, & the Sioux north."[34]

While Bradley scoured the Republican River and the peace commission concluded its tasks, the generals mustered their resources for a strong offensive. All believed that Indian transgressions justified immediate retribution. Augur, who, according to Sherman, leaned "to the side of forebearance and moderation," held that "these In-

33. Taylor to President, Oct. 9, SI, AR, 831–32; Athearn, *William Tecumseh Sherman*, 226–28.

34. Diary, Sept. 13, 1868, U.S. Army Hist. Res. Coll., Bradley Papers (quotation); Sheridan to Bradley, Sept. 22, 1868, ibid.

The Offensives of 1868 and 1869

Source: Adapted from Utley, *Frontier Regulars*, pp. 151, 171

dians must be terribly whipped before they can appreciate kindness."
Sherman argued that "either the Indians must give way, or we must
abandon all west of the Missouri River, and confess . . . that forty
millions of whites are cowed by a few thousand savages." Grant
wanted the army to "squelch the Indians" and advised that it should
"push after their villages and families."[35]

Despite objections from "old hunters, old frontiersmen, and old
officers," who believed a winter campaign would be a disaster for
the government, plans for a strong offensive were completed by
October 15.[36] Hazen offered food and protection to all Indians who
came in to Fort Cobb. Those who did not seek out Hazen were
considered hostile. When the cold weather killed the grasses on the
southern plains and forced the scattered bands of Indians together,
columns struck from New Mexico, Colorado, and Kansas. Because
of the winter campaign's experimental nature, Sheridan accompanied
the Kansas force as an observer. Sherman viewed the expedition as
an opportunity for total warfare. "I want you all to go ahead, kill
and punish the hostiles, . . . capture and destroy the ponies, lances,
carbines, &c., &c., of the Cheyennes, Arapahoes, and Kiowas," he
ordered.[37]

The winter campaign, fraught with hardships for both sides, was
a military success. From New Mexico, Maj. Andrew W. Evans led

35. Sherman to Tappan, Sept. 24, 1868, LC, Sherman Papers, 90, reel 45
(first and second quotations); Grant to Sherman, Sept. 25, 1868, ibid., 24, reel
13 (third and fourth quotations).

36. Sheridan to Bradley, Sept. 28, 1868, U.S. Army Hist. Res. Coll., Bradley
Papers; Sheridan to Sherman, Apr., 1878, Box 19, LC, Sheridan Papers (quotation);
Sheridan, *Personal Memoirs* 2:307.

37. Sheridan to Sherman, Nov. 1, 1869, Box 75, LC, Sheridan Papers; Sherman
to Hazen, Sept. 26, 1868, LC, Sherman Papers, 90, reel 45; Sheridan to Sherman,
Oct. 15, SW, AR, 1868, 21; Sherman to Sheridan, Oct. 15, 1868, Senate Ex.
Doc. No. 18, 40th Cong., 3rd sess., 1869, ser. 1360, 4; Utley, *Frontier Regulars*,
154–55; Lonnie J. White, "Winter Campaigning with Custer and Sheridan," 68–
98; Sheridan, *Personal Memoirs* 2:308–9; Taylor, "Carr-Penrose Expedition," 159–
76; Sheridan to Sherman, Nov. 1, SW, AR, 1869, 45; Sherman to Sheridan,
Hazen, and Grierson, Dec. 23, 1868, LC, Sherman Papers, 25, reel 14 (quotation).

563 men out of Fort Bascom eastward down the South Canadian River. Major Carr and about 650 troops moved southeast from Fort Lyon, Colorado, toward the Antelope Hills and the Red River. These two columns pushed the Indians toward a third force led by General Sully and accompanied by Sheridan. Sully's column included eleven troops of the Seventh Cavalry under Lieutenant Colonel Custer, five infantry companies, and the Nineteenth Kansas Volunteer Cavalry. Custer's Seventh Cavalry destroyed Black Kettle's Cheyenne villages and engaged a large Indian force at the Battle of the Washita. Major Evans razed a Nakoni Comanche village at Soldier Springs in December. The following July, Carr reached the Cheyenne Dog Soldier village at Summit Springs, Colorado, destroying their camp equipment and supplies; and breaking the Dog Soldiers as a cohesive fighting group. Large groups from the Kiowa, Comanche, and Arapaho tribes eventually gathered at Fort Cobb. The troops established Fort Sill and Camp Supply, which were to become important bastions of army power in Indian Territory.[38]

Although the battles were not of a decisive nature, the campaign shattered Indian morale and left thousands destitute. Sheridan reported that "the Indians for the first time begin to realize that winter will not compel us to make a truce with them." The offensives also affected conditions in the North. "Sheridan's operations," said Augur, "have had a good effect upon the northern Indians generally, and at present I see no indications of anything like a war on their part."[39]

The converging winter columns of 1868–69 did not emerge unscathed. Supply failures were the rule rather than the exception. Horses and mules died by the hundreds, victims of inadequate stockpiles of food and a lack of winter forage. Snow, mud, and bitter

38. Utley, *Frontier Regulars*, 155–64; Sherman to Hazen, Sheridan, and Grierson, Dec. 23, 1868, LC, Sherman Papers, 25, reel 14; Ambrose, *Crazy Horse and Custer*, 290–94, 298.

39. Sheridan to Nichols, Dec. 19, 1868, Senate Ex. Doc. No. 18, 40th Cong., 3rd sess., 1869, ser. 1360, 40–41 (first quotation); Augur to Sherman, Mar. 10, 1869, LC, Sherman Papers, 25, reel 14 (second quotation).

cold revealed startling deficiencies in army equipment and clothing.[40] Leadership was also lacking. Many officers were unwilling to
push themselves and their commands with the vigor necessary to
hunt down their foes. An even greater problem arose from the scheme
to assemble peaceful Indians at Fort Cobb. Hazen, the shepherd of
the flock, found himself in an impossible situation. Responsible for
an estimated six thousand Indians ranging from twenty to one
hundred miles from the fort, he had no way of keeping up with all
of his charges. The resulting Sheridan-Hazen dispute was only one
of many that poisoned interarmy relations during the Indian wars.[41]

While the exhausted soldiers and Indians of the southern plains
slowly recovered from the arduous campaigns of 1868–69, the military reshuffled its command structure in the wake of Grant's presidential election. Sherman, promoted to commanding general,
moved from his offices in St. Louis to Washington, D.C. Sheridan
inherited Sherman's old job as head of the Missouri division; John
Schofield took control of the newly vacated Department of the Missouri. By June 1869, Schofield was busily securing reinforcements
"for a new and decisive winter campaign" against nonreservation
Indians. Reductions of military expenditures and the Grant administration's newly launched peace initiative, however, scuttled Schofield's plans.[42]

The years from 1865 to 1869 had a fundamental impact on the
nation's efforts to destroy Indian resistance. Action taken during
the Civil War against Indians had not solved the strategic dilemmas
in the West. Early postbellum plans calling for "points of rendez-
vous" and armed, organized emigrant trains were ineffective in end-
ing frontier conflicts, as Indians refused to leave their homelands in
favor of lands far from the heavily used overland trails. Hancock's
spring campaign of 1867 was an expensive failure that strengthened

---

40. Chappell, *Search for the Well-Dressed Soldier*, 27–32; Sheridan to Sherman,
Nov. 29, 1868, LC, Sherman Papers, 24, reel 13; Utley, *Frontier Regulars*, 155.
41. Hazen to Sheridan, Nov. 10, 22, 1868, Box 76, LC, Sheridan Papers.
42. Townsend to Sheridan, June 16, 1869, LS, AGO, 50, reel 37.

Indian resentment. Only the Sheridan winter offensive of 1868–69, using converging columns directed at Indian villages and resources, had produced tangible results. These large scale campaigns on the southern plains were effective not through combat but in exhausting Indian supplies and destroying morale. Crook's experience in Oregon reinforced this lesson. Still, subsequent campaigns would show that not all officers adopted these methods.

The most acclaimed Civil War generals of the North had dominated these efforts to subdue the western Indians. Grant, Sherman, Sheridan, Augur, Schofield, Hancock, Pope, Crook, and Custer headed the list of those who had first made their reputations fighting Confederates. Noting this common group of soldiers, historians have emphasized the connection between the Civil and Indian wars, arguing that Civil War experiences conditioned strategists to pursue a deliberate policy of terror against their Indian enemies.[43]

General Grant and President Abraham Lincoln eventually recognized that the Confederate armies must be annihilated. Grant, concentrating his forces, stripped garrisons and put all available soldiers in the field to destroy the enemy. Developing his plans more fully as he moved to Virginia, he brought Sheridan to the eastern theater. In August 1864, Grant requested that Sheridan take command of troops in the Shenandoah Valley "with instructions to put him south of the enemy and follow him to death. Wherever the enemy goes let our troops go also." Furthermore, Sheridan was to destroy the Valley as an economic base for the Confederacy. Sheridan later noted, "I do not hold war to mean simply that lines of men shall engage each other in battle. . . . War means much more, and is far worse than this. . . . Reduction to poverty brings prayers for peace more surely and more quickly than does the destruction of human life."[44]

43. Weigley, *American Way of War*, 153–63; Utley, "Frontier and the American Military Tradition," in Tate, ed., *American Military on the Frontier*, 11.

44. Grant to Halleck, Aug. 1, 1864, U.S. War Dept., *OR*, ser. 1, 37, pt. 2, 558 (first quotation); Weigley, *American Way of War*, 141–43; Foote, *Civil War* 3:135–36, 868–74; Sheridan, *Personal Memoirs* 1:487–88 (second quotation).

While Grant hounded Robert E. Lee's Army of Northern Virginia, Sherman wreaked havoc on the western front. Sherman captured Atlanta after a series of flanking movements, avoiding major conflicts and costly frontal assaults in the process. Pressing ahead, threatening key resource and communications centers, he forced his Confederate foes to make several unsuccessful attacks at Atlanta and a disastrous offensive thrust into Tennessee. His subsequent March to the Sea became a classic example of psychological and economic warfare. By striking at material possessions, Sherman made it difficult for the enemy to gather the means with which to fight; by destroying his opponent's homeland and spreading terror and confusion through bold action, he struck at the enemy's will to continue the war.[45]

In time, direct moves against the homes and villages of enemy tribes became a common strategem in the postwar West. As the winter campaign of 1868–69 had shown, commanders directed these economic and psychological attacks with devastating results. Sheridan pointed out the connection when he explained: "If a village is attacked and women and children killed, the responsibility is not with the soldiers but with the people whose crimes necessitated the attack. During the war did any one hesitate to attack a village or town occupied by the enemy because women or children were within its limits? Did we cease to throw shells into Vicksburg or Atlanta because women and children were there?"[46]

Although a direct connection between the Civil and Indian wars appeals to those who stress the continuity of American military strategy over the nineteenth and twentieth centuries, evidence suggests that it has been greatly exaggerated. During the Civil War, President Lincoln faced strong criticism of his effort to restore the Union by force. Peace Democrats opposed the war itself; radical Republicans urged Lincoln to make a more aggressive stance on

45. Williams, *History of American Wars*, 298–99; Hart, *Sherman*, 428–30; Sherman, *Memoirs* 2:266.

46. Hutton, *Phil Sheridan*, 185.

slavery; a variety of critics charged that the president's suspension of the writ of habeas corpus had violated the Constitution. Yet, in spite of a strong campaign for the presidency in 1864, Lincoln's opponents never gained control of the government. Likewise, congressional critics of the war effort sniped at northern generals, some harassing alleged Confederate sympathizers and others jabbing at commanders who seemed overly enthusiastic about establishing military rule in reoccupied southern districts. As was the case in the race for the presidency, however, the pro-Lincoln and pro-war majority retained control.

Although politics had been a nuisance to generals during the Civil War, it virtually handcuffed army brass in the Indian wars after 1865. Critics of the military gained congressional predominance in the decade that followed the war. Political considerations made it impossible to concentrate small garrisons into powerful strike forces needed to defeat the tribes rapidly. Furthermore, the peace commissions of 1867 and 1868 halted army offensives; Civil War campaigns, with minor exceptions (such as Lincoln's veto of Grant's proposed raid on North Carolina in 1864), met few obstacles of a similar magnitude.[47]

Environmental perceptions also reveal differences in the civil and Indian conflicts. Almost all military men had deemed the South worth retaking. But officers saw little immediate need to seize the vast regions of the Plains, initially considered by many to be unfit for farming. As settlers and explorers pronounced increasing amounts of land suitable for white settlement, army objectives had to be changed accordingly to guarantee control over areas once judged to be "Indian."

Racism surfaced as well. In simple terms, most soldiers found dispatching Indian men, women, and children far easier than killing white Southerners. The Sherman-Sheridan raids through Georgia, the Carolinas, and the Shenandoah Valley devastated the economic

47. See Hattaway and Jones, *How the North Won*, 683–704, for an account of civil-military relations during the Civil War.

heart of the Confederacy. Many Yankee soldiers had little sympathy for their Southern foes, whom they blamed for having started the civil conflict. Cities were burned and civilians shelled.[48] Yet in light of the hundreds of thousands of casualties suffered during the war between the states, a relatively small number of noncombatants were killed or wounded. By contrast, Indian women and children regularly comprised a sizable percentage of casualties in Indian-white conflicts after 1865. These deaths were at times murders resulting from motives of revenge or racism; in other instances, they were the product of the confused nature of trans-Mississippi warfare.[49] To Southerners, terror meant the destruction of economic resources and of the will to resist; to Indians, it more often meant death.

The use of railroads might suggest direct connections between strategy as employed in the Civil War and Indian wars. Rail lines had been important in shaping Civil War strategy, as both Union and Confederate generals moved large numbers of men and material via such means. Similarly, expanding rail routes merited protection and led planners to seek removal of Indians who threatened safe passage after 1865. Yet recognition of the importance of railroads to military affairs cannot be attributed to Civil War lessons alone. Farsighted observers had long predicted that such arteries would aid western settlement and improve frontier defense. As early as 1838 Gen. Edmund Gaines had urged the War Department to build railroads connecting extended posts with supply bases. By the 1850s war secretaries Charles Conrad, Jefferson Davis, and John Floyd enthusiastically supported federally sponsored railroads to the Pacific.[50]

48. Glatthaar, *March to the Sea*, 78–80.

49. Hutton, *Phil Sheridan*, 100.

50. Gaines, "A Plan for the Defence of the Western Frontier," Feb. 28, 1838, House Doc. No. 311, 25th Cong., 2nd sess., ser. 329, 1–12; Conrad to Johnson, Stanton, Scurry, Howard, and Williams, June 29, 1852, LS, SW, 33; Davis to Sandridge, Jan. 29, 1856, ibid., 37; Report of Davis, Dec. 1, SW, AR, 1853, 23; Floyd to Pope, May 5, 1857, LS, SW, 39; Floyd to Shields, Mar. 16, 1858, ibid., 40; Floyd to Brown, June 9, 1858, ibid.

Frontier conditions made traditional military tactics and techniques ineffective, further calling into question the Civil War-Indian wars connection. Particularly significant in the Indian conflicts were winter campaigns, Indian scouts, and mounted troops. In New Mexico and Arizona, winter campaigns were used to good effect both before and during the Civil War. In 1854–55 Capt. Richard Ewell and Lt. Samuel Sturgis used the winter elements to assist in their pursuit of separate groups of Mescalero Apaches. Five years later, Secretary of War John Floyd pressed Thomas Fauntleroy, commander of the Department of New Mexico, to use infantry during the winter to chastise hostile tribesmen. Kit Carson had dealt successfully with the Navajos following a winter assault in 1863–64.[51] Three years after the Carson expedition, Brig. Gen. John Mason conducted a midwinter campaign from forts Grant and Goodwin. Likewise, Sheridan had conducted his campaigns of 1868–69 during the winter season.[52]

The army's greater logistical capabilities were crucial in these winter operations against Indians. As food grew scarce during the cold weather, the army drew upon stocks of supplies, animals, and equipment assembled in anticipation of its offensive thrusts. In addition, its horses could eat grain rather than having to depend upon forage. The Indians, on the other hand, saw their resources dwindle as the bluecoats saturated tribal homelands. Limited stocks of surplus food and clothing vanished as the chase continued. Ponies dependent upon grazing grew progressively weaker as range grasses died and the demands of constant movement mounted. The army's logistical system was far from perfect; nonetheless, it was greatly superior to anything the tribes might muster.

Winter campaigning during the Indian wars was clearly more

51. Report of Ewell, Feb. 10, SW, AR, 1855, 59–61; Report of Garland, Jan. 31, Mar. 31, ibid., 56; Floyd to Nichols, July 9, ibid., 1860, 60; Fauntleroy to Scott, Aug. 26, ibid., 63; Cooper to Fauntleroy, Oct. 29, ibid., 68; Trafzer, *Kit Carson Campaign*, 96–168.

52. Report of Mason, Apr. 29, SW, AR, 1867, 97; Report of Sheridan, Nov. 1, SW, AR, 1869, 44–50.

important to the United States Army than it had been during the
Civil War. In the Indian conflicts, this strategy often proved crucial.
By contrast, it gave neither side such an enormous advantage in the
war between the states, when comparatively less fighting took place
in the winter months. The Confederacy's limited resources did cause
great hardships for her soldiers, with the image of James Longstreet's
barefooted soldiers leaving bloody tracks in the snow during his East
Tennessee campaign (1863–64) not easily overlooked. Yet these
disadvantages were not comparable to those western Indians faced
after 1865. Confederate troops at least knew that their families were
relatively safe from the fighting, and did not have to undergo the
horrors of a torturous winter chase; furthermore, as witnessed at
Fredericksburg, the southerners proved dangerous in winter combat.

Indian scouts and mounted troops were also crucial to post–1865
western strategy, when department and division commanders repeatedly sought to raise more Indian auxiliaries. These leaders had
not done so during the Civil War. Masses of Indian scouts were
indispensable to the conflicts after 1865; their unique services had
little influence during the civil conflict. And cavalry, although not
a prerequisite for success, was extremely important in tracking and
pursuing many hostile tribes. Such troops had far less impact in the
Civil War, when their roles were limited to reconnaissance, minor
raids, and screening operations.[53]

Such differences belie a direct correlation between the Indian wars
and Civil War experiences. Logistic imbalances and the special demands for cavalry and Indian scouts, along with perceptions of the
environment and of the opposition's racial differences, created a
situation in the West far different from that encountered in fighting
the Confederacy. Although the army's leaders profited from the
confidence and experience they had gained during the Civil War,

53. In the fighting between Federals and Confederates, Hattaway and Jones,
How the North Won, 44–46, 684, stress the importance of Civil War cavalry in
raids against enemy logistics in the West. On the battlefield, however, they argue
that such troops were "obsolete."

they did not simply apply established theories to new terrain. Rather, they sought by trial and error to formulate strategies suitable for use against trans-Mississippi Indians.

Furthermore, it must be emphasized that total war against an Indian enemy was not new to the United States. English speaking peoples in North America had conducted total warfare against the Pequots as early as 1637. More commonly known to nineteenth-century military men were the Second (1835–42) and Third (1856–58) Seminole wars. During these bitter conflicts, a series of commanders attempted to remove the scattered Indian bands from Florida. The Seminoles eluded the army's strike forces, and, led by such fighters as Osceola and Billy Bowlegs, conducted masterful guerrilla campaigns. Only by applying the principles of total warfare, in which enemy leaders were taken prisoner under flags of truce, women and children killed and captured, and crops, homes, and possessions ruthlessly destroyed, did the army force the Seminoles into submission. Among the junior officers receiving firsthand experience in the conflicts were Sherman, Schofield, and Ord.[54]

As individuals, Sheridan and Sherman eventually came to see that total war could be used against Indians after 1865. Sheridan in particular applied it as forcefully as possible. Sherman, however, personally adopted a policy of total warfare only after trying other methods. His reports of 1865 and 1866 do not reveal his intention to pursue such a strategy; instead, he suggests that Indians be dealt with in a much different fashion. Removal, "railroad belts," and armed emigrant trains were a far cry from total warfare. Sherman had often avoided battles during the Civil War; direct conflicts with the Indians were his ultimate objectives by 1868.[55]

54. Williams, *History of American Wars*, 312; Utley, "Frontier and American Military Tradition," 11. On the Florida conflict, see Mahon, *History of the Second Seminole War*. On the Pequot War, see Malone, "Indian and English Military Systems," 256–64.

55. See particularly Sherman's early letters and reports, including Sherman to Grant, Aug. 31, 1866, House Ex. Doc. No. 23, 39th Cong., 2nd sess., VI, ser. 1288, 9; Sherman to Rawlins, Sept. 12, 21, ibid., 13, 15–16; and report of Nov.

Despite the tremendous influence of Sheridan and Sherman, their gradually developed theories of total warfare did not win the universal acceptance of fellow officers, most of whom continued to see Indian warfare as being almost totally different from Civil War combat. Hancock's Plains offensive of 1867 resembles not his actions against the Confederates but rather a series of moves long used on the Indian frontier, seen most clearly in Col. Stephen Kearny's ninety-nine day march onto the Plains with five companies of the First Dragoons in 1845.[56]

John Schofield's 1881 article, "Notes on 'The Legitimate in War,' " clearly illustrates that the doctrine of total, indiscriminate warfare against Indians failed to win full approval within the armed forces. In his essay Schofield admitted that civilized peoples might be forced to exterminate "incorrigible savages." Yet most American Indians, he believed, did not fall into that category. "Hence, even in our dealings with them we have no right to disregard the rules of civilized warfare, although we may have to modify their application according to the character of the enemy." Schofield went on to argue that "the end of war is not destruction, but peace and profitable friendship." He maintained further that "the only legitimate objects of attack are the military power and resources of the enemy. We have no right to destroy either life or property in mere wantonness," he concluded. While no more a summation of army policy than anything contributed by Sheridan or Sherman, the Schofield essay, written by a future commanding general, shows that the idea of total warfare against American Indians had not gained universal acceptance, even by 1881.[57]

Despite military achievements on the southern plains and in Or-

---

5, SW, AR, 1866, 20–21. Contrast also the secondary accounts of Foote, *Civil War* 3:833, and Utley, *Frontier Regulars*, 51.

56. Report of Kearny, Sept. 15, SW, AR, 1845, 210–12.

57. Schofield, "Notes on 'The Legitimate in War,'" For a similar example, see the revised edition of Bigelow's *Principles of Strategy*, 263–64, as noted by Gates, *Schoolbooks and Krags*, 83.

egon, the army had reached no clear consensus by 1869 as to how Indians could best be defeated, and numerous obstacles prevented the military from achieving this goal. Even the best laid plans remained subject to changes resulting from supply foul-ups, misinformation, and unexpected Indian initiatives. The costs of winter attacks were quite heavy, especially in terms of animals and supplies. Troops could not campaign constantly, and the nagging questions of concentration or dispersal of frontier forces remained unresolved. Aggressive leadership essential for success was often lacking. The more realistic military planners also realized that political realities often prevented the army from launching its vaunted offensives.[58]

More conflict loomed ahead, the most dangerous of which included attempts to destroy Indians whose inter-tribal cooperation the army had so long feared. A few formal guidelines had been established. Sherman and Sheridan encouraged railroad expansion with escorts and protection. Better mobility, converging columns, and determined pursuit regardless of season or terrain helped the army confront Indian warriors with better results. Commanders in the field as well as in department and division headquarters nonetheless continued to rely largely on personal experience when implementing broad military objectives in the West. Specific instructions had been and would continue to be vague. Their methods were often distinct from those practiced between 1861 and 1865. Despite the absence of cogent strategic guidelines, intermittent but determined army action reduced the resources Indians had at their disposal and, in time, decimated the tribes.

58. Sheridan, *Personal Memoirs* 2:327.

Chapter Five
"To Conquer a Lasting Peace": The Frontier, 1869–1877

"The whole Indian question is in such a snarl, that I am utterly powerless to help you by order or advice," wrote General Sherman to Schofield, commander of the Department of the Missouri, in June 1869. "Do the best you can."[1] Despite the concerted efforts of men like Sherman, Schofield, Sheridan, and Pope—all battle-tested veterans of the Civil War—little development of military policy or strategy regarding Indians occurred in the immediate postwar years. The army, lacking sustained congressional or popular support, could rarely afford to launch costly efforts such as those undertaken on the southern plains between 1867 and 1869. More significant, Grant's

1. Sherman to Schofield, June 9, 1869, LS, AGO, 50, reel 37.

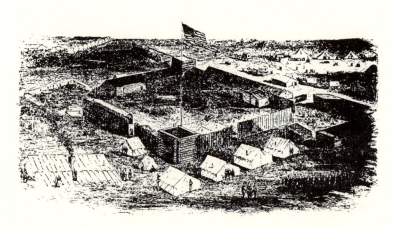

controversial peace policy discouraged offensive campaigns, relying on good works rather than military conquest to bring peace to the American West.

Events in Montana during the winter of 1869 further eroded support for military action in the West. On October 21, 1869, Sheridan suggested a surprise attack on the winter camps of the Piegan Indians, who had been suspected of numerous depredations over the years. Sherman gave his permission two weeks later, having first sent copies of plans for the proposed strike to the Indian bureau, which issued no protest. Following these directions, Major Baker attacked a camp of Piegans on January 23 and decimated the unprepared Indians.[2] An elated Sheridan predicted that the Baker affair would "end Indian troubles in Montana"; Commissioner of Indian Affairs Parker, although crediting the attack with "completely subduing the Indians," found the killing of fifty-three women and children "deplorable." Subsequent attempts by the military to justify Baker's attack were ineffectual, and the episode reinforced the image many Americans held of bloodthirsty bluecoats wantonly slaughtering innocent Indian noncombatants.[3]

The army, confronted with a nation weary of war, a Congress eager to cut military expenditures, and a president seeking to initiate a more pacific policy toward American Indians, assumed a defensive posture. Until the Interior Department permitted troops to enter Indian reservations, major offensives against the Plains tribes were prohibited. In this atmosphere, John Pope, who had taken over the Missouri department from Schofield in 1870, proposed to concen-

2. Sheridan to Townsend, Oct. 21, 1869, Senate Ex. Doc. No. 49, 41st Cong., 2nd sess., II, ser. 1406, 7; Townsend to Sheridan, Nov. 4, ibid.; Report of Hancock, Nov. 1, SW, AR, 1870, 29–30; Sherman to Sheridan, Mar. 24, 1870, LS, AGO, 51, reel 38.

3. Sheridan to Sherman, Jan. 29, 1870, Box 53, LC, Sheridan Papers (first quotation); Report of Parker, Oct. 31, SI, AR, 1870, 467 (second and third quotations). See also Sully to Parker, Feb. 10, 1870, House Ex. Doc. No. 185, 41st Cong., 2nd sess., VII, ser. 1418, 6; Hutton, "Phil Sheridan's Pyrrhic Victory," 32–43.

trate troops in large garrisons. Sheridan disagreed, arguing that, as Pope's current duties were passive, his troops should be dispersed along the frontiers and travel routes. Commanding General Sherman urged the restless Sheridan to try to cope with the forced inactivity, and to trust that the country's innate wisdom would ultimately prevail. In the meantime, the army had to satisfy itself with guarding the railroads, reorganizing its administrative structure (transferring the Department of Texas to the Division of the Missouri and merging the departments of the Platte and the Missouri), and dealing with minor problems as they occured.[4]

While officers stationed on the grasslands of middle America fretted about their enforced inactivity, those serving in the Far Southwest and the Pacific Northwest enjoyed greater freedom of action, since Indians in these two regions attracted less public attention than did the more notorious Plains tribes. Although department commander Ord perceived Arizona and New Mexico as largely unsuitable for white settlement, he asserted that the Apaches had to be crushed nonetheless. Ord labeled them a collection of "robbers and murderers" whose "hands have always been bloody, . . . their favorite ornaments the finger & toe nails, the teeth, hair, and small bones of their victims." Ord established new forts and sent out expeditions with instructions "to capture and root out the Apache by every means, and to hunt them as they would wild animals." He argued that this "fear of extermination" forced Apache warriors to protect their families and remain on the defensive.[5]

4. Belknap to Clarke, Feb. 15, 1870, LS, SW, 63, reel 60; Report of Pope, Oct. 31, SW, AR, 1870, 11–13; Report of Sheridan, Nov. 4, ibid., 1871, 24; Sherman to Sheridan, Mar. 24, 1870, LS, AGO, 51, reel 38 (quotation); Sherman to Townsend, June 11, 1871, LC, Sherman Papers, 90, reel 45; Sherman to Sheridan, Oct. 31, 1871, ibid.; Sherman to Schofield, ibid.

5. Ord to Logan, Dec. 29, 1869, LC, Logan Papers (first two quotations); Report of Ord, Sept. 27, SW, AR, 1869, 121–22 (third and fourth quotations).

On his views of the environment, see Ord to Sherman, Mar. 30, 1870, LC, Sherman Papers, 27, reel 15. For examples of Sherman's attitudes, see Sherman to Schofield, July 16, 1869, LS, AGO, 50, reel 37; Sherman to Belknap, Jan. 7, 1870, ibid., 51, reel 38.

Despite Ord's determined efforts, complaints about Apache depredations continued. Hoping to ease administrative difficulties, War Department officials created a separate Department of Arizona in April 1870. Colonel George Stoneman, formerly head of the District of Arizona, assumed command of the newly upgraded department. Stoneman had no desire to live in the wilds of Arizona, however, and maintained "temporary" headquarters at Drum Barracks, near Los Angeles. He finally launched an offensive in December 1870, in which he vowed to "prosecute a vigorous, persistent and relentless winter campaign against the Pinal and Tonto" Apaches.[6]

These vaunted attacks were less effective than expected. Stoneman advised Sherman confidentially that the campaign "was intended for the Arizona market" and hoped that peace commissioners would "take this arduous and dangerous duty out of our hands, and protect the lives of the People of Arizona by an exercise of moral and religious influence." Stoneman's claims undoubtedly came in response to Sherman's warning to abide by Grant's peace policy. In any event, Arizonians, especially Governor Anson P. K. Safford, blamed Stoneman for the continued Apache depredations. Safford and Senator William M. Stewart (R–Nev.) convinced Grant to replace Stoneman with Crook.[7]

Before Crook could arrive, a group of Tucson citizens took matters into their own hands. On April 30, 1871, the vigilante group, bolstered by a number of Papagos Indians, slaughtered at least eighty-five Indians at nearby Camp Grant. Despite a storm of eastern

6. Thian, comp., *Military Geography*, 52, 54, 76–77; Utley, *Frontier Regulars*, 199; Altshuler, *Chains of Command*, 162–63, 188. Stoneman's order quoted in Sherman to Schofield, Feb. 2, 1871, LS, AGO, 53, reel 40; Schofield to Townsend, Dec. 15, 1870, Box 81, LC, Schofield Papers.

7. Quoted from Altshuler, *Chains of Command*, 189. For Schofield's opinions of Stoneman, see Schofield to Sherman, Apr. 1, 1871, Box 49, LC, Schofield Papers; Sherman to Schofield, Feb. 2, 1871, LS, AGO, 53, reel 40; Altshuler, *Chains of Command*, 190–96; Sherman to Schofield, Sept. 22, 1871, LS, AGO, 54, reel 41.

protest, a Tucson jury acquitted all participants in the massacre after only nineteen minutes of deliberation. The enraged Apaches struck back as frontier violence escalated amid cries of protest from Indian reformers. Crook delayed preparations for a winter offensive scheduled for late 1871 in order to allow first Vincent Colyer and then Howard opportunities to extend the government's olive branch. Although Colyer and Howard convinced large numbers of Apaches and Yavapais to move to reservations, these efforts failed to bring lasting peace to the Southwest. Crook cooperated with both men; privately, he always maintained that he must be allowed to "conquer a lasting peace" with the Apaches. With strong support from the territorial populace, the federal government finally assented to military action.[8]

Crook was one of the few army officers with a genuine understanding of Indian warfare. He advised subordinates to familiarize themselves with the terrain and environment in which they worked. He also believed that they should attempt to understand the distinctive habits of the various tribes and pointed out the benefits of cooperating with friendly Indians. Crook instructed one officer to give Indian allies surplus arms and ammunition "to convince them of our friendly regard, so that their separation from hostile parties may be rendered more assured and complete." Such treatment might also lure them into signing up for army scouting duties. Most important, Crook realized that troops must pursue hostiles relentlessly with swift thrusts to keep them from scattering. With his troops sweeping through Indian haunts regardless of season, Crook

8. Schofield to Sherman, Sept. 14, 1871, National Archives, LS, Dept. of Mo., Box 49, LC, Schofield Papers; Schofield to Crook, Feb. 8, 1872, ibid.; Sherman to Schofield, Sept. 22, 1871, LS, AGO, 54, reel 41; Delano to Howard, Feb. 29, 1872, Bowdoin Library, Howard Papers; Grant to Schofield, Mar. 6, 1872, LC, Grant Papers, series 2, 1, reel 3; Schofield to Sherman, Mar. 25, 1872, LC, Sherman Papers, 32, reel 17; Crook to AG, Sept. 19, 1871, Hayes Library, Crook Papers (quotation); Utley, *Frontier Regulars*, 200–1.

On the Camp Grant massacre, see Langellier, "Camp Grant Affair," 17–30.

forced the recalcitrants onto reservations by late 1873. Civil and military authorities alike applauded his efforts.[9]

A different situation plagued officers in Oregon. In 1872–73, about sixty Modoc warriors led by Kintpuash (Captain Jack) created a defensive stronghold in the jagged terrain of the lava beds south of Tule Lake that was unequaled in the Indian wars. Agents pressured the army to take action against the Modocs, who surrendered only after inflicting several embarrassing defeats on hapless army detachments and murdering Brig. Gen. E. R. S. Canby while under a white flag of truce.[10] The Modoc War won few plaudits for the army. The regulars' firepower had failed to drive the Modocs from their rock strongholds. Although one officer asserted that this was the first time in his twenty-three years of service against Indians in which artillery had been necessary, only two small mountain howitzers were available for much of the campaign.[11] Officers rarely coordinated their attacks. Furthermore, most were unable to deploy skirmishers properly, thus inviting Modoc sharpshooters to pick off vulnerable troopers. "Those men dont [sic] know how to fight Indians," wrote one critic, who concluded that "Crook appears to be about the only good Indian fighter we have." Enlisted men acquitted themselves no better, exhibiting poor marksmanship and unsteadiness under fire. In the end, those Indians remaining loyal to Kint-

9. Crook to AG, Sept. 4, 1871, National Archives, LS, Dept. of Arizona (quotation); Crook to Commander, Apache Camp, Sept. 12, ibid.; Crook to AG, Sept. 4, 1871, Hayes Library, Crook Papers; Crook to Schofield, Mar. 12, 1872, Box 39, LC, Schofield Papers; Report of Crook, Sept. 28, SW, AR, 1871, 78; Report of Schofield, Nov. 3, ibid., 1873, 51; Report of Williams, Sept. 1, SI, AR, 1873, 656.

10. Primary accounts are in House Ex. Doc. No. 122, 43rd Cong., 1st sess., IX, ser. 1607, 33–113; Canby to AAG, Feb. 3, 1872, Jan. 15, 1873, National Archives, LS, Dept. of the Columbia; Canby to Meacham, Feb. 5, 1872, ibid.; AAAG to Caziarc, Feb. 16, 1872, ibid.; Canby to Gillem, Jan. 29, 1873, ibid.; Canby to Sherman, Jan. 30, 1873, ibid. For secondary accounts, see Murray, *Modocs and Their War*, and Utley, *Frontier Regulars*, 205–7.

11. Frank Wheaton to Schofield, May 10, 1873, Box 9, LC, Schofield Papers.

puash were convinced to surrender not by army regulars but by deserters from their own tribe. The entire episode exposed the army's poor training, inadequate planning and preparation, and dearth of innovative thinking.[12]

While the soldiers in the Northwest battled Modocs, Colonel Mackenzie took decisive action along the Rio Grande. Citizens in south and west Texas had long been victimized by Indians who crossed the border, raided settlements in the United States, and retired to their homes in Mexico. Acting on the verbal instructions of division chief Sheridan, Mackenzie led a powerful column across the Rio Grande into Mexico in May 1873, destroying three Indian villages. Both Sheridan and department commander Augur applauded Mackenzie's unlawful raid, and the number of Indian depredations declined in the following months.[13]

Crook's experiences in Arizona, the army's haphazard conduct in Oregon, and Mackenzie's expedition south of the border encouraged the aggressive inclinations of military leaders. Crook and Mackenzie had produced positive results. Rather than merely reacting to Indian offensives, they had seized the initiative. There were of course obvious differences in their methods. Crook harassed his Apache counterparts into surrender by dogged pursuit; Mackenzie struck directly at their homes and villages. Yet each had gained the upper hand by moving decisively. By contrast, Canby's inaction in Oregon allowed a few Modoc warriors to tie up several hundred regulars for almost six months. The events of 1872–73 thus strengthened the army's resolve to scrap the peace policy, which hampered offensives, and reinforced the impression that the army alone could not affect government In-

12. Van Vliet to Sherman, May 4, 1873, LC, Sherman Papers, 35, reel 19 (quotation); Utley, *Frontier Regulars*, 213.

13. Sheridan to Augur, May 22, 1873, Box 58, LC, Sheridan Papers; Augur to Mackenzie, May 29, 1873, U.S. Army Hist. Res. Coll., Mackenzie Papers. See also chapter 3.

dian policy. In each case, only after citizen complaints became especially impassioned or local Indian agents summoned military support had the army been able to take the offensive.

Although the reformers' attempts to secure peace did not prevent armed conflict in the Southwest or Pacific Northwest, they had kept the army from launching major expeditions on the Plains, where the most powerful tribes lived. Because of their large numbers and growing mystique in the minds of many Americans, Plains Indians remained in the public eye much more than the less numerous Apaches and less well-known Modocs. As a result, government officials, whether in the War Department or the Indian bureau, could not afford to openly violate the spirit of the peace policy, even when dealing with Indians who committed crimes outside their reservations. Depredations along the Texas, Kansas, and Dakota frontiers grew as the impact of the 1868–69 winter campaigns faded. The army found it impossible to punish fractious Indians who retreated to the immunity of their reservations after each raid. Fighting between Plains Indians and regulars was as a result desultory and indecisive from 1869 to 1874.

Especially galling were the actions of tribes in the Indian Territory. This area was under the control of Quaker agents, who had been assigned their tasks as part of Grant's peace initiative. Army officers believed that the Friends were gullible and easily duped by raiders. In May 1871, Sherman himself narrowly escaped death at the hands of a Kiowa raiding party eight miles west of Fort Richardson, Texas. Sherman and Colonel Grierson arrested the most blatant offenders, Satank, Satanta, and Big Tree, when they brazenly demanded arms and supplies at Grierson's house at Fort Sill later that month. Satank was killed while attempting to escape; a Jacksboro civil court convicted Satanta and Big Tree of murder, only to have Governor Davis of Texas commute their sentences as a show of the government's good faith. Furor over Davis's action and the alleged inaction of the Quakers led military officers to assert that only disarming and dismounting the Indians would restore peace.

To do this, the army needed permission to hunt down guilty Indians wherever they were found.[14]

Sheridan planned several offensives in the early 1870s. He explained that, although he supported the government's efforts to "civilize and Christianize the wild Indians, . . . the principle [sic] error . . . is that, while efforts are being made to teach the Indian what is right, and to induce him to do right, sufficient importance has not been given to teaching him what is wrong." To inflict such punishment, officers in the departments of the Missouri and Texas joined Sheridan in planning for winter campaigns. Yet due to the implementation of the peace plan, Schofield's proposed expedition of 1869 never really earned serious consideration; Augur's plans for 1871 met a similar fate. Sheridan pushed hard for a winter offensive the next year but failed to convince Interior Secretary Delano to abandon the peace policy.[15]

By 1873, Sheridan's plans had matured more fully. He wanted powerful infantry and cavalry columns to invade the Indian Territory during the winter, for "that is the time they can be caught." Many officers were convinced that a winter campaign was indeed forthcoming, as patrols were stepped up and orders issued to break up illicit trade with the Indians on the Staked Plains. All awaited Delano's permission for the operation. On December 11, a still hopeful Sheridan lamented that the Interior Secretary had been "slow" in authorizing the movement. A month later Sherman testified that action would begin in February 1874, "when the Indian

14. Rister, "Significance of the Jacksboro Indian Affair." Schofield to Sheridan, Feb. 4, 1870, Box 78, LC, Schofield Papers; Belknap to Clarke, Feb. 15, 1870, LS, SW, 68, reel 60; Reynolds to AG, Aug. 15, 1870, National Archives, LS, Dept. of Texas; Mackenzie to Sherman, June 15, 1871, LC, Sherman Papers, 30, reel 16; Sheridan, endorsement of July 11, 1872, Box 7, LC, Sheridan Papers.

15. Report of Sheridan, Oct. 12, SW, AR, 1872, 35 (quotation); Davis to Schofield, Nov. 20, 1869, Box 4, LC, Schofield Papers; Augur to Sheridan, Dec. 9, 1871, National Archives, LS, Dept. of Texas; Sheridan, endorsement of July 16, 1872, Box 7, LC, Sheridan Papers; Belknap to Sheridan, July 27, 1872, LS, SW, 70, reel 64.

ponies are all poor." But when spring came troops continued their normal duties. Again, the army's role in shaping federal Indian policy had been minimal.[16]

Sheridan's plans could not change Delano's mind about the peace policy, but subsequent Indian raids did. Indians of the southern plains grew increasingly restive as buffalo hunters continued their annual slaughter. Comanche, Kiowa, and Cheyenne warriors, forced to move from their traditional homelands to arbitrary reservations in Indian Territory, now saw their very way of life threatened, and struck with bitter vengeance along the Kansas and Texas borders. Sherman advised Belknap to take action. "Defensively it will require ten thousand cavalry to give even a partial protection; but offensively, a thousand cavalry can follow them and punish them as they surely merit." On July 16, 1874, Belknap informed Delano that he agreed with Sherman's views, requesting an "early reply of the Honorable Secretary of the Interior." Delano authorized the army to pursue hostile parties onto reservations two days later; the change in attitudes of civil policymakers clearly resulted from increased Indian raids rather than army influence.[17]

Sheridan had anticipated Delano's decision. Throughout July he had urged Augur, chief of the Texas department, to prepare for an immediate offensive. Sheridan also encouraged Pope, in the Missouri department, to cooperate. Pope, however, was reluctant, advising that the army should instead remain on the defensive until "the cold weather shuts up the Indians so that they cannot escape, and then

16. Sheridan to Sherman, Nov. 12, 1873, Box 10, LC, Sheridan Papers (first quotation); Woodward to Grierson, Oct. 10, 1873, Ill. State Hist. Library, Grierson Papers; Sheridan to Pope, Dec. 4, 11 (second quotation), 1873, Box 92, Sheridan Papers; Testimony of Sherman, Jan. 7, 1874, House Rpt. No. 384, 43rd Cong., 1st sess., ser. 1624, 13 (third quotation).

17. Reports of Sheridan, Oct. 1, SW, AR, 1874, 26; Pope, Sept. 7, ibid., 29–30; and Augur, Sept. 28, ibid., 40; Sherman, endorsement of July 16, 1874, in Taylor, comp., *Indian Campaign on the Staked Plains*, 113 (first quotation); Belknap to SI, July 16, 1874, LS, SW, 75, reel 68 (second quotation); Belknap to SI, July 20, 1874, ibid.

The Red River War, 1874–1875

Source: Utley, *Frontier Regulars*, pp. 171, 228

Note: From July 10, 1874, to March 11, 1875, the Department of Texas consisted of the state of Texas and that part of the Indian territory south of the main branch of the Canadian River. The Department of the Missouri included the states of Missouri, Kansas, and Illinois, the territories of New Mexico and Colorado, and those parts of Texas and the Indian territory north of the Canadian. Thian, *Military Geography*, pp. 77, 100

strike them effectually as was intended last winter. We can make a complete finish up of the whole concern by waiting, and I fear if we begin now we shall only use up our cavalry." Pope's opposition infuriated Sheridan, who promptly complained to Sherman that Pope "is so taken with the idea of a defensive line that he does not see the absurdity of using cavalry that way." Apparently, Sheridan decided that the army could not afford to wait for winter. Other Indians might go on the warpath if guilty tribesmen were not soon punished. Westerners demanded immediate action, and the Interior Department might withdraw its permission at any moment. Sheridan also pointed out that a second campaign could come the following winter.[18]

Despite Pope's sluggishness, vague plans for a late summer offensive slowly materialized in July. Except for the season, the movements resembled those undertaken five years earlier on the southern plains. Several mixed columns of cavalry and infantry marched across the Texas Panhandle and the western Indian territory with freedom to pursue hostiles wherever they fled. As commander of the Division of the Missouri, Sheridan concerned himself chiefly with relaying interdepartmental communications and securing supplies. "I will not sketch out any plan of operations for your cavalry," he wrote Pope, "leaving you to exercise your good judgment in this respect." Department commanders Pope and Augur could thus conduct and coordinate their actions as each saw fit. In practice, however, this meant that each knew little about the other's intentions. To com-

18. Sheridan to Augur, July 21, 1874, National Archives, LS, Dept. of the Missouri; Pope to Sheridan, July 10, 16 (first quotation), 22, 1874, ibid.; Sheridan to Sherman, July 16, 1874, Box 56, LC, Sheridan Papers (second quotation); Sheridan to Pope, ibid.; Sheridan to Sherman, July 18, 1874, ibid.; Sheridan to Pope, July 18, 1874, ibid.; Sheridan to Pope, July 24, 1874, ibid.

Sheridan later noted that someone had "stupidly allowed to be published" his July 16 letter critical of Pope's lack of energy. While this angered Pope, Sheridan concluded that "I claim the right to criticize the military actions of subordinate commanders in confidential communications to my superior" (Sheridan to Sherman, Sept. 7, 1874, ibid., Box 11).

pound the problem, Sherman had moved his headquarters from Washington to St. Louis two months earlier to protest War Secretary Belknap's interference in army affairs. Although Sherman had just cause for complaint, the move effectively removed him from any role he might otherwise have played in the upcoming campaign.[19]

The lack of coordination extended below the departmental level. Pope organized columns from his sector under Colonel Miles and Maj. William R. Price, but his instructions to these field leaders were at least as vague as those he had received from Sheridan. Their mobile commands should attack hostile Indians wherever located, but "must be guided by circumstances as they arise." It was "desirable" that Miles go south from Fort Dodge, Kansas, to Fort Sill, and then operate west of the Wichita Mountains. "If the circumstances will permit," Price was to join Miles after marching down the Canadian River from Fort Bascom, New Mexico.[20]

In Texas, Augur made his plans with the assumption that the northern operations would drive hostile Indians into his department. Increasingly vigorous Mexican policing efforts along the Rio Grande allowed him to transfer Mackenzie and his battle-tested Fourth Cavalry to the northern frontier to spearhead the offensive. "In carrying out your plans," he instructed the aggressive Mackenzie, "you need pay no regard to Department or Reservation lines. You are at liberty to follow the Indians wherever they go, even to the Agencies." Lieutenant Colonels George Buell and John W. Davidson were assigned to work to the north of Mackenzie.[21] Augur expected a long

---

19. Sheridan to Pope, July 22, LC, Sheridan Papers, Box 11 (quotation); see also numerous letters from Sheridan to Pope and Augur, Aug.-Dec. 1874, in ibid., Box 56. Those of Aug. 2, Nov. 18, and Dec. 1 are especially instructive.

20. Pope to Sheridan, July 22, 1874, National Archives, LS, Dept. of Mo.; Pope to Miles, July 29, 1874, ibid. (first two quotations); Pope to Miles, Aug. 3, Sept. 15, 1874, ibid.; Pope to Miles, Aug. 5, 1874, ibid.; Pope to Price, Aug. 12, 1874, ibid.

21. Sheridan to Augur, July 21, 23, 1874, Box 56, LC, Sheridan Papers; Sheridan to Augur, Aug. 24, 1874, Box 11, ibid., (quotation); Augur to Mackenzie, July 23, 1874, National Archives, LS, Dept. of Texas; Augur to Sheridan,

campaign, warning Mackenzie not to count on success "in a day" and advising Sheridan that these subordinates must be allowed to continue their efforts throughout the upcoming winter. That was the extent of Augur's instructions; it was clear that he placed great faith in Mackenzie's celebrated skill in Indian warfare.[22]

Davidson's black troopers of the Tenth Cavalry saw action first. He had been assigned the thankless task of separating friendly and hostile Indians at Fort Sill. The job was maddening. Davidson's sanity had already been questioned by fellow officers. A subordinate had noted the previous May that "Davidson is, without doubt, crazy at times. He says himself he has had a sunstroke which seriously effects his brain. . . . I must confess it aint [sic] pleasant to serve under a lunatic." Whatever Davidson's mental condition, his duties in this situation were enough to try even the sanest of men. Many Cheyennes, Kiowas, and Comanches refused to report to reservation officials. In August 1874, troops and Indians began long-range skirmishing. Sheridan blamed Davidson for not pursuing the hostiles more vigorously (as he had charged Hazen five years earlier) but was satisfied that justice had been served. The Indians had been given a chance to surrender and the reformers had been quieted; now Sheridan's columns could hunt to the death hostile Kiowas, Comanches, and Cheyennes.[23]

July 28, 1874, ibid.; Sheridan to Augur, Aug. 24, 1874, Box 11, Sheridan Papers; Woodward to Grierson, Aug. 8, 1874, Ill. State Hist. Library, Grierson Papers; Augur to Mackenzie, Aug. 28, 1874, in Wallace, ed., *Ranald S. Mackenzie's Official Correspondence Relating to Texas*, 80–82 (quotation) (hereafter cited as *Mackenzie Corr.*); Mackenzie to Augur, Aug. 28, 1874, ibid., 82–83; Davidson to AAG, Oct. 10, 1874, ibid., 130; Sheridan to Sherman, Sept. 5, 1874, Box 11, Sheridan Papers.

22. Augur to Mackenzie, Aug. 28, 1874, National Archives, LS, Dept. of Texas; Augur to Sheridan, July 28, 1874, ibid.; Sheridan to Augur, Sept. 2, 1874, Box 11, LC, Sheridan Papers.

23. Report of Augur, Sept. 28, 1874, Wallace, *Mackenzie Corr.*, 103–11; Sheridan to Pope, Sept. 2, 1874, Box 11, LC, Sheridan Papers. Quoted in S. L. W. [Woodward] to Grierson, Fort Concho Res. Library, Texas Letters of Benjamin Grierson.

To the west, Miles, Price, Buell, and Mackenzie scoured the Staked Plains in separate columns, each having scant knowledge of what his colleagues were doing. Severe drought, heat, and a locust plague made the late summer combatants—white, black, and Indian—suffer terribly. Actual combat was sporadic; most important were sharp fights led by Miles at Tule and by Mackenzie at Palo Duro Canyons. The latter encounter, in which Mackenzie surprised a group of Kiowas, Comanches, and Cheyennes, was particularly significant. The Indians escaped but left behind their winter stores, lodges, and ponies. After selecting the finest mounts for his own beleaguered command, Mackenzie ordered the slaughter of the one thousand remaining horses that had been captured, thus crippling the mobility of the affected tribes.[24]

As winter breathed its icy winds over the Staked Plains, dissension prevailed among both regulars and Indians. Augur complained that "the contractors [suppliers] have failed us." Davidson gave up the chase in late November; Buell returned to Fort Griffin in December; Mackenzie's exhausted troops retired later that month. Miles accused Pope of failing to secure supplies. "I do not think he has much sympathy with this movement," he wrote to Sherman. Yet after briefly refurbishing his troops in the fall of 1874, Miles again sent his columns into the field, the last expedition returning to base on the Washita River on February 3, 1875.[25]

24. Miles to AAG, Mar. 4, SW, AR, 1875, 78–79; Miles to AAG, Sept. 1, 1874, Wallace, *Mackenzie Corr.*, 84–88; Price to AAG, Sept. 23, 1874, ibid., 94–103; Drum to Whipple, Oct. 24, 1874, ibid., 144; Buell to Mackenzie, Nov. 8, 1874, *Indian Campaign*, 81–82; Mackenzie's Journal of Campaign, Sept. 20–29, 1874, Wallace, *Mackenzie Corr.*, 119–24. For a secondary account, see Leckie, "Red River War."

25. Augur to Mackenzie, Sept. 13, 1874, National Archives, LS, Dept. of Texas (quotation); Augur to Sheridan, Nov. 26, 1874, ibid.; Mackenzie to Augur, Nov. 16, 27, Dec. 2, 1874, Wallace, *Mackenzie Corr.*, 164–67, 173–76, 181–83; Mackenzie's Journal of Campaign, Nov. 22–Dec. 19, 1874, ibid., 188–90; Miles to AAG, Mar. 4, SW, AR, 1875, 79–83; Pope to Drum, Sept. 1, ibid., 73–74; Miles to Sherman, Sept. 27, 1874, LC, Sherman Papers, 37, reel 20 (second quotation).

In terms of combat casualties, the 1874–75 offensives had produced meager results for the army. But the large columns of regulars that overran the Staked Plains demoralized the Indians. The long forced marches exhausted Indian supplies, ponies, and fighting spirit, whereas the detested reservations at least offered security. Amid bitter internal struggles, increasing numbers of Indians surrendered throughout the winter and spring, the last band of resisters straggling in the following June. To prevent future troubles, the army shipped seventy-four of the most notable chiefs and a few arbitrarily selected warriors to Florida. Indian military power in the southern plains had been forever broken.[26]

Serious trouble was also brewing in the north, where the projection of the Northern Pacific Railroad into lands claimed by the Sioux boded ill for future Indian-white relations. The Fort Laramie Treaty of 1868 had created a huge Sioux reservation comprising much of present-day South Dakota west of the Missouri River and had called for the government to issue annuities at designated agencies. Although many officers opposed the treaty's provision that closed the Bozeman Trail (and thus forced the army to abandon forts Phil Kearny and C. F. Smith), the new restrictions on the emigrant line would at least make frontier defense more manageable. The army, too small to engage in simultaneous fighting over all the Plains,

The severity of the winter is shown in Davidson to Augur, Nov. 23, 1874, in *Indian Campaign*, 109, in which he notes that an ice storm killed 100 animals and inflicted frostbite on 26 of his 160 effective troops.

On the Pope-Miles controversy, see also Pope to Miles, Sept. 13, 18, 24, 1874, LS, Dept. of Mo., 87; and Sheridan to Pope, Nov. 11, 1874, Box 11, LC, Sheridan Papers. On Price, see Drum to Miles, Nov. 3, 1874, LS, Dept. of Mo., 87.

26. Neill to AAG, Oct. 4, 1874, *Indian Campaign*, 88–90; Whipple to AG, Nov. 7, 1874, ibid., 102; Pope to Drum, Feb. 23, 1875, ibid., 180–82; Neill to AAG, Mar. 7, 1875, ibid., 190–92; Henely to Post Adjutant, Apr. 26, SW, AR, 1875, 89–91; Pope to Drum, Sept. 1, ibid., 74–75; Sheridan, endorsement of Feb. 25, 1875, *Indian Campaign*, 178–79; Sherman to SW, Mar. 1, 1875, ibid., 179; Delano to Belknap, ibid., 185–86; Pratt to Sheridan, Apr. 26, 1875, ibid., 279–80; Pratt to AG, May 23, 1875, ibid., 285–89.

could concentrate on the Indians to the south, limiting itself in the north to a more passive defense of railroad construction teams. Other officers acknowledged that the land returned to the Sioux seemed to be of little immediate value to white settlers, further easing the acceptance of the Bozeman Trail closure. Military men generally agreed, however, that the restless Sioux and Northern Cheyennes, especially those led by Sitting Bull, would have to be dealt with in the future.[27]

The army's responsibilities in the north became increasingly difficult as progress on the railroads continued. Large escorts accompanied railroad surveying parties in 1871, 1872, and 1873. Realizing that the railroads would encourage white hunters and settlers and menace traditional Sioux lifestyles, the Sioux opposed the 1873 escort in force. During the winter of 1873–74 the Sioux wreaked havoc at the Red Cloud and Spotted Tail agencies. In response to the agents' calls for military protection, Sheridan ordered Col. John Smith and nearly one thousand troops into the field with instructions to "strike the first blow, always saving women and children" if he found the Indians meditating an attack. Smith drove some of the more troublesome Indians from the Red Cloud and Spotted Tail bases, establishing camps Robinson and Sheridan in the process.[28]

The Northern Pacific Railroad went bankrupt in 1873, thus temporarily removing the threat from that source. However, the Sioux

27. Sherman to Sheridan, July 15, 1869, LS, AGO, 50, reel 37; Sherman to Sheridan, May 18, 1870, ibid., 52, reel 39; Sherman to Belknap, Apr. 21, 1870, ibid.; Sherman to Sheridan, Apr. 25, 1870, ibid.; Sherman to Hancock, Aug. 5, 1870, ibid.; Townsend to Hancock, Nov. 23, 1870, ibid., 53, reel 40; Sherman to Sheridan, July 28, SI, AR, 1871, 850; Sheridan to Sherman, Aug. 3, ibid., 850; Sherman to SW, Aug. 7, ibid., 850; Belknap to SI, Aug. 10, 1871, LS, SW, 67, reel 62.

28. Sheridan to Hancock, Jan. 31, 1872, Box 7, LC, Sheridan Papers; Utley, *Frontier Regulars*, 243–50; Reports of Ord, Sept. 9, SW, AR, 1874, 32; Saville, Aug. 21, SI, AR, 1874, 559; and Howard, Sept. 30, ibid., 561; Belknap to SI, Jan. 29, 1874, LS, SW, 75, reel 68; Sheridan to Ord, Feb. 18, 1874, Box 10, LC, Sheridan Papers (quotation).

faced an even greater menace the following year when new rumors of gold strikes in the region reached the public. To investigate the gold claims and the possibility of placing a fort in the Black Hills, Custer led a strong force into the area in July 1874. Two miners accompanied the expedition. If Custer deemed that the hostile tribes posed a threat to settlers, military positions, or friendly Arikara or Mandan Indians, he was authorized to launch a "sharp and decisive" blow. As his expedition continued, he surveyed a good location for a fort in the northeast section of the hills and reported favorably on the potential for fishing, hunting, grazing, and lumbering. More significant, some of his men found gold. The press quickly turned Custer's somewhat restrained official reports on the discovery into a new gold rush.[29]

The Black Hills lay in the heart of the Great Sioux Reservation and were among the best hunting grounds still available to the Sioux. Nevertheless, hundreds of miners swarmed into the hills in a frantic quest for gold, defying treaty lines in the process. Many in the army, including recently reappointed Dakota department chief Terry, sympathized with the Sioux and made sincere if ineffectual efforts to prevent white intrusions. Others, most notably Custer, believed that "a sound drubbing" was a surer way to end Sioux depredations and to secure the Black Hills.[30] The army was unable to stop the increasing number of gold seekers, and the government

29. Sheridan to Sherman, May 1, 1874, Box 11, LC, Sheridan Papers; Townsend to Sheridan, May 11, 1874, LS, AGO, 57, reel 44; Terry to Custer, May 26, 28 (quotation), 1874, National Archives, LS, Dept. of Dakota; Forsyth to Sheridan, July 15, 1874, Box 11, LC, Sheridan Papers; Report of Sheridan, Sept. 25, 1874, ibid. For a secondary account, see Jackson, *Custer's Gold.*

30. Terry to Clark, Aug. 29, 1874, National Archives, LS, Dept. of Dakota; Terry to Custer, Sept. 3, 1874, ibid.; Terry to commanders of Fort Lincoln, Rice, Cheyenne, etc., Dec. 23, 1874, ibid.; Terry to AAG, Mar. 9, 1875, ibid.; Bailey, *Pacifying the Plains*, 109.

Custer's plans are outlined in Custer to Sheridan, Feb. 28, 1875, Box 13, LC, Sheridan Papers (quotation). Opposition to his scheme is in Terry to AG, May 17, 1875, LS, Dept. of Dakota; Townsend to Terry, May 17, 1875, LS, AGO, 58, reel 45; Sheridan to Belknap, June 7, 1875, Box 13, Sheridan Papers.

failed to persuade the Sioux to sell the Black Hills. Debate over the agricultural potential of the northern plains further enlivened the controversy. In an extraordinary executive meeting on November 3, 1875, President Grant, Belknap, Chandler, Commissioner of Indian Affairs Edward Smith, Crook, and Sheridan decided to halt the army's anti-miner patrols and to force the Indians onto their reservations.[31]

Sioux-white relations had been deteriorating all year. While whites trespassed in the Hills, Sitting Bull and his confederates openly defied reservation lines, harassing settlers, miners, emigrants, and other Indians. By November 9, the situation led U.S. Indian Inspector E. C. Watkins to call for a thousand-man force to engage the hostiles in a winter offensive. Twenty days later, Interior Secretary Chandler sent copies of the Watkins proposal to the War Department; it was forwarded to Sheridan on December 13. In the meantime, Chandler, bowing to pressure from his subordinates, issued an ultimatum on December 3: the Sioux were to be given until January 31, 1876, to return to their reservations. If they had not complied by that time, the Interior Department would turn the matter over to the army.[32]

Not wanting to waste this unforeseen boon, officials in the Division of the Missouri began preparing secret plans in readiness for the deadline. Crook, recently appointed to head the Department of the Platte, assured superiors that "military operations may be commenced against them whenever . . . in the opinion of the Department such action becomes necessary." In the Department of Dakota, Terry, whose desire for secrecy prevented him from informing even

---

31. Anderson, "Challenge to Brown's Sioux Indian Wars Thesis," 46–49; Utley, *Frontier Regulars*, 253–54. For a different view, see Brown, "New Focus on the Sioux War," 76–85; Hutton, *Phil Sheridan*, 299. See also Kroecker, *Great Plains Command*, 120–42; and Hazen, "Great Middle Region of the United States."

32. Watkins to Smith, Nov. 9, 1875, Box 91, LC, Sheridan Papers; Smith to Chandler, Nov. 27, 1875, ibid.; Chandler to SW, Nov. 29, 1875, ibid.; McCook endorsement, Dec. 13, 1875, ibid.; Chandler to SW, Dec. 3, 1875, ibid. Extracts may also be found in Cameron to President, July 8, 1876, LS, SW, 79, reel 72.

his own staff of the situation, believed that columns could reach the hostile Sioux "in ordinary winter weather." An eager Sheridan agreed with their optimism, as did Sherman. Despite a last-minute plea from the Standing Rock agent to grant an extension, Commissioner of Indian Affairs John Q. Smith recommended on January 31 that offensives begin. The next day Chandler advised Belknap to let loose the army, thus signaling a crucial change in the government's stance. Again, military influence in determining federal Indian policy had been minimal. Only after Inspector Watkins filed his report favoring army action did the Interior Department consent to relinquish control.[33]

Sheridan advocated immediate action. The army must surprise the Sioux in their winter camps before they split up for spring and summer buffalo hunts. Using the precedents of the southern plains campaigns of 1868–69 and 1874–75, two columns would converge on the Black Hills. Crook would come from the west (Fort Fetterman), and Terry from the east (Fort Abraham Lincoln). Sheridan again refused to participate directly in planning, although the operations included the separate departments of the Platte and Dakota. "I am not well enough acquainted with the character of the winter and early springs in your latitude to give any directions," he wrote to Terry. "I am of the belief that the operations under your directions and those under Gen. Crook should be made without concert, but if you and he can come to any understanding about concerted movements, there will be no objections from me."[34]

Crook left Fort Fetterman March 1, accompanying 883 men under

33. Crook to AAG, Dec. 22, 1875, Box 91, LC, Sheridan Papers; Terry to AAG, Dec. 28, 1875, ibid.; Sheridan to Sherman, Jan. 3, 1876, Box 14, ibid.; Crosby to SI, Jan. 12, 1876, LS, SW, 79, reel 72; Smith to SI, Jan. 21, Box 91, Sheridan Papers; Belknap to SI, Jan. 26, LS, SW, 79, reel 72; Smith to Chandler, Jan. 31, 1876, Box 91, Sheridan Papers; Chandler to SW, Feb. 1, 1876, ibid.

34. Sheridan to Mrs. John Sherman, Feb. 25, 1876, Box 58, LC, Sheridan Papers; Sheridan to Terry, Feb. 25, 1876, ibid. (first quotation); Sheridan to Terry, Feb. 8, 1876, ibid., Box 14 (second quotation); Bailey, *Pacifying the Plains*, 125–26.

Campaigns on the Northern Plains

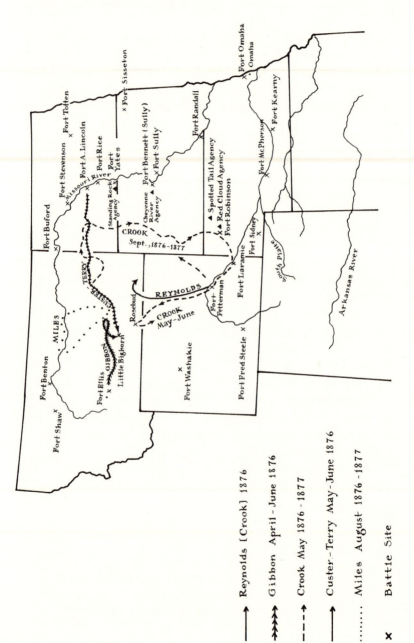

Sources: Adapted from Bailey, *Pacifying the Plains*, p. 165; and Utley, *Frontier Regulars*, p. 257

the direct charge of Colonel Reynolds. As Sheridan had done in 1868–69, Crook served as advisor and analyzed the feasibility of this winter move from a firsthand perspective. After less than a month in the field, Reynolds retired to Fort Fetterman. He commented to Sherman, "These winter campaigns in this latitude should be prohibited. Cruelty is no name for them. The month of March has told on me more than any five years of my life." Crook agreed but judged that Reynolds had performed poorly, having allowed the Indians to recapture a number of ponies in a night raid. Terry, deeming the winter snows too heavy, remained at Fort Abraham Lincoln.[35]

Sheridan, determined to end the threat of the Sioux and Northern Cheyennes, pressed Crook, Terry, and Colonel Gibbon to renew their attacks. The division commander respectfully vetoed Sherman's suggestion that the Department of the Platte be enlarged to include all the Sioux country, arguing that the people of the Old Northwest would oppose most vigorously even the partial transfer of federal patronage from St. Paul to Omaha that such a move entailed. In an effort to maintain control, Sheridan also directed Terry and Crook to communicate with each other through his office. Once again, he left the field commanders to their own devices, assuring them of "the impossibility of any large numbers of Indians keeping together as a hostile body for even a week."[36]

Experience supported his final assertion. Large groups of Indians usually scattered shortly after discovering bluecoats nearby. Officers

35. Reynolds to Sherman, Apr. 11, 1876, LC, Sherman Papers, 43, reel 22 (quotation); Crook to AAG, May 7, 1876, National Archives, LS, Dept. of the Platte; Sheridan, endorsement of May 17, 1876, Box 15, LC, Sheridan Papers; Report of Sherman, Nov. 10, SW, AR, 1876, 28–29; Bailey, *Pacifying the Plains*, 126–27. For longer secondary accounts, see Vaughn, *Reynolds Campaign*; and Bradley, *March of the Montana Column*.

36. Sheridan to Crook, Mar. 25, 1876, Box 58, LC, Sheridan Papers; Sherman to Sheridan, Apr. 1, 1876, LC, Sherman Papers, 43, reel 22; Sheridan to Sherman, Apr. 3, 1876, ibid.; Sheridan to Reno, Apr. 17, 1876, Box 58, Sheridan Papers; Sheridan to Terry, May 16, 1876, ibid. (quotation).

consequently found it extremely difficult to force Indians to fight pitched battles, where the army's discipline and organization could be decisive. To preclude the possibility of such dispersals, ambitious officers sought to surprise, encircle, and attack large Indian camps when discovered. While this often meant dividing one's forces in the face of the enemy, most officers agreed that the risk was justified.

In light of such experience, Custer led his Seventh Cavalry in a detached column from Terry's main force toward a Sioux-Cheyenne village near the Little Bighorn River on June 25, 1876. As he had done seven and a half years earlier at the Battle of the Washita, Custer divided his command, sending three companies under Capt. Frederick W. Benteen to reconnoiter and another three troops led by Maj. Marcus A. Reno to encircle the village. The decision was fatal, for this huge encampment, including Oglalas, Hunkpapas, Sans Arcs, Blackfeet, Cheyennes, and a smattering of warriors from additional tribes, was more than willing to fight. Unknown to Custer, these Indians of the northern plains had whipped George Crook's column at the Battle of the Rosebud only eight days earlier and remained eager to crush any intruders. The 263 troopers remaining with Custer fell to a man; Reno and Benteen narrowly escaped a similar fate. Badly shaken, Crook, Terry, and Gibbon withdrew to refit and await reinforcements.[37]

The disaster at the Little Bighorn shocked the country. Congress appropriated funds to establish two big new forts on the Yellowstone that had long been sought by Sheridan and authorized twenty-five hundred new cavalry privates. The army acted less decisively. Crook and Terry, still smarting from the defeat at the Rosebud, waited a month while reinforcements poured in. Their efforts to locate hostile Indians throughout the late summer and early fall were marked by tremendous feats of physical endurance but little innovative thought. Crook was later charged with having failed to cooperate effectively.

37. Report of Sheridan, Nov. 25, SW, AR, 1876, 444–45; Reno to Sheridan, July 4, 1876, Box 15, LC, Sheridan Papers; Finerty, *War-Path and Bivouac*, 203.

In exasperation, the army dismounted and disarmed Indians at the Red Cloud, Standing Rock, and Cheyenne River agencies. Winter found Crook, now supported by Mackenzie, pursuing Crazy Horse's Oglalas and Cheyennes. Miles led his beleaguered troops through the snows of Montana, doggedly pursuing a coalition of Sioux tribes under Sitting Bull's leadership.[38]

Several fierce skirmishes resulted from the long campaigns, but, as frequently happened in the Indian wars, the chase itself proved to be more devastating in the long run than actual combat. By May 1877, the remarkable northern plains coalition lay in a shambles. Most of its diverse elements, scattered and lacking supplies after constant flight and numerous skirmishes, surrendered with key leaders Crazy Horse and Spotted Tail. Remnants of the coalition followed Sitting Bull across the Canadian border. Miles ended the campaign by forcing a few diehard Miniconjou to surrender after a determined pursuit in the summer of 1877.[39]

38. Reports of Sherman, Nov. 10, SW, AR, 1876, 37; and Townsend, Oct. 1, ibid., 73. On the reinforcements, see Sheridan to Sherman, July 7, 1876, LS, SW, 79, reel 72; Sherman to Sheridan, July 15, 1876, LS, AGO, 59, reel 46; Sherman to Pope, July 23, 25, 1876, Box 58, LC, Sheridan Papers. On the disarmament, see Sheridan to Mackenzie, Aug. 1, 1876, ibid.; Sheridan to Sherman, Aug. 22, 1876, ibid.; Sheridan to Crook, Aug. 23, 1876, ibid.; Crook to Merritt, Sept. 25, 1876, National Archives, LS, Dept. of the Platte; Crook to AAG, Oct. 30, 1876, ibid.; Sheridan, endorsement of Nov. 6, 1876, Box 15, Sheridan Papers.

The Terry, Crook, and Miles campaigns are discussed in Sheridan to Terry, Aug. 18, 1876, ibid.; Sheridan to Sherman, Aug. 30, 1876, ibid.; Sheridan to Crook, Aug. 17, 1876, Feb. 5, 1877, Box 58, ibid.; Sheridan to Terry, Sept. 11, 1876, ibid.; Report of Crook, Sept. 25, SW, AR, 1876, 499; Miles to Sherman, Oct. 2, 16, 23, 27, Nov. 18, 1876, Jan. 20, Feb. 10, 1877, LC, Sherman Papers, 44–45, reel 23; Report of Sheridan, Nov. 25, SW, AR, 1876, 445–47; Crook to AAG, Jan. 18, 1877, LS, Dept. of the Platte. Greene, *Slim Buttes, 1876*, stresses the importance of the Crook–Anson Mills strike at Slim Buttes.

39. Sheridan to Terry, Mar. 15, Apr. 14, 1877, Box 58, LC, Sheridan Papers; Sheridan to Sherman, Mar. 17, 1877, Box 17, ibid.; Crook to Sheridan, Apr. 9, 1877, Box 91, Sheridan Papers; Terry to Sherman, June 9, LC, Sherman Papers,

High-level military officials had begun the 1870s with little strategic consensus on a military policy for coping with Indians. Fighting in Oregon, California, Arizona, Texas, the Indian Territory, New Mexico, Nebraska, Dakota, and Montana from 1870 to 1877 brought about few new strategic techniques. Several commanders sought to gain advantages by attacking their Indian foes during the winter. These cold-weather campaigns yielded long-range benefits by exhausting Indian supplies and lowering their morale. The campaigns were not, however, the panacea their advocates had once predicted. All officers now stressed the need for vigorous pursuit; adherence to this simple principle raised Miles to the heights of army glory.

Sheridan had noted that Miles's conduct during 1874–75 in the Texas Panhandle met with his "decided approval" and "exceeded my expectations." Three years later Sherman credited Miles with "extraordinary pluck and talents" and "untiring industry and skill."[40] Miles attributed his success to "a perfect spy system" and "a properly organized command" but neglected to give further details of his methods.[41]

No other commander matched Miles's performance. Custer lay dead at the Little Bighorn. Mackenzie did well in Texas and the southern plains but arrived too late to make an impact in the north. Although Crook temporarily calmed Arizona, he seemed flustered throughout the Sioux campaign, especially after his fight at the

---

46, reel 24; Report of Lee, Aug. 10, SI, AR, 1877, 462; Report of Sheridan, Oct. 25, SW, AR, 1877, 55. The best secondary account, on which this summary depends heavily, is in Utley, *Frontier Regulars*, 275–99.

40. Sheridan to Williams, Oct. 6, 1874, Box 11, LC, Sheridan Papers (first two quotations); Sherman to McCrary, Aug. 3, 1877, LS, AGO, 60, reel 47 (third and fourth quotations).

41. Miles to Sherman, Feb. 5, 1877, LC, Sherman Papers, 45, reel 23. On Feb. 1, Miles had written Sherman, "Some time when I get time, I will write you my plan of Indian campaigning for it may interest you, and as it enables me to know the strength & design of my enemy, to always find, defeat & follow him" (Ibid.).

Rosebud. Sheridan and Sherman both criticized Crook's lack of cooperation with Terry and Gibbon in their summer campaigns. Sheridan also condemned Crook's "march around the Black Hills" of autumn 1876. By depleting supplies, Crook's foray had made winter cavalry action impossible. Sheridan added Terry to the blacklist, arguing that the commander of the Department of Dakota had troops and supplies sufficient to have handled the Sioux problem with much less difficulty. It was clear that neither Terry nor Crook had conducted affairs capably. Sheridan concluded that his "only thought has been to let them sleep."[42]

In reality, neither Sheridan nor Sherman had acquitted themselves any better. Sherman's dispute with Secretary of War Belknap and subsequent move to St. Louis effectively removed him from the 1874–75 campaign to the south. Sheridan had stressed on at least two occasions the erroneous belief that large groups of hostile Indians could not remain in a body for more than a week to ten days.[43] More serious was Sheridan's explicit refusal to redraw departmental boundaries. The resulting situation, for which he bore full responsibility, divided the area occupied by most of the nonreservation Indians between the departments of Dakota and the Platte. As a consequence, neither Terry nor Crook ever had full authority. In February 1877, Sherman pointed out the error to Sheridan. The presence of two different department commanders in the field was "always a bad thing" for which "you and I are responsible." "One officer should have unlimited control of all the troops," Sherman

42. Sheridan to Sherman, Feb. 10, LC, Sherman Papers, 45, reel 23 (first quotation); Sheridan to Sherman, Feb. 10, 1877, Sherman Papers, 45, reel 23 (second quotation). See also his letter to Crook, Jan. 27, 1877, Box 15, LC, Sheridan Papers, and endorsement of Nov. 6, 1876, ibid., and Jan. 24, 1877, Box 16, ibid. Sherman and Miles also attacked Crook. See Sherman to Sheridan, Feb. 21, 1877, LS, AGO, 60, reel 47; Sherman to Sheridan, Feb. 17, 1877, Sherman Papers, 90, reel 45; and Miles to Sherman, Mar. 29, 1877, ibid., 46, reel 24.

43. Sheridan to Terry, May 16, 1876, Box 58, LC, Sheridan Papers; and Sheridan to Sherman, May 29, 1876, Box 15, ibid.

continued, ". . . with power to draw supplies from any of the Posts or Cantonments on or near the Border of the country where these operations are in progress."[44]

Considering the disorganized nature of the American military, Sheridan's refusal to issue specific orders to field commanders was also detrimental to the campaigns of the 1870s. This is not to suggest that a lack of detailed instructions alone caused the problems encountered by Crook, Custer, Reynolds, and Terry. A brief comparison with the Prussian army, that most admired fighting force of the latter nineteenth century, which Sheridan had seen in action, shows that even the Prussian general staff did not dictate comprehensive orders to its generals in the field; instead, it sought to monitor and coordinate independent commands. Company commanders became increasingly important. As chief of the general staff, Helmut von Moltke realized that even the technological advances of the railroad and the telegraph could not give him effective centralized control of scattered columns.[45]

The decentralization of tactics made effective strategy crucial. Herein lay the fundamental flaws in the United States army of the era. Like von Moltke, Sheridan employed a loose command system that depended on several fundamentals: a sound overall strategic plan; capable leadership by independent regimental and company officers; and some degree of cooperation among the various columns in the field. In contrast to the Prussians, however, the Americans never achieved these essential elements. The cooperation, as has been noted, was often nonexistent. And the American army, little concerned with strategy and more interested in fighting conventional wars with conventional enemies, never developed a consistent strategic doctrine effective in Indian warfare. While individual officers achieved success, their methods were not made official policy, nor were these select individuals called upon to give strategic advice to less able or less experienced officers.

44. Sherman to Sheridan, Feb. 21, 1877, LS, AGO, 60, reel 47.
45. Van Creveld, *Command in War*, 103–47.

To make matters worse, many officers seemed to pay more attention to the treatment they received in the memoirs written by their former Civil War comrades than in how to fight Indians. Rather than developing new strategies or tactics, they refought Gettysburg, Petersburg, or Chancellorsville. While such reflection was understandable, it did little to ease conditions on the western frontiers.[46]

Although the army was plagued by strategic failures, the near extermination of the American bison during the 1870s helped to mask the military's poor performance. By stripping many Indians of their available resources, the slaughter of the buffalo severely reduced the Indians' capacity to continue an armed struggle against the United States. The military's role in this matter is difficult to assess. Sheridan and Sherman recognized that eliminating the buffalo might be the best way to force Indians to change their nomadic habits. The editors of the *Army and Navy Journal* supported the proposition, comparing such an effort with Civil War campaigns against Confederate supplies and food sources. Nelson Miles agreed, arguing that the buffalo "occupy a pastoral country which should be covered with domestic stock." Forts provided de facto support for hunters, who used the civilian services often found near army bases. Officers and enlisted personnel also killed buffalo for food and sport, though the impact of their hunts was minute when compared to the organized efforts of the professionals.[47]

In 1874, Secretary of the Interior Delano testified before Congress, "The buffalo are disappearing rapidly, but not faster than I desire. I regard the destruction of such game as Indians subsist upon as facilitating the policy of the Government, of destroying their hunting habits, coercing them on reservations, and compelling them to begin to adopt the habits of civilization."[48]

46. Hutton, *Phil Sheridan*, 145.

47. *Army and Navy Journal* 6 (Jan. 26, 1869); Sherman to Sheridan, Apr. 30, 1870, LC, Sherman Papers, 90, reel 45; Report of Miles, Mar. 4, SW, AR, 1875, 84; Barker Archives, Evans Papers, Jan. 1931.

48. Testimony of Delano, Jan. 10, 1874, House Rpt. No. 384, 43rd Cong., 1st sess., ser. 1624, 99 (quotation).

Two years later, reporter John F. Finerty wrote that the government's Indian allies "killed the animals in sheer wantonness, and when reproached by the officers said: 'better kill buffalo than have him feed the Sioux.' "[49]

Although Sheridan added that "if I could learn that every buffalo in the northern herd were killed I would be glad," some indications point to a groundswell of military opposition to the killing. In 1873 Secretary of War Belknap was forwarded a letter from Maj. R. J. Dodge, endorsed by Pope and Sheridan, that addressed the problem. Belknap also approved Sheridan's request which seemed to indicate the general's own ambivalence on the subject, to authorize Col. De L. Floyd Jones "to put a stop to their wholesale destruction." Several officers protested the wanton destruction to Henry Bergh, president of the American Society for the Prevention of Cruelty to Animals. In the late 1870s, Terry protested "the wholesale slaughter of buffalo on Indian reservations by white men"; his efforts to halt the practice won Sheridan's support. The army, while anxious to strike against the Indians' ability to continue their resistance, did not make the virtual extermination of the American bison part of its official policy; in some cases, individual officers took it upon themselves to try and end the slaughter.[50]

Army-Indian affairs were clarified while Grant was president. Although Sitting Bull's temporary northern plains alliance had been broken, its very existence terrified military authorities, who had long feared such a tribal confederation. With large numbers of warriors collected in Indian Territory and Sitting Bull defiantly

49. Finerty, *War-Path and Bivouac*, 121 (quotation). See also Report of Delano, Oct. 31, SI, AR, 1873, vi.

50. Sheridan is quoted from Hutton, *Phil Sheridan*, 246; Sheridan, endorsement of Nov. 3, 1873, Box 10, LC, Sheridan Papers; Belknap to SI, Nov. 14, LS, SW, 83, reel 66; Potts to Sheridan, June 22, 1872, ibid., 69, reel 63; Branch, *Hunting of the Buffalo*, 174–84; McCrary to SI, Nov. 3, 1879, LS, SW, 85, reel 78 (quotation); Sheridan to Townsend, Oct. 31, 1879, Box 58, Sheridan Papers. Congressional efforts to halt the slaughter are described in Branch, *Hunting of the Buffalo*, 178–80.

remaining in Canada, the future appeared cloudy. President Grant's peace program showed clearly the army's lack of impact on overall federal Indian policy. Unfortunately, government Indian agents often demanded that the army enforce unfair treaties, broken promises, and what amounted to the destruction of Indian culture. The army's subservient position in policy-making—clearly a civilian function—restricted its military choices. Rarely could it assume the strategic initiative. Instead, the military had the unenviable task of responding to calls from outside agencies to restore the peace or to force unwilling tribes to live on unattractive reservations.

Chapter Six
The Twilight of the Old Army
1877–1903

Historians, with the advantage of hindsight, now know that the defeat of the Plains tribes in the mid–1870s was decisive in Indian-army confrontations. Subsequent Nez Percé, Bannock, Ute, Apache, and Sioux struggles against the awesome strength of the United States seem to the modern observer even more futile than earlier efforts to retain tribal freedom. Yet such conclusions were rarely evident to contemporary Americans, who read only of recurring battles with Indians. Indeed, scattered confrontations continued throughout the 1890s. Military officials thus kept a sizable percentage of the regular army in western stations well into the twentieth century, ready to take action if reservation In-

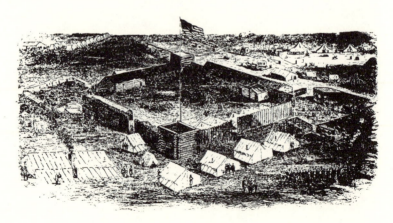

dians should become openly hostile. In conjunction with this show of force, the army continued to grasp for policies and strategic guidelines that would be effective against western Indians until turn of the century conflicts forced the army to accept new international obligations.

In March 1877, the Department of the Interior requested army aid in forcing nontreaty Nez Percé under the leadership of Chief Joseph to enter an Idaho reservation. Discussions with Department of the Columbia head Howard proved to be futile, and the Nez Percé determined not to cooperate. A sharp fight erupted at White Bird Canyon on June 17, in which Capt. David Perry's detachment of volunteers and regulars was routed and nearly annihilated. Soon after this, some eight hundred Indians began an epic three-month flight that eventually covered seventeen hundred miles across much of Idaho and Montana.[1]

Howard himself led the pursuit. But Howard stopped to reorganize after a sharp encounter at the Battle of the Clearwater on July 11 and 12, 1877, while Joseph continued to move. Seeking to block the Indian flight, Colonel Gibbon and a mixed force of two hundred regulars and volunteers surprised the Nez Percé camp at the Big Hole River in early August, only to be badly whipped by the more capable enemy marksmen. As Howard's troops continued their pursuit, Col. Samuel D. Sturgis, having failed in his first attempt to bottle up the Nez Percé, was eluded again at Canyon Creek on September 13. Only after the exhausted Indians slowed their pace did Colonel Miles, in command of yet another army column, force Chief Joseph to surrender short of the Canadian border in early October.[2]

The army's conduct during the Nez Percé campaign is difficult to evaluate. As was so often the case, the military was placed in a

1. Utley, *Frontier Regulars*, 250–63; Carpenter, *Sword and Olive Branch*, 250–63. For Howard's account, see his *Nez Percé Joseph*. For other secondary accounts, see Beal, *I Will Fight No More Forever*, and Josephy, *Nez Percé Indians*.

2. Utley, *Frontier Regulars*, 250–63.

Military Conflicts in the West, 1877–1903

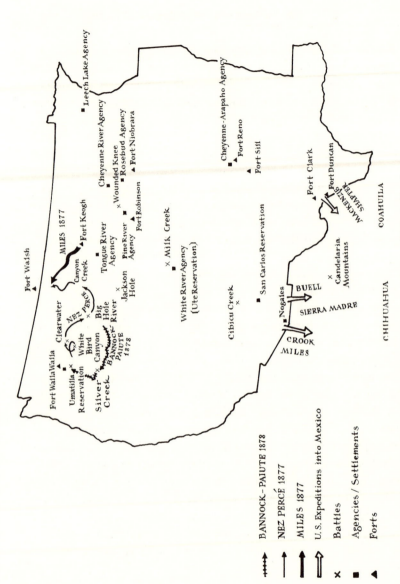

BANNOCK – PAIUTE 1878

NEZ PERCÉ 1877

MILES 1877

U.S. Expeditions into Mexico

× Battles

■ Agencies / Settlements

▲ Forts

Sources: Utley, *Indian Frontier*, pp. 68–69, 152–53, 194–95; and Matloff, ed.,
American Military History, pp. 302–03

dians should become openly hostile. In conjunction with this show of force, the army continued to grasp for policies and strategic guidelines that would be effective against western Indians until turn of the century conflicts forced the army to accept new international obligations.

In March 1877, the Department of the Interior requested army aid in forcing nontreaty Nez Percé under the leadership of Chief Joseph to enter an Idaho reservation. Discussions with Department of the Columbia head Howard proved to be futile, and the Nez Percé determined not to cooperate. A sharp fight erupted at White Bird Canyon on June 17, in which Capt. David Perry's detachment of volunteers and regulars was routed and nearly annihilated. Soon after this, some eight hundred Indians began an epic three-month flight that eventually covered seventeen hundred miles across much of Idaho and Montana.[1]

Howard himself led the pursuit. But Howard stopped to reorganize after a sharp encounter at the Battle of the Clearwater on July 11 and 12, 1877, while Joseph continued to move. Seeking to block the Indian flight, Colonel Gibbon and a mixed force of two hundred regulars and volunteers surprised the Nez Percé camp at the Big Hole River in early August, only to be badly whipped by the more capable enemy marksmen. As Howard's troops continued their pursuit, Col. Samuel D. Sturgis, having failed in his first attempt to bottle up the Nez Percé, was eluded again at Canyon Creek on September 13. Only after the exhausted Indians slowed their pace did Colonel Miles, in command of yet another army column, force Chief Joseph to surrender short of the Canadian border in early October.[2]

The army's conduct during the Nez Percé campaign is difficult to evaluate. As was so often the case, the military was placed in a

1. Utley, *Frontier Regulars*, 250–63; Carpenter, *Sword and Olive Branch*, 250–63. For Howard's account, see his *Nez Percé Joseph*. For other secondary accounts, see Beal, *I Will Fight No More Forever*, and Josephy, *Nez Percé Indians*.

2. Utley, *Frontier Regulars*, 250–63.

position of carrying out Indian policies that it had not formulated. Howard himself believed that the government erred in stripping the Nez Percé of a large chunk of their original reservation. The Nez Percé were also capable foes, who, as Sherman concluded, "fought with almost scientific skill, using advance and rear-guards, skirmish lines and field-fortifications."[3]

In addition, the campaign occurred while many of the army's best officers were engaged in other duties—most notably watching Sitting Bull and quelling eastern labor disputes. The high command's usual practice of giving field commanders much freedom of action failed in this instance, as Howard lacked the drive and aggressiveness essential to defeat Indians. In fact, Howard kept his command only because Lt. Col. Charles Gilbert, sent by Sherman in late August to assume field leadership, could not find Howard's column.[4] Only after Miles shifted his attention from Sitting Bull to Joseph did the army block the Nez Percé escape to Canada. Miles performed with his customary competence, aggressiveness, and eye to public opinion, claiming all the fruits of the campaign without crediting Howard's stubborn yet unlucky forces for their efforts.[5]

Howard redeemed himself the following year. Hunger, white

3. Howard, *Nez Percé Joseph*, 24–32; Report of Sherman, Nov. 7, SW, AR, 1877, 15 (quotation).

4. Sherman to McDowell, July 29, 1877, LS, AGO, 60, reel 47; Sherman to McCrary, Aug. 3, 1877, ibid.; Sherman to Howard, Aug. 24, 28, SW, AR, 1877, 13; Howard to Sherman, Aug. 27, ibid.; Sherman to Howard, Aug. 29, 1877, Bowdoin Library, Howard Papers; Gilbert to AG, Sept. 23, 1877, ibid.; Crosby to SI, Sept. 8, 1877, LS, SW, 81, reel 74.

5. Sherman to McCrary, Aug. 3, 1877, LS, AGO, 60, reel 47; Howard to Miles, Aug. 12, SW, AR, 1877, 73; McCrary to SI, Oct. 8, 1877, LS, SW, 81, reel 74; Gibbon to Miles, Oct. 21, 1877, LC, Miles Collection, ser. 1, Box 2; Miles to Sherman, Oct. 28, 1877, LC, Sherman Papers, 46, reel 24; Report of Hayt, Nov. 1, SI, AR, 1877, 409; Report of Sherman, Nov. 7, SW, AR, 1877, 15. For the resulting controversy between Miles, Gibbon, and Howard, see McCrary to SI, Oct. 12, 1877, LS, SW, 81, reel 74; Sherman to Howard, Mar. 29, 1877, Bowdoin Library, Howard Papers; Gibbon to Howard, Nov. 12, 1877, ibid.; Miles to Howard, Jan. 8, 31, 1878, ibid.

that the Cheyennes merely wanted to leave the Indian Territory to return to their traditional homelands to the north, reports in early 1879 that two thousand Indians had left Fort Sill alarmed the War Department.[8]

The Cheyennes in fact remained calm, but conflict seemed imminent in Colorado. Tension mounted as Agent Nathan C. Meeker attempted to transform the Utes into solid agriculturalists overnight. His call for the army to enforce his decrees resulted in disaster. In a confused encounter at Milk Creek, Colorado, on September 29, 1879, Indian warriors killed Maj. Thomas "Tip" Thornburgh and ten other soldiers. The same afternoon, another party murdered Meeker and nine employees. Sheridan, warned of possible problems a year and a half earlier, rushed colonels Wesley Merritt, Edward P. Hatch, and Ranald Mackenzie to the scene with powerful supporting forces. As the military prepared to crush Ute resistance, Interior Secretary Schurz stepped up his last-ditch efforts to restore the peace. By October 26, 1879, after several late-night visits with Sherman, Schurz convinced the commanding general to delay planned winter offensives until a peace commission had met with Ute representatives. Schurz, special agent Charles Adams of the Interior Department, and Ute chief Ouray, negotiating with a spirit of delicate compromise rarely matched in Indian-white relations, hammered out a new agreement that precluded further bloodshed.[9]

The Ute "war" of 1879 exemplified many of the intricacies of army Indian policy after 1865. As usual, the army did not initiate policy but answered civilian calls for action. Using railroads to speed

8. Sheridan to Townsend, Feb. 25, 1879, Box 21, LC, Sheridan Papers; Sheridan to Sherman, Oct. 14, 19, 1878, Box 20, ibid.; Report of Crook, Sept. 27, SW, AR, 1879, 78; McCrary to SI, Jan. 10, 1879, LS, SW, 85, reel 78.

9. Report of Hayt, Nov. 1, SI, AR, 1879, 83–96; Crook to Sheridan, Apr. 23, 1878, Hayes Library, Crook Papers; Sherman to Sheridan, July 19, Oct. 26, 1879, LC, Sherman Papers, 91, reel 45; Sheridan to Sherman, Oct. 17, Box 59; LC, Sheridan Papers; Sheridan to Crook, Oct. 19, 1879, ibid.; Schurz to President, Dec. 26, 1879, LC, Schurz Papers, reel 87; Reports of Schurz, Nov. 15, SI, AR, 1879, 16–18, and Nov. 1, ibid., 1880, 20–22.

nearly three thousand troops to the area, commanders then faced the problems of feeding their men, implementing a government policy that they did not control, and planning a military campaign. That those involved represented two departments (the Missouri and the Platte) caused further complications. Sheridan summed up the dilemma: "We went to the agency at the solicitation of the Indian Bureau, whose agent was murdered and our men killed and wounded, and now we are left in the heart of the mountains with our hands tied and the danger of being snowed in staring us in the face. I am not easily discouraged, but it looks as though we had been pretty badly sold out in this business."[10]

On the northern plains, Sitting Bull's open defiance had worried political and military officials since the 1860s. His presence in Canada, they feared, would lure restless tribes such as the Nez Percé from their reservations and might spark yet another Indian confederation. Sitting Bull also threatened white settlement in the region. Canadian authorities at Fort Walsh recognized that the buffalo herds north of the border could not feed Sitting Bull's people and suspected that hunger might lead to criminal activities. The North West Mounted Police thus supported General Terry's council with Sioux leaders at Walsh in October 1877. But efforts to coax the Sioux south failed dismally, as the Indians ignored U.S. officials and claimed that they were and had always been subjects of the British Crown.[11]

The continuing threats along the Canadian border gave Miles the opportunity to renew his campaign for promotion. In so doing, he revealed two major problems in the army's policy-making efforts.

10. Sheridan to Sherman, Oct. 17, 1879, in Senate Ex. Doc. No. 30, 46th Cong., 2nd sess., I, ser. 1882, 90 (quotation). See also Merritt to Crook, Oct. 21, 1879, ibid., 96.

11. Anderson, "Sioux Pictorial Account," 95–97; Report of Gibbon, Oct. 4, SW, AR, 1878, 71; Report of Sherman, Nov. 1, ibid., 1879, 5; McCrary to Terry, Sept. 6, 1877, LS, SW, 80, reel 74; Report of Schurz, Nov. 1, SI, AR, 1877, iv–v; McCrary to SI, Jan. 29, 1878, LS, SW, 84, reel 77; Sherman to Sheridan, Apr. 13, 1879, LC, Sherman Papers, 91, reel 45.

First, he demanded a military department, noting that he had "fought and defeated larger and better armed bodies of hostile Indians than any other officer since the history of Indian warfare commenced, and at the same time have gained a more extended knowledge of our frontier country than any living man."[12] Never guilty of self-effacement, Miles had indeed performed brilliantly. Using mixed forces of light artillery, cavalry, mounted infantry, and Indian scouts, he had forced most of the Sioux and Northern Cheyennes to return to their reservations despite Sitting Bull's defiance. Yet because of slow promotion and rules of seniority, this difficult but capable man remained a colonel until 1880, thus betraying a creaky army bureaucracy that rewarded excellence only after maddening delays.[13]

The second major complication concerned Miles's suggestion that he be granted authority to cross the Canadian border and capture Sitting Bull. Miles asserted that the Indians "have used the British territory as a recruiting depot and arsenal." He hoped "to move up to the line and in conjunction with the British authorities compell [sic] that miserable savage to choose his country and abide by its laws." Sherman rebuked Miles sharply for suggesting that international boundaries be ignored and warned him not to cross the border without a direct presidential order.[14]

Although Sherman deserves credit for his determined stance in this case, Miles's aggressiveness and willingness to interpret his instructions in the broadest possible terms seems a natural result of

12. Miles to Sherman, Feb. 1, 1877, LC, Sherman Papers, 45, reel 23 (quotation); see also Jan. 8, 27, 1878, ibid., 46, reel 24. For Miles's view of the Canadian system, see Miles, "Indian Problem," 309, 314.

13. See Miles, "My Forty Years of Fighting," 106, 109, 110, 251, and *Serving the Republic*, 123, 146–47, 153, 163–64; Rickey, "Battle of Wolf Mountain," 45, 47–48, 54; Stegmaier, "Artillery Helped Win the West," 71–72.

14. Miles to Sherman, Jan. 8, 1878, LC, Sherman Papers, 46, reel 24 (quotation); Sherman to Miles, Feb. 9, 1878, ibid., 90, reel 45; Sherman to Sheridan, July 19, 25, 1879, ibid., 91, reel 45; Sherman to Sheridan, July 24, 1879, Box 59, LC, Sheridan Papers.

post–Civil War army practices. For the last fifteen years senior officers had been issuing vague directives to subordinates. Sherman and Sheridan both claimed that they did so to allow field commanders enough leeway to react to changing conditions. With trusted, experienced subordinates, the practice worked reasonably well. In other cases, however, one suspects that the high command worded orders vaguely in order to escape criticism if events turned out badly.

Apparently unruffled by Sherman's rebuke, Miles remained eager to destroy the northern Indian threat. He believed that another major campaign was necessary—a sentiment that Sherman echoed. Tensions ran especially high in July 1879, when Miles encountered Sitting Bull searching for food and game near the Milk River. Miles forced the Sioux back into Canada after lengthy skirmishing, reiterating his government's demand for unconditional surrender. Although Sherman feared another major Sioux war, he again warned his nephew-in-law against precipitating trouble with Dominion authorities. Surprisingly, the pugnacious Sheridan astutely assessed the situation as early as March 30, 1878, when he proclaimed that "Sitting Bull and his outfit . . . have had enough of Indian hostilities." Some "will sneak back to their agencies," but he believed that tribes friendly to the government would not join a general uprising. True to Sheridan's prediction, hunger, fear, and the realization that the bluecoats would never give up the chase ultimately forced even the most defiant Indians to return to the United States. Sitting Bull himself surrendered in July 1881.[15]

Despite the surrender, United States and Canadian officials

15. McCrary to SS, Jan. 26, 1878, LS, SW, 83, reel 76; Sheridan endorsement, Mar. 21, 1878, Box 19, LC, Sheridan Papers; Terry to Sherman, June 12, 1879, LC, Sherman Papers, 50, reel 26; Sherman to Sheridan, July 25, 1879, ibid., 91, reel 45; Report of Miles, Sept., SW, AR, 1879, 74; Report of Sherman, Nov. 1, ibid., 4–5; Sherman to Sheridan, Aug. 2, 1879, Box 59, Sheridan Papers; Sheridan to Sherman, Mar. 30, 1878, Box 19, ibid. (quotations). See also Sheridan, endorsement to Sherman, Feb. 8, 1879, Box 21, ibid.; Sheridan to Sherman, Dec. 21, 1880, Sherman Papers, 54, reel 28; Sheridan to Terry, Jan. 16, 1881, Box 59, Sheridan Papers.

kept a wary eye on border Indian problems throughout the next decade. The Americans complimented the North West Mounted Police for their efforts to prevent cross-border raids and were especially pleased with the removal of troublesome Crees from their homes near the boundary line in 1883. Still, the small size of the Canadian military establishment bothered the United States Army. Also in 1883, Secretary of War Lincoln pressed for a "hot pursuit" agreement with Canada similar to the one between the United States and Mexico. Two years later, Canadians feared that supporters of Louis Riel would invade the North West Territory and commit depredations. The border Indians were less eager for battle than nervous officials predicted, although authorities continued to monitor the situation carefully. The American propensity for territorial expansion undoubtedly contributed to Canadian security concerns along the forty-ninth parallel. Sherman attempted to define a purely defensive border policy; Miles nonetheless inaccurately opined that the citizens of British Columbia were ready for an American takeover in 1881.[16]

Although relations remained uneasy in the north, the resolution of the Ute and Sioux crises enabled the army to begin in earnest its long-awaited and much debated concentration program. This did not mean that military men considered the country's Indian wars to have ended. Rather, officers recognized that the new western railroads would allow them to group sizable forces into larger, more economical forts accessible to supplies and communications. The

16. Lincoln to SS, Apr. 12, May 12, 1883, LS, SW, 102, reel 87; Report of Ruger, Sept. 10, SW, AR, 1883, 124; Crosby to SI, Sept. 30, 1880, LS, SW, 88, reel 80; McKeever to Commander, Dept. of Dakota, Aug. 12, 1884, LS, AGO, 72, reel 57; Endicott to SS, Apr. 22, 1885, LS, SW, 110, reel 94; Kelton to Commander, Dept. of Dakota, May 3, 1886, LS, AGO, 78, reel 56; Endicott to SS, May 22, 1886, ibid., 113, reel 96; Drum to Commander, Div. of Missouri, Oct. 2, 1886, LS, AGO, 79, reel 60; Endicott to SS, June 21, 1887, LS, SW, 117, reel 100; Sherman to Sheridan, Jan. 15, 1881, LC, Sherman Papers, 91, reel 45; Miles to Sherman, Dec. 12, 1881, ibid., 67, reel 30.

troops so stationed could use the railways to meet emergencies hundreds of miles away quickly and efficiently, providing effective defense at reduced cost. Proponents theorized that the bigger garrisons would also improve morale and training.

Sherman recognized these possibilities better than most. He had not always believed that concentration was a practical goal. Responding to Rep. Henry Banning's [D–Ohio] December 1878 request that the War Department study the feasibility of concentration, Sherman warned that political considerations would probably interfere with the orderly redistribution of western positions. But observations while on extensive western tours in the early 1880s convinced Sherman of the advisability of abandoning more isolated posts, and he saw with even greater clarity the close relationship between military defense and railroads. "I would have every Post [in the Southwest] if possible on the bank of the Rio Grande or on the Railroad. The Southern Pacific Railroad will be the best possible picket line we could have along our Southern border." Sherman urged that numerous posts be abandoned in the interests of economy, morale, and security.[17]

Sherman's forced retirement in 1883 meant that his personal recommendations were not followed precisely.[18] The general policy of concentration nonetheless retained favor in army circles. Sheridan never displayed his former chief's enthusiasm for the

17. Report of Sherman, Nov. 7, SW, AR, 1878, 7; McCrary to Speaker of the House, Apr. 19, 1878, LS, SW, 88, reel 76; McCrary to Banning, Jan. 21, 1878, ibid.; Testimony of Sherman, Nov. 22, 1877, House Misc. Doc. No. 64, 45th Cong., 2nd sess., 1878, VI, ser. 1820, 36–38; Sherman to Terry, July 20, 1880, LC, Sherman Papers, 91, reel 45; Report of Sherman, Nov. 10, SW, AR, 1880, 5; Sherman to Sheridan, July 31, 1881, Sherman Papers, 95, reel 47; Sherman to Huntington, Jan. 17, 1882, ibid.; Sherman to Augur, Mar. 26, 1882, ibid. (quotation); Sherman to Lincoln, Mar. 18, 30, Apr. 14, 1882, ibid. For an example of other responses to Banning's request, see Crook to AG, Jan. 24, 1878, National Archives, LS, Dept. of the Platte.

18. Sherman to Lincoln, Apr. 14, 1882, LC, Sherman Papers, 95, reel 47; Sherman to Sheridan, Mar. 7, 1883, ibid., 96, reel 47; Sherman to Lincoln, July 2, 1883, ibid.; Frazer, *Forts of the West*, passim.

project, but in 1882 he reversed his earlier skepticism about the practicality of abandoning large numbers of isolated positions. Support from Crook, Pope, Gibbon, Schofield, Inspector General D. B. Sacket, war secretaries Lincoln, Alexander Ramsey, William Endicott, and Redfield Proctor, along with President Grover Cleveland, led the War Department to abandon as a major policy goal its former practice of using smaller posts for western defense. The newly accepted directive resulted from the increased concentration of Indians on reservations, as well as the mobility afforded the army by railroads.[19] Of course, pork-barrel politics and a general shortage of barracks influenced final decisions about which forts would be discontinued.[20]

Renewed conflict along the Mexican border and in the Far Southwest in the late 1870s slowed implementation of the concentration policy and forced Americans to realize that the Indian wars were not over. Repeated crossings into Mexico by Lieutenant Colonel Shafter and Lieutenant Bullis in 1876 and 1877 followed Mackenzie's 1873 expedition. Relations between the United States and Mexico

19. Testimony of Sheridan, Dec. 12, 1877, in House Misc. Doc. No. 64, 45th Cong., 2nd sess., 1878, VI, ser. 1820, 68–69; Report of Sheridan, Oct. 23, SW, AR, 1880, 53; Report of Sheridan, Oct. 20, ibid., 1882, 80; Crook to Sheridan, Mar. 3, 1879, Hayes Library, Crook Papers, Crook to AAG, May 15, 1881, ibid.; Report of Pope, Sept. 15, SW, AR, 1877, 63–64; Report of Gibbon, Oct. 4, ibid., 1878, 66; Schofield to SW, Mar. 6, 20, 1890, LC, Schofield Papers; Report of Lincoln, Nov. 14, SW, AR, 1882, iv; Report of Sacket, Oct. 10, ibid., 69; Report of Ramsey, Nov. 19, ibid., 1880, vi; Lincoln to SI, July 24, 1884, LS, SW, 107, reel 91; Tweedale to President, July 13, 1885, ibid., 110, reel 94; Macfeely to Bogert, Sept. 17, 1888, ibid., 124, reel 107; Report of Endicott, Nov. 30, SW, AR, 1886, 6; Endicott to Hawley, Feb. 11, 1888, LS, SW, 121, reel 104; Proctor to McCook, Oct. 3, 1890, Proctor Library, Proctor Papers; Cleveland, Annual Message, Dec. 3, 1894, in Richardson, comp., *Messages and Papers of the Presidents* 9:534.

20. Harmon to Ramsey, Nov. 26, 1880, Minn. State Hist. Soc., Ramsey Papers, reel 25; Macfeely to Crain, Oct. 8, 1887, LS, SW, 120, reel 103; Proctor to Harrison, Sept. 26, 1889, ibid., 127, reel 110; Ruger to Gov. of Montana, Aug. 30, 1890, National Archives, LS, Dept. of Dakota; Drum to Smith, Oct. 4, 1888, LS, AGO, 83, reel 62.

deteriorated as border banditry continued; the Hayes administration announced its unilateral policy of hot pursuit across the border on June 1, 1877. Tension heightened during the following June when Mackenzie led over a thousand men into Coahuila. Sheridan believed that the expedition was a failure, but the ostentatious show of force encouraged the Mexican army under General Treviño to take action against border Indians. The aggressive United States campaigns in Mexico, although probably illegal, reduced depredations along the Rio Grande and, in so doing, defused military proposals that the army occupy northern Mexico.[21]

Open warfare again erupted in Arizona and New Mexico in 1877. Poor land, fraud, quarrels between civil and military authorities, and the intense factionalism among the varied Apache tribes at the San Carlos reservation made violence almost inevitable. Rugged terrain, the safe haven often provided by the international boundary, and the skilled leadership of Victorio transformed the Warm Springs, Chiricahua, and Mescalero Apaches who followed him into particularly difficult opponents. Regular troops from both countries hunted the recalcitrants without success through New Mexico, Arizona, and Chihuahua until 1880. Finally, Victorio, seeking to avoid the army which he knew would await him to the west as he recrossed into the United States, became entangled with troops stationed at a series of subposts established by Colonel Grierson in West Texas. Grierson, commanding the Tenth Cavalry, adopted a defensive position rather than devoting his energies to futile pursuit, as he had done while cooperating with Colonel Hatch in New Mexico earlier that year. Grierson's plan worked; baffled by the scattered outposts

21. McCrary to Sherman, June 1, 1877, LS, SW, 82, reel 75; Sheridan to Sherman, June 24, 1878, Box 19, LC, Sheridan Papers; McCrary to SS, June 28, 1878, LS, SW, 83, reel 76; Ord to Sherman, Jan. 30, 1879, LC, Sherman Papers, 46, reel 25; Clendenen, *Blood on the Border*, 75–82. Valuable are the Edward O. C. Ord Papers (Bancroft Library); Samuel B. M. Young Papers (U.S. Army Hist. Res. Coll.); and William R. Shafter Papers (Stanford Univ. Library). For examples, see Sheridan to Sherman, July 2, 1878, Box 19, Sheridan Papers; Young to Gov. of Pennsylvania, July 16, 1878, Young Papers.

at strategic waterholes along the West Texas–Mexico border, Victorio pulled back into Chihuahua.[22]

The United States government, in an effort to secure a cooperative solution to the international threat posed by Victorio, had granted Mexican troops permission to pursue Victorio's band into Texas. As Victorio retraced his steps into Mexico, colonels Buell and Carr followed him in a reciprocal crossing. The tortuous trail led deep into the Candelaria Mountains. General Terrazas, commanding Mexican troops in the area, suddenly informed Buell that continued Yankee presence "would be objectionable" as Terrazas prepared to pounce on Victorio. Far from supplies and reinforcements, Buell withdrew; Terrazas's troops cornered and killed the Apache leader in October 1880.[23]

Victorio's death did not end the turmoil in the Southwest. Conditions at San Carlos again deteriorated; in 1881, Carr was handed a particularly embarrassing defeat at the Battle of Cibicu Creek. A number of small bands left their reservations, spreading destruction in southern New Mexico and northern Chihuahua. By September, Sherman had lost all patience. "I want this annual Apache stampede to end right now," he demanded, "and to effect that result will send every available man in the Army if necessary."[24]

Reinforcements poured into Arizona and New Mexico. To improve the quality of leadership, Sherman moved Mackenzie from Colorado to head the District of New Mexico. Sherman acknowledged the problems resulting from the artificial division of authority between commanders in Arizona and New Mexico; he sought to remedy them by creating a new "Division of the Border." The proposed change, including Texas, New Mexico, and Arizona, seemed a logical way to handle the continuing Indian problems

22. Utley, *Frontier Regulars*, 369–72.

23. Report of Buell, Dec. 20, 1880, in Crimmins, ed., "Colonel Buell's Expedition," 133–42.

24. Utley, *Frontier Regulars*, 381–83; Sherman to McDowell, Sept. 16, SW, AR, 1881, 144 (quotation).

along the nation's southwestern border. At the same time, however, it meant a diminution of responsibilities for those in the Pacific and Missouri divisions, which would suffer substantial territorial reductions. As commander of the threatened Division of Missouri, Sheridan strenuously opposed the change as "another piece of jugglery." The plan was squelched after meetings between Sherman, Sheridan, Secretary of War Lincoln, and President Garfield. Sherman still wanted to give Mackenzie command of a consolidated department encompassing both Arizona and New Mexico, but Mackenzie's poor health soon removed him from consideration. Sherman appointed Crook, who, to avoid the bureaucratic infighting that might result from official consolidation of New Mexico with Arizona, would serve as chief of the Department of Arizona, with implicit authority over regional field operations.[25]

Crook prepared to take the field in 1883, enlisting Indian auxiliaries and appointing capable subordinates to oversee local affairs. With Mexican support for a reciprocal crossing agreement, Crook met with Sonoran and Chihuahuan officials to coordinate plans before leading two hundred fifty scouts and bluecoats into Mexico. Fighting was rare as the army drove into the heart of Apache strongholds in the Sierra Madre, but Crook convinced Geronimo to return to his reservation after a series of parleys. Crook described his negotiations: "Being personally acquainted with almost all of the Apaches, I was fortunate enough to make them see that the war to the death, which they admitted having in contemplation, would no doubt cost our Government many lives and much money for its suppression, but

25. Sherman to Tourtellotte, Sept. 11, 1881, LC, Sherman Papers, 95, reel 47; Sherman to McDowell, Sept. 29, SW, AR, 1881, 145; Sherman to Lincoln, Mar. 10, 1881, Sherman Papers, 94, reel 46 (first quotation); Sherman to Schofield, Apr. 27, May 3, 4, 1881, ibid.; Schofield to Sherman, May 3, 1881, ibid.; Sheridan to Pope, Mar. 12, 1881, Box 59, LC, Sheridan Papers (second quotation); Benjamin to Commander, Fort Bowie, Jan. 20, 1882, National Archives, LS, Dept. of Ariz.; Lincoln to Sherman, Apr. 29, 1882, Sherman Papers, 57, reel 30; Sherman to Lincoln, Apr. 29, ibid., 95, reel 47; Sheridan to Sherman, Dec. 28, 1883, Box 43, Sheridan Papers; Report of Sherman, Nov. 6, SW, AR, 1882, 5.

for all that, it would finally result in wiping off the face of the earth the whole Apache race."[26]

Army involvement did not end with Geronimo's surrender. In July 1883 meetings with War Secretary Lincoln, Interior Secretary Henry Teller, and Commissioner of Indian Affairs Hiram Price, Crook secured authority to police the Chiricahua at the San Carlos reservation and to impose his own Indian policy. Every male was to wear a numbered tag and to attend frequent roll calls. Indian spies would appraise white officers of the moods and actions of the Indians. Predictably, officers and civilian agents soon feuded over how far to extend the army's police power. "The same hand that feeds should punish," maintained Crook, who sought to concentrate all authority under one military leader. While Washington officials delayed their decision on who should rule the reservation, aggrieved Indians fled the scene and made their way into Mexico, leaving in their wake a path of destruction.[27]

Two columns followed the Apaches into the Sierra Madre while Crook organized a series of outposts in southern Arizona and New Mexico. These efforts failed, as did schemes to induce friendly Mescalero Apache warriors "to go out & join the [hostile] Apaches & then kill them & bring in their heads" at fifty to one hundred dollars apiece. At War Secretary Endicott's request, Sheridan inspected

26. Kelton to Schofield, May 4, 1883, Box 12, LC, Schofield Papers; Schofield to AG, June 21, 1883, Box 51, ibid.; Crook to AAG, July 23, SW, AR, 1883, 173–78; Report of Crook, Sept. 27, ibid., 165–69; Report of Lincoln, Nov. 15, ibid., 5; Crook to Reyes, Nov. 14, 1882, National Archives, LS, Dept. of Ariz.; Crook to AAG, Mar. 26, 1883, ibid.; Crook to Lomelo, Mar. 28, 1883, ibid.; Crook to Maj. Gen. Commanding Mexican Troops, Mar. 28, June 13, 1883, Hayes Library, Crook Papers; Crook to AG, Apr. 30, 1883, LS, Dept. of Ariz.; Report of Crook, Sept. 27, SW, AR, 1883, 160 (quotation); Utley, *Frontier Regulars*, 389–90; Crook to AAG, July 23, SW, AR, 1883, 173–78.

27. Report of Lincoln, Nov. 15, SW, AR, 1883, 5; Report of Crook, Sept. 27, ibid., 165–69; Report of Atkins, Oct. 5, SI, AR, 1885, 46; Crook to AAG, June 5, 1885, National Archives, LS, Dept. of Ariz. (quotation); Report of Crook, Sept. 9, SW, AR, 1885, 170–75. Harte, "Conflict at San Carlos," is critical of the army takeover.

operations in Arizona in late November 1885. He temporarily combined the District of New Mexico with the Department of Arizona and proposed that all Chiricahua and Warm Springs Apaches be removed from the Southwest. Crook rejected the removal plan, explaining that another major Indian campaign was imminent. President Cleveland remained concerned and wrote to Endicott on December 22, "I go to bed tonight very much dejected and wondering if something cannot be done to better protect our citizens on the frontier and put a stop to these dreadful murders."[28]

The following year's campaign in the Sierra Madre was even more difficult than previous ones. Crook finally caught Geronimo after an exhausting chase, but the wily Indian leader refused to surrender unconditionally. After some confusion, during which Crook's Indian scouts refused to obey orders, Geronimo and his followers escaped. The impatient Sheridan, already complaining about Crook's infrequent communications and heavy dependence on Indian allies, suggested that he concentrate troops for defense in a letter obviously designed to alienate his subordinate. Crook responded on April 1, demanding that the offensives be continued and offering his resignation if they were not.[29]

28. Crook to Bradley, Sept. 7, 1885, U.S. Army Hist. Res. Coll., Bradley Papers (first quotation); Utley, *Frontier Regulars*, 393; Report of Sheridan, Oct. 4, SW, AR, 1885, 61–62; Endicott to Sheridan, Nov. 20, 1885, LS, SW, 111, reel 95; Endicott to Lamar and Cleveland, Nov. 21, 1885, LC, Cleveland Papers, ser. 2, reel 24; Sheridan to Endicott, Nov. 30, Dec. 3, 1885, Box 44, LC, Sheridan Papers; Cleveland to Endicott, Dec. 22, 1885, Cleveland Papers, ser. 2, reel 26 (second quotation).

29. Roberts to Lockett, Nov. 26, 1885, National Archives, LS, Dept. of Ariz.; Crook to Sheridan, Dec. 30, 1885, ibid.; Report of Crook, Apr. 10, SW, AR, 1886, 149; Report of Sheridan, Oct. 10, ibid., 72; Report of Endicott, Nov. 30, ibid., 11; Sheridan to Crook, Dec. 29, 1885, Mar. 12, 30, Apr. 1, 1886, Box 44, LC, Sheridan Papers; Crook to Sheridan, Apr. 1, 1886, in Davis, *Truth about Geronimo*, 217.

For other criticism of Crook's methods, see Endicott to Parkman, Feb. 4, 1886, LC, Cleveland Papers, ser. 3, reel 102. Britton Davis, veteran of many Apache

Two days later, Sheridan replaced Crook with Miles. Sheridan did "not wish to embarrass" Miles with specific instructions, but suggested "the necessity of making active and prominent use of the Regular troops of your command." Although Miles infused more regulars into the chase, his techniques closely paralleled those of his predecessor. In September, continued military pressure forced Geronimo and his weary band to surrender. An angry Cleveland ordered that, "if we cannot hang him which I would much prefer," then Geronimo should be treated as a prisoner of war, regardless of any promises Miles might have made.[30]

As Crook and Miles tracked Apaches in the Southwest, an uneasy calm settled over affairs on the Plains. Although still wary of reservation flare-ups, several army officers used the comparative quiet to review their policies or to renew their personal quests for promotion. In his final annual report before retiring, Sherman concluded that "the recent completion of the last of the four great transcontinental lines of railway has settled forever the Indian question." While admitting that sporadic violence might continue, he perceived that the railroads and the progression of white immigrants and soldiers had made the outcome inevitable. Sherman's successor, Sheridan, had acknowledged in a rare moment of candor in 1878 that "the government made treaties, gave presents, made promises, none of which were fulfilled." Motivated by compassion, as well as by the awareness of potential hostilities caused by starvation among

---

campaigns, defended Crook, arguing that "Sheridan . . . was hopelessly at sea in his knowledge of these people, their mode of warfare, or the problem of catching them" (Davis, *Truth about Geronimo*, 74).

30. Drum to Miles, Apr. 3, 1886, in Report of Sheridan, Oct. 10, SW, AR, 1886, 72–73 (first and second quotations); General Field Orders No. 7, Apr. 20, ibid., 166; Report of Endicott, Nov. 30, ibid., 11–13; Drum to Endicott, Dec. 24, LC, Cleveland Papers, ser. 2, reel 43 (third quotation). See also Drum to Howard, Sept. 9, 1886, LS, SW, 116, reel 99; Drum to Endicott, Sept. 10, 1886, Cleveland Papers, ser. 2, reel 38; Drum to Miles, Sept. 25, 1886, ibid. On Capt. Henry Lawton's campaign, see Box 4, LC, Lawton Papers.

Indians, numerous army men stressed the need to feed reservation tribes properly.[31]

Neither the congresses nor the presidents took effective steps to solve the tragic problem. Opening additional western lands to white settlers and making grandiose schemes to transform all Indians into agriculturalists were more romantic and yielded bigger political dividends than did the mundane task of supplying Indians with adequate food and clothing. The military was in some ways even guiltier than civilian leaders. Whereas army men were in a position to recognize the problems rampant among Indians in the 1880s, few officers did more than lodge an occasional complaint; official recognition of their respective military genius seemed to warrant more of their attention. Even the most well-intentioned individuals preferred the politics of promotion and transfer to the thankless task of formulating and promoting an enlightened or effective Indian policy.[32]

Sporadic outbreaks still marred frontier relations. Pope believed that the Indians living on immigration routes should be moved to ranges parallel to but removed from these routes in order to allow unimpeded movement of whites north and south of the tribes. Commissioner of Indian Affairs Ezra A. Hayt agreed that consolidating

31. Report of Sherman, Oct. 27, SW, AR, 1883, 46 (first quotation); Report of Sheridan, Oct. 25, ibid., 1878, 34–35 (second quotation); McCrary to SI, June 21, 1877, LS, SW, 81, reel 74; Report of Pope, Sept. 15, SW, AR, 1877, 60; Report of Sherman, Nov. 7, ibid., 1878, 6; Report of Gibbon, Oct. 9, ibid., 1884, 117; Report of Schofield, Oct. 14, ibid., 104.

32. For proposed department changes, see Sherman to Sheridan, Nov. 29, 1877, LC, Sherman Papers, 90, reel 45; Sheridan to Lincoln, Sept. 25, Oct. 7, 1883, Box 34, LC, Sheridan Papers; Grierson to Schofield, July 28, 1888, LC, Schofield Papers; Proctor to Miles, Apr. 13, July 2, 1889, Proctor Library, Proctor Papers. For examples of politics, see Sheridan to Sherman, Mar. 17, 1877, Box 17, Sheridan Papers; Harrison to Grierson and Endicott, June 22, 1885, LC, Harrison Papers, ser. 2, reel 47; Miles to Lamont, Mar. 19, 1887, LC, Cleveland Papers, ser. 2, reel 47; Miles to Schofield, Jan. 26, 1889, Box 41, LC, Schofield Papers; Stanley to Schofield, Apr. 14, 1889, Box 42, ibid.; Proctor to Pres., Sept. 16, 1889, Harrison Papers, ser. 1, reel 22.

tribes on fewer reservations would reduce potential conflict between settlers and Indians. Others proposed less overt steps, arguing that forces large enough to overawe possible hostiles should remain within quick striking distance of the reservations.[33]

This policy of cautious readiness was implemented in 1885, when Indian Agent D. B. Dyer called upon the army to use "overwhelming force" in disarming rebellious Cheyennes at the Cheyenne and Arapaho Agency. Schofield, commanding the Division of the Missouri, thought the measures were "extreme" and advised that, if such action was necessary, the army had best wait "until winter, when the Indians can not go on the war path." Nonetheless, the Interior Department insisted upon forceful measures. Strong forces, commanded by Miles, prepared to move by rail to the threatened areas. In a last-minute quest for peace, Sheridan went to Fort Reno, where he found the difficulties "complicated" but the Cheyennes eager to avoid violence.[34]

More serious trouble arose five years later at the Rosebud, Cheyenne River, and Pine Ridge agencies of South Dakota. Inexperienced agents, crop failures, unfulfilled treaty agreements, and excitement surrounding the increasingly popular Ghost Dance brought affairs to the brink of disaster by the late fall of 1890. The army mobilized large forces in response to calls from agents for military support. On the scene, Brig. Gen. Thomas H. Ruger, commanding the Department of Dakota, hoped the show of force would intimidate

33. Report of Pope, Sept. 22, SW, AR, 1881, 122–23; Report of Hayt, Nov. 1, SI, AR, 1878, 445; Reports of Schofield, Oct. 9, SW, AR, 1885, 129–30, and Oct. 25, ibid., 1888, 69; Endicott to SI, June 8, 1886, LS, SW, 116, reel 99.

34. Drum to Endicott, June 28, 1885, LC, Cleveland Papers, ser. 2, reel 15; Armstrong to SI, July 5, 1885, Box 72, LC, Schofield Papers (first quotation); Schofield to Augur, July 7, 1885, Box 51, Schofield Papers (second and third quotations); AG to Schofield, July 7, 1885, LS, AGO, 75, reel 58; Armstrong to SI, July 8, 1885, Cleveland Papers, series 2, reel 16; Sheridan to Schofield, July 8, 1885, Box 72, Schofield Papers; Endicott to President, July 11, 1885, LS, SW, 110, reel 94; Sheridan to Cleveland, July 16, 1885, Cleveland Papers, ser. 2, reel 16 (fourth quotation); Hodgkins to President, July 18, LS, SW, 61, reel 95.

the Indians. Brig. Gen. John Brooke, commanding the Department of the Platte, foresaw open warfare the next spring and prepared his cavalry to launch a "decisive" attack.[35]

Among the Sioux, the peaceful doctrine espoused in the Ghost Dance of the mystic medicine man, Wovoka, was transformed into an antagonistic belief in a vengeful Messiah who would destroy the white intruders. Tension mounted as Big Foot, influential leader of the Miniconjou tribe of the Cheyenne River agency, first joined and then defected from the Ghost Dance. Miles and Ruger pegged Big Foot as a troublemaker despite his rejection of the Ghost Dance. After some hesitation, Big Foot accepted a request from several chiefs to mediate the growing internal struggles at the Pine Ridge agency. He and his tribe moved south, eluding several columns before being intercepted at Wounded Knee Creek.[36]

The Miniconjou, fearful of white betrayal, naturally unwilling to give up their best rifles, and influenced by the religious pronouncements of the fiery medicine man, Yellow Bird, refused to cooperate with demands that they give up their weapons to Colonel Forsyth's Seventh Cavalry. Whether by accident or design, the disarmament efforts turned into a bloody brawl on December 29, 1890, with Indian casualties totalling over two hundred men, women, and children. White losses numbered twenty-five killed and thirty-nine wounded.[37]

Almost half of the entire army participated in the campaign that followed Wounded Knee. Combining overwhelming force with overtures to important chiefs, Miles eventually coerced the panic-stricken Indians to return to their reservations.[38] Charles G. Sey-

35. Belt to SI, Apr. 14, 1890, LC, Harrison Papers, ser. 1, reel 26; Ruger to AG, Apr. 14, ibid.; Noble to Harrison, Apr. 15, ibid.; Brooke to AAG, Aug. 16, 1890, National Archives, LS, Dept. of the Platte; Report of Miles, Sept. 14, SW, AR, 1891, 133–42. Outstanding is Utley's *Last Days of the Sioux Nation*.

36. Utley, *Last Days of the Sioux Nation*, passim.

37. Ibid.

38. Ruger to AAG, Nov. 13, 16, National Archives, LS, Dept. of Dakota; Brooke to AAG, Nov. 16, 22, 1890, LS, Dept. of the Platte; Brooke to Carr,

mour, writing for *Harper's Weekly*, described the final review at the
Pine Ridge Agency, where General Miles assembled thirty-five
hundred men:

> When the sun came up, the ridges . . . were fringed with Indians,
> who looked like Arab sheiks in their white sheets and hooded
> heads. . . . Statuesque and haughty, the warriors stood watching
> the flying columns of cavalrymen and the explosive efforts of the
> cannoneers as they urged their animals into line. Down in the
> same valley, where the troops were hurriedly preparing for their
> manoeuvers, but nearly a mile away, were the great Indian vil-
> lages, with the squaws corralling their thousands of ponies, as a
> precautionary measure against any possible hostile demonstration
> of the part of the army. . . .
>
> The column was almost pathetically grand, with its bullet-pierced
> gun-carridges, its tattered guidons, and its long lines of troopers
> and foot soldiers facing a storm that was almost unbearable. It
> was the grandest demonstration by the army ever seen in the
> West; and when the soldiers had gone to their tents, the sullen
> and suspicious Brulés were still standing like statues on the crests
> of the hills.[39]

Few army officers on the scene suspected that this assemblage
would indeed be the "final review" of Indians and bluecoats. Miles
warned some months later that "the old theory that the destruction
of vast herds of buffalo had ended Indian wars, is not well-founded."
To avert future problems, he renewed the campaign for complete
army authority over troubled reservations. Captain William E.
Dougherty warned that "permanent quietude and contentment are
not apparent to me" in 1891. Commanding general Schofield and
war secretaries Stephen B. Elkins and Daniel S. Lamont predicted

---

Dec. 14, 1890, ibid.; Brooke to Miles, Dec. 16, 1890, ibid.; Utley, *Last Days of
the Sioux Nation*, 200–85.

39. Seymour, "Sioux Rebellion," 106 (quotation).

that Indian warfare had nearly ended, but trouble with "The Kid," a San Carlos renegade, seemed to belie such contentions. Brig. Gen. Alexander McD. McCook, commanding the Department of Arizona, recommended that irrigation and stock water supplies be established to pacify the Navajo in 1892. "A conflict with the Navajoes [sic], who are in great numbers and are well armed," warned McCook, "could be a serious business."[40]

Schofield's retirement in 1895 meant that Miles could finally take charge of the army. Miles noted that "only a few years have elapsed since the country was threatened by the most serious hostile conspiracy ever known in its history" and credited the subsequent decrease in violence to the army's practice of stationing troops near potential trouble spots and to the use of army officers as agents in the most dangerous areas.[41]

Sporadic confrontations between Indians and the army continued through the 1890s. In 1895, army units quieted what could have become a serious conflict between civilians and Indians near Jackson Hole, Wyoming. Brigadier General Wheaton called attention the following year to "the extraordinary amount of field service and laborious scouting" performed by troops from his Department of Colorado while pursuing still another group of Apaches in Mexico. Disturbances at the Tongue River Agency in Montana also required an army presence. In 1899, several companies of soldiers investigated unrest at the Leech Lake Agency in Minnesota.[42]

40. Report of Miles, Sept. 14, SW, AR, 1891, 144 (first quotation); Dougherty, "Recent Indian Craze," 578 (second quotation); Reports of Schofield, Oct. 23, SW, AR, 1890, 44, and Oct. 1, ibid., 1894, 60–63; Report of Elkins, ibid., 1892, 5–6; Reports of Lamont, Nov. 27, ibid., 1893, 5, and Nov. 26, ibid., 1894, 3–4; Report of McCook, Sept. 1, ibid., 1892, 130–31 (third quotation). See also Report of Wheaton, Aug. 25, ibid., 1895, 137.

For yet another confrontation, see Svingen, "Case of Spotted Hawk and Little Whirlwind." For opposing views, see Morgan to SI, Feb. 24, 1891, LC, Harrison Papers, ser. 1, reel 30.

41. Report of Miles, Nov. 5, ibid., 1895, 63–64 (quotation). See also his Report of Nov. 6, ibid., 1896, 75.

42. Reports of Coppinger, Aug. 28, ibid., 1895, 163; Lamont, Nov. 26, ibid.,

The discovery of gold in the Yukon renewed army interest in yet another area of potential turmoil—Alaska. Brigadier General Elwell S. Otis had stated after an inspection tour that, as the native population was peaceful, the navy and treasury coastal patrol vessels already present provided sufficient measures of government authority. The following year, however, Miles disagreed with Otis's report. Miles argued that as the Alaskan Indians and Eskimos "are supplied with modern arms they may become turbulent and troublesome. Such has been the history of nearly all the tribes in other Territories." He called for three posts to be established in Alaska. Some troops were sent north, but spent most of their time rescuing beleaguered gold seekers.[43]

Despite the white intrusions, America's Indian wars did not extend to Alaska. The Alaskan natives—Indians and Eskimos—were more receptive to many of the new ways imported by the outsiders than the Indians of the western plains had been. Most significant, the sparse native population (fifty to seventy-five thousand in the late nineteenth century) and the slow influx of immigrants (about seven thousand non-natives lived there in 1890) meant that each group had more time and space to adapt to changing conditions, in sharp distinction with the situation in the remainder of the country. As a result, the army was not forced to assume its usual position as arbiter of the unequal struggle for dominance.[44]

In contrast with affairs in Alaska, the Spanish-American War and the subsequent American occupation of the Philippines radically altered the size and composition of the United States Army. Although these changes affected garrisons still on Indian service, the army did not consider the Indian threat suddenly eliminated. Well over ten thousand troops remained in the departments of Alaska,

4; Wheaton, Sept. 30, ibid., 1896, 142 (quotation), 145–48; and Wade, Aug. 29, 1899, House Doc. No. 2, 56th Cong., 1st sess., IV, ser. 3901, 23–24.

43. Report of Otis, Aug. 25, ibid., 1896, 162; Report of Miles, Oct. 21, ibid., 1897, 90–91 (quotation).

44. Utley, *Indian Frontier*, 266–68.

California, Colorado, Columbia, Dakota, Missouri, and Texas—
approximately two-thirds the number stationed in those areas during
the 1870s.[45] Bolstered by volunteers and total naval supremacy, the
expanded regular army defeated the Spanish in Cuba and the Philippines; Emilio Aguinaldo and other Filipino insurgents, however,
rebelled against the new foreign presence in a bloody war of occupation that lasted for four years.

Although the Philippine insurrection involved larger numbers of
men than the Indian wars did, the conflicts had a number of similarities. Again the army was placed in a virtually impossible position; this time, it was to enforce President McKinley's policy of
"benevolent assimilation" against native peoples who sought independence from all outside authority. Experienced Indian fighters
such as Elwell Otis, Henry Lawton, Arthur MacArthur, Jacob H.
Smith, and Adna R. Chaffee carried out the policy with mixed
results. As they had done with the Indians, they tried to foster
support among the Filipinos through a mixture of gifts, threats,
and intimidation. Friendly native scouts and policemen were enlisted
in large numbers. Efforts to isolate the hostiles from the the remainder of the population also resembled methods used against
Indians. And although the Filipinos conducted their guerrilla defensive more systematically than did the American tribes, the army's
mobile columns and destruction of property in the Philippines may
also be compared to tactics used during the North American conflicts. As Secretary of War Elihu Root noted, troops were "utilizing
the lessons of the Indian wars."[46]

45. For army returns, see SW, AR, 1899, 6–7; ibid., 1900, 38d; ibid., 1901,
74B; ibid., 1902, 300B; ibid., 1903, 438B.

46. Report of Root, SW, AR, 1902, 16 (quotation); Mills to Mother, Sept.
18, 1880, U.S. Army Hist. Res. Coll., Mills Papers; Duvall to AG, Dec. 13,
1909, ibid.; Gates, *Schoolbooks and Krags*; and Miller, *"Benevolent Assimilation,"*
196–218. Gates emphasizes the army's basic benevolence; Miller should be used
to document army atrocities and the battle between imperialist and anti-imperialist
newspapers. Neither Miller's "'Injun Warfare' under Chaffee and Roosevelt," nor

Other elements of the conflicts also bear comparison. In each conflict, combatants on both sides committed numerous atrocities. Records of the Philippine conflict are especially illuminating. Casualty reports claimed as many as fifteen Filipinos dead for every one wounded, a sharp reversal of the one killed to four or five wounded ratio more common to the era. Like reformers during the Indian wars, critics charged that the high death rate reflected the American practice of giving no quarter. But again not all army officers were bloodthirsty killers. "Let us so work that the more enlightened Filipino may, as did the savage Indian, look upon the army as an honorable and generous adversary when forced into war, and one always ready to be a staunch friend," wrote the acting military governor of the Philippines in 1901.[47]

As many regulars moved to the Philippines or the Caribbean, new officers commanded troops that were still on Indian duty. Rumors of trouble west of Nogales, Arizona, and around forts Sill, Robinson, and Niobrara prompted Brig. Gen. Edwin V. Sumner to send small detachments to preserve the peace in 1898. Brigadier General James F. Wade took similar actions the following year in response to disturbances among the Chippewa in the Department of Dakota. Brigadier General Henry C. Merriam of the Department of Colorado warned that the drains of foreign obligations upon western garrisons might have serious results: "This depletion has been carried possibly to the danger limit, considering the large numbers of Indians (about 55,000) residing within the department, and others domiciled in Mexico." Commanding general Miles concurred in 1901: "There is no doubt that the presence of military stations within a reasonable distance of their reservations has had a restraining influence upon them. These stations will have to be

---

Roth's *Muddy Glory* gives an adequate scholarly comparison of large-scale policies in the Indian and Philippines conflicts.

47. Miller, *"Benevolent Assimilation,"* 189; Leonard, *Above the Battle*, 68 (quotation).

maintained for some years to come or during the time that they are in a state of transition from a nomadic, uncivilized condition to that of a peaceful, industrious life."[48]

Organizational debacles exposed during the Spanish-American War clearly reflected the army's structural inability either to anticipate areas of possible conflict or to plan for war once those areas had been identified. The Military Information Division, formed in 1889 as part of the Adjutant-General's Office, had been assigned the task of securing information on the geography, economic resources, and armed forces of the United States and foreign powers. Although its official staff eventually included twelve officers, ten clerks, two messengers in Washington, forty officers on National Guard duty, and sixteen overseas attachés, it had not prepared the army for war against Spain.[49]

As the Spanish-American War began, President McKinley turned a White House office into a war room, replete with telegraph and telephone wires to army commanders and up-to-date situation maps of Cuba and the Philippines. Unfortunately, he found the War Department and the army poorly equipped to handle the rapidly changing situation. Growing disillusionment with his mediocre Secretary of War, Russell A. Alger, and the pompous Miles, led the president to seek out the recently retired Schofield; quickly giving up on Schofield, McKinley turned to Adjutant-General Henry C. Corbin, whose growing influence in the capital was a great boon to military efficiency. Even considering Corbin's input, however, McKinley made most of the key strategic decisions of the war himself. Considering the army's lack of strategic initiative, the chief executive could have done little else.[50]

48. Reports of Sumner, Sept. 2, 8, SW, AR, 1898, 192, 194; Wade, Aug. 25, ibid., 1899, 23–24; Merriam, Aug. 25, ibid., 25–26 (first quotation); and Miles, Oct. 1, ibid., 1901, 6 (second quotation).

49. Cosmas, *Army for Empire*, 30–31; Report of Elkins, n.d., SW, AR, 1892, 7; Trask, *War with Spain*, 72, 148. The military's failure to learn from experience against Indians is examined by Gates, "Indians and Insurrectos."

50. Gould, *Spanish-American War and President McKinley*, 55–90.

The logistical improvements made by the army during the course of the war are clear. Chaos gradually became order as officials coped with changing national policy—the decision to annex the Philippines, for example—and the demands of equipping and supplying a rapidly expanding military force. Little evidence, however, suggests that the War Department was capable of making similar strides in strategic planning.[51]

Although Miles had personally conducted the Puerto Rican campaign with much success, his failure to provide McKinley with sound strategic advice against Spain had been disappointing. Himself a product of mid-nineteenth-century America, Miles' army service and background had been geared to opponents far different from the Spanish and Filipinos. His continued concern with the Indian threat was understandable. Yet his inability to grasp the intricacies of the nation's new global involvements seriously undermined effective planning. Miles's public pronouncements regarding the infamous "embalmed beef" scandal, during which he falsely charged the War Department with having sent beef spoiled by harmful chemicals to United States troops in the Caribbean, caused further embarassment to successive Republican administrations.[52]

Secretary of War Elihu Root, appointed in 1899, was determined to reform the old army. To solve the strategic problems, Root created the Army War College and asked Congress to replace the position of commanding general with that of a chief of staff, who would act as adviser to the secretary of war. Miles fought the Root program with all of his considerable energies. Dismayed by Miles's egotistical nature and opposition to army policy in the Philippines, President Theodore Roosevelt gave his wholehearted support to Root. As the battle lingered, Roosevelt came to despise the old Indian fighter, describing his nemesis as "an element of great mischief . . . and the

51. Trask, *War with Spain*, 167–70, 484–85.

52. Weigley, *Towards an American Army*, 172–76; Keuchel, "Chemicals and Meat," 249–64; *New York Times*, Apr. 4, 1902; Alger to Spooner, May 2, 1902, LC, Spooner Papers.

most serious obstacle that Root has encountered in his efforts to put the army on a serious plane." In the end Root won, and in 1903 Miles was forced to retire.[53]

The creation of a general staff meant that strategic military planning could be conducted on a systematic basis in the future. In Root's view, the object was to ready the army "to provide for war" rather than merely providing for "present utility." The reorganization was timely, for the occupation of Cuba, Puerto Rico, and the Philippines had forced the United States to accept new responsibilities of an international nature. Thousands of troops were hence to be stationed overseas; the reforms orchestrated by Secretary of War Root institutionalized this increased army concern for non-Indian affairs. No longer could the army afford to be satisfied with maintaining scattered garrisons to keep peace in the western United States; it now needed to meet its obligations as a world power.[54]

53. Jessup, *Elihu Root*, passim; Roosevelt to Harvey, Jan. 22, 1904, in Morison, ed., *Letters of Theodore Roosevelt* 3:705 (quotation); *New York Times*, Mar. 23, Apr. 4, 1902. In 1910, Miles charged Roosevelt with being "guilty of treason" (*New York Times*, Oct. 4, 1910).

54. See Root's reports of 1899–1901, in his *Military and Colonial Policy*, 349–82 (quotations). On the creation of the General Staff, see William H. Carter, "Creation of American General Staff," Sen. Misc. Doc. No. 119, 68th Cong., 1st sess., II, ser. 8254.

Conclusion

The Spanish-American War had exposed the lack of strategic military planning in the United States as well as the inability of any organization within the army to rectify this liability. The Root reforms of the early 1900s thus addressed problems fundamental to America's armed forces. Root's general staff assembled information, supervised education, and planned future actions involving the military. Although the new arrangement did not solve all the army's problems, it was at least an attempt to organize the nation's armed forces systematically. General staff officers prepared reports on various strategic issues. In the new Army War College, students grappled with large-scale problems. As a result, America's strategic military policy no longer depended solely on intuition, individual experience, and random chance. It followed, albeit somewhat belatedly, the general trend among European military systems after Prussia's stunning successes of the 1860s and 1870s, which had revealed the benefits of a well-organized, well-trained staff and efficient management.[1]

1. Nenninger, *Leavenworth Schools*, 63–65. For examples, see the report of Hugh Drum, Fox Conner, and Leroy Eltinge, "A Strategical Study of the Employment of the A.E.F. against the Imperial Government," Sept. 25, 1917, as discussed in ibid., 136; and Matthew F. Steele's lectures, "The South African War" and "The Conduct of War," plus his Strategy (n.d.), all located in U.S. Army Hist. Res. Coll., Steele Papers.

The professional approach to strategy was new to the United States Army. Before 1900, staff and line officers had frequently remained at odds. Line officers performed field duties and ran frontier forts; staff officers procured supplies, dealt with administrative problems, and handled congressional relations. This division of authority severely hurt strategic planning during the Indian wars. Sherman, Sheridan, and the war secretaries did not have at their disposal a cadre of younger officers trained in the art of military strategy. Instead, they had a small number of aides whose poorly defined roles rarely included offering strategic advice to their superiors. The most successful Indian fighters, Miles and Crook, developed their methods of warfare in response to field experience rather than from academic instruction. At a lower level, many officers did no more than carry out routine garrison duty. Many older men claimed that books and military education could add little to one's abilities and that actual combat and field service provided the only means by which one could learn about war. This demanding on-the-job training provided no room for failure and, as a consequence, little opportunity for experimentation. It also needlessly endangered the lives of soldiers.[2]

Not surprisingly, officers remained largely unaware of international developments in military structure and theory. Although a few noticed the exploits of British commanders such as Sir Garnet Wolseley, the majority of senior American officers, perceiving the Indian wars as less important than possible confrontations with European foes, failed to study the contemporary colonial wars. Had they done so, they might have recognized a number of similarities between the respective conflicts, noting and perhaps profiting from the successes and failures of other European nations in fighting nomadic and tribal peoples. Both the French and the British, for example, used native troops earlier and more effectively than did their American counterparts, many of whom—with the notable exceptions of Crook and Miles—never recognized that such levies could perform effectively in battle as well as on the trail. Of course,

2. Nenninger, *Leavenworth Schools*, 3–52.

Spain had used native troops in the Americas for many years; to analyze that country's military seemed ludicrous to the proud Americans.[3]

In fairness to United States military men, it should be noted that most of their European counterparts were also unable to resolve problems of a similar nature. A few dynamic Europeans—Wolseley, Louis Lyautey, and Horatio Herbert Kitchener, for example—were successful. Less qualified commanders, often blinded by racism and ignorance, found it impossible to deal with the diverse peoples they faced in combat. The litany of problems encountered by Europeans after 1865 seems familiar to the student of America's Indian conflicts. Realistic British officers, for instance, knew that many of their troops were pitiful marksmen plagued by chronically inadequate mounted troops. Supplies were a constant headache. The proper size and composition of the ideal strike force was never fully resolved, and the ideal balance between training, firepower, reconnaissance, and speed within a column remained tenuous. Faced by a well-led, determined foe, any expedition could meet with disaster. Custer's Seventh Cavalry found this out at the Little Bighorn in 1876; Brevet Lt. Col. Henry Burmester Pulleine's six companies of the Twenty-fourth Regiment and the Natal Kaffirs discovered it too late at Isandhlwana in southern Africa nearly three years later.[4]

Other similarities abound, but the majority of Americans and

3. Merritt, "Some Defects of Our Cavalry System"; Worcester, "Apaches in the History of the Southwest," 28–29.

For an insightful account of British colonial wars, see Farwell, *Queen Victoria's Little Wars*. For examples of the French use of native troops, see Cohen, "Malaria and French Imperialism," 30–31. Increasing substitution by England of colonial troops for British regulars is explained by Bond in the introduction to his *Victorian Military Campaigns*, 8; and Killingray, "Idea of a British Imperial African Army." Exceptions to the lack of attention by American officers may be seen in Seaman, "Native Troops for Our Colonial Possessions" and "Zulu War," 297–300. See also Luvaas, *Education of an Army*, 187 n. 26.

4. Bond, *Victorian Army*, 18–27; Keegan, "Ashanti Campaign," in *Victorian Military Campaigns*, 195; Bond, "South African War," ibid., 210–37. Lyautey's views are in his "Du rôle colonial de l'armée," 308–22.

Europeans were rarely willing or able to learn from the experiences of their international rivals. C. E. Callwell's classic account, *Tirah*, described the campaign of Anglo-Indian troops against the Afridi and Orakzais tribes on the northwestern frontier of India. Callwell's observations that a well-defined objective was rarely apparent and that numerous columns were often necessary could have described the United States Army's experience on the Great Plains, as well as the British colonial efforts in Africa and India. In 1879, Wolseley complained that "the howling Societies at home" would not allow him to punish the Zulus as he deemed necessary. Sherman and Sheridan might well have understood Wolseley's dilemma. Several British officers, failing to force a decisive battle with indigenous tribes by conventional methods, resorted to the destruction of enemy villages, crops, herds, and families. As in the United States, conventions that might have prevented wholesale slaughters of "civilized peoples" often held no force in Africa or India.[5]

European problems of politics and policy also resemble those in the United States. Governments of the late nineteenth century raced to control more land and resources and were willing to fight the native inhabitants to secure their gains. In addition, they wanted to further causes that they believed to be just—Christianity, western-style government, and European settlement, for example. Military force often seemed the easiest way to establish or guarantee such principles. With so much at stake for the respective governments, struggles broke out among those who sought authority over the military. In the United States, debate centered on the efforts of the War and Interior departments to control the Indian bureau, and on the efforts of the secretary of war and commanding general to control the army. In Britain, the fight raged between the commander-in-chief, the secretary of state for war, and the Colonial Office for control of the army and its use in colonial wars. In both cases, the lack of administrative clarity made cooperation between agencies

5. Callwell, *Tirah 1897*, 10–20, 154; James, *Savage Wars*, 174 (quotation), 184–86.

rare; the political infighting made long-term planning exceedingly difficult.[6]

Naval strategists gained the upper hand in both countries, further impeding the efforts of their land-based counterparts to make policy. Recent breakthroughs in naval technology challenged traditional assumptions about seapower in Britain and the United States. In London, changes in technology and international politics threatened England's naval dominance; discussion focused on the ability of the British navy to protect the far-flung empire. Although army theorists continued to pronounce their judgements, politicians found naval matters to be of increasing interest and importance. Across the Atlantic, congressional support for a revamped fleet dimmed the United States Army's hopes for increased funding, as naval theorists championed the value of seapower to national defense. Beset by such challenges, the army's role in the new order remained poorly defined.[7]

The shortsightedness of political and military leaders seemed to be reinforced almost daily in the United States, hampering the development of strategic thought in the army between 1865 and 1903 in the process. Those strategic debates that did occur almost always concerned conventional warfare more applicable to the battlefields of Europe than to those of the American West.[8] The absence of routine meetings, regular correspondence, or open discussion of military strategy toward Indians also discouraged individual initiative. And in a larger context, the army's failure to define clear strategic concepts for use against Indians was symptomatic of the federal government's failure to define the means through which its general Indian policy was to be implemented. Whites generally

6. See Bond, *Victorian Army*, 13–19.

7. For the strategic debates in Britain, see Luvaas, *Education of an Army*, 244, 429; and Gooch, *Plans of War*, 11, 20, 28. For the U.S. Army's lack of strategic doctrine, see Trask, *War with Spain*, 72, 148.

8. Cosmas, *An Army for Empires*, stresses the strategic thought within the army. See especially his excellent bibliography of articles published in the *Journal of the Military Service Institution*.

accepted the twin goals of suppressing Indian military power and assimilating Indians into American society. There was no such consensus, however, as to the means through which these goals could be effected. Military and civilian leaders thus succumbed to the temptation to word their reports concerning Indian affairs in vague, rhetorical terms rather than outlining specific recommendations.

A variety of factors influenced military attempts to effect the nation's haphazard Indian policies. Military leaders' perceptions of the western environments significantly influenced their actions. Most officers had at least toured their commands, although their views of western lands and resources usually remained superficial. The department commander who perceived his region as one that welcomed white settlement or offered lucrative natural resources tended to take an aggressive military posture against Indians. Such a commander generally had little patience with hostiles. In contrast, the division chief or commanding general who saw his domain as being unfit for white habitation frequently adopted a much more tolerant attitude toward the local peoples and used his most capable subordinates in other, more promising departments. Positive reactions to the environment may be seen in the determination to crush Indian resistance on the Great Plains; negative perceptions help explain the army's general reluctance to station its most effective leaders in the Far Southwest before the 1880s. Somewhat surprisingly, few senior officers openly expressed a desire to use the armed forces to exterminate the buffalo. Aware of the devastating effects such a slaughter would have on Plains tribes, several officers formally protested the wanton destruction of these animals.

Prejudice against Indians also affected the implementation of military policy. The overwhelming majority of strategists after 1865 believed that Indians were inferior savages unequal to the white man. The Indian barbarians, they argued, needed to be removed to reservations, where a few of the more advanced might progress if given sufficient time. Other officers, less certain of the Indians' fate, preferred to separate those tribes already on the pathway to "civilization" from those that had clung to their "barbaric" ways. Some subscribed to reformist principles and pointed out that the tribes had suffered repeated injustices at the hands of unscrupulous whites. All, however, allowed paternalism to influence their convictions. While few showed tangible evidence of having accepted the pseudoscientific racism increasingly prevalent during the nineteenth century, even the most generous believed that Indians were less human than whites.[9] The continual underestimation of Indians made it difficult to respect them as worthy opponents and as a consequence discouraged the development of military techniques to be used against them. This attitude combined with the confused nature of combat with Indians to encourage military commanders to disregard traditional rules of warfare. Many simply rationalized that they could use whatever tactics they deemed necessary to crush the resistance of an inferior people.

Personal disputes further hampered military effectiveness. Men accustomed to rapid, even mercurial rises through the ranks during the Civil War found the ten-, fifteen-, and twenty-year intervals between promotions after 1865 almost insufferable. Impatience, age and educational differences, and petty jealousies turned army officers into fractious individuals seeking preferment rather than into a smoothly operating team. Miles despised Crook and voiced his opinions loudly and repeatedly to superiors. Hazen and Grierson justifiably believed that Sheridan had stunted their careers. Pope refused to serve under wartime nemesis Halleck. Sheridan and Pope both distrusted Ord's intentions in the Department of Texas. Sheridan accepted Crook's resignation of the Arizona department over a dispute concerning the proper use of Indian allies. A number of officers disliked Custer. In practice, these antipathies precluded effective cooperation. Although most officers understood their general frontier duties and objectives, the open dialogue that might have helped them achieve their goals more smoothly was practically nonexistent.

9. See the debate between Prucha, "Scientific Racism and Indian Policy," in his *Indian Policy in the United States*, 180–97; and Horsman, "Scientific Racism and the American Indian."

No single factor determined military policy or attitudes. Most officers dealt with problems as they arose rather than according to well-defined doctrine. Moreover, the impact of continually changing perceptions of Indians and western environments varied according to the individual. Although a select minority remained above the pettiness of their peers, the cumulative effects of military infighting can scarcely be ignored. An awareness of the cultural beliefs and personal idiosyncrasies that pervaded the nineteenth-century United States Army is thus essential to any accurate understanding of the army's Indian policies.

The army's relations with other government agencies also affected its conduct of western affairs. War and State department contacts were on the whole cordial. The lack of rivalry between the two offices meant that problems along the nation's southwestern and northern international borders could usually be handled with a minimum of interdepartmental rancor. The army recognized the complexities of the borderlands Indian issue and eventually tried to cooperate with Mexican and Canadian authorities. In contrast, the tangled web of divided authority over Indians led to an open breach between the War and Interior departments for control of the Bureau of Indian Affairs. Each department was loath to accept any suggestions or recommendations from its rival. In the end, the bureau remained in the Interior Department. The bitter conflict was significant nonetheless, as it blocked any meaningful exchange of ideas and information regarding Indians between the two departments most concerned.

The army's relations with Congress were even more confused. Debates concerning the federal government's proper role in Reconstruction, along with traditional controversies about the merits of a regular army as opposed to a volunteer or militia force, and the proper size of the defense budget, were often indistinguishable from debates over the army's role in Indian affairs. Sherman's stubborn determination to keep the army out of partisan politics severely limited its congressional influence. The navy won huge congressional appropriations; its land-based counterpart never mounted a comparable campaign to win popular support for military actions against Indians. Attempts to transfer the Indian bureau to the War Department failed, as did efforts to significantly increase the size and efficiency of the standing army. This political impotence hurt the army's overall effectiveness and limited its strategic choices in the West.

The unresolved question of who was to make general Indian policy spawned further confusion. Post–Civil War presidents, with the exception of the unpredictable Grant, took comparatively little interest in Indian affairs. They wanted the westward movement of white settlers to continue as smoothly as possible, with a minimum of controversy between social reformers and diehard expansionists. In the absence of presidential leadership, the secretaries of war and the interior battled each other and Congress for dominance over Indian policy. On the whole, the Interior Department must be judged the most influential, as the secretary of the interior could veto military schemes to enter reservations. Without such permission, army officers in the field had little chance of tracking down their Indian enemies, who could simply flee to their reservation havens.

The army's role in implementing policy should not be ignored. The lack of specific guidelines frequently gave department commanders and their subordinates control over Indian policy in fact if not in theory. With the active support of the commanding general and division chiefs, these officers repeatedly interpreted their instructions as they saw fit. No established routine existed for making policy at this level, either; annual reports, sporadic personal tours, and random inspiration were most influential. The army's jumbled command structure gave its junior officers additional leeway; conflicts between staff and line officers, as well as between the commanding general and secretary of war, prevented the army from establishing strict mandates of its own.

Problems of military strategy against Indians compounded those of policy. Junior officers were instructed in the art of strategy only after the Indian wars had ended. As a result, young staff members could rarely offer valuable suggestions to their superiors. Among the higher ranks, slow promotions and the seniority system encouraged excesses; some officers were overcautious, others overaggressive. Petty quarrels forestalled cooperation. Reconstruction, coastal defense, scientific responsibilities, natural disasters, the so-called Mormon threat, and labor disputes drained manpower and further impeded effective strategy. The army was therefore never free to concentrate its full military efforts against Indians even if it had so desired.

Despite the obstacles, a few military leaders conducted successful campaigns against Indians, with some consensus on proper techniques. For instance, officers agreed on the need for converging columns to strike at the camps and villages of Indians that they labeled hostile. In spite of support from various quarters for concentrating garrisons at key forts or for organizing roving columns intended to subdue Indians, most commanders also recognized that such defensive measures failed to limit violence between Indians and whites.

Little other agreement existed, and the least successful officers failed to grasp even these basic points. No consensus was reached concerning the optimal composition and timing of offensives. Officers like Crook sought to increase mobility by leaving cumbersome wagons behind and relying on pack mules to carry supplies. Miles, on the other hand, emphasized the need to equip his command with adequate firepower in the form of Gatling guns and mountain howitzers. Disagreement with Sheridan on the proper use of Indian auxiliaries resulted in Crook's ouster from Arizona. The most effective season for offensive strikes was also disputed. Following tradition, some officers held that offensives should begin in the spring or summer, thus easing the army's need to gather forage for animals and reducing hardships for man and beast in the field. Critics argued that such conditions guaranteed failure and claimed instead that winter campaigns held the key to success against Indians. These planners pointed out that winter offered Indians less natural forage and game; while admitting that the regulars would suffer, the planners believed that the corresponding reduction of Indian mobility and morale more than compensated for the temporary agony of the troops.

Whatever their preferences, few commanders were unaware of the logical outcome of any of these plans. The grinding campaigns, when conducted effectively, brought upon Indians a form of warfare much different from that seen in Georgia, the Carolinas, or Virginia during the Civil War campaigns of 1864 and 1865. Offensives directed at Indian villages of noncombatants culminated, if the commander was skillful, determined, and lucky, in a confused melee of warriors, soldiers, and dependents. Indian women and children as a consequence were often killed in the fighting, whether by accident or design. Noncombatants did not represent a significant percentage of the casualties incurred during the Civil War; they did, however, make up a sizable portion of those killed in the Indian wars.

Military success against Indians was thus not attributable to a national strategic doctrine understood and practiced by officers in the field. It was instead the result of a commander's personal experiences in the West, his perceptions of Indians and the natural environment, the abilities of his subordinates, and simple good fortune. Strategic thought in the United States had admittedly undergone fundamental changes as a result of the Civil War. The dominance of Jominian ideas, emphasizing limited offensives and limited wars, gave way to the concepts of total warfare, foreseen to some degree by Clausewitz. The nation's twentieth-century strategists have used overwhelming power to annihilate the enemy's armed forces in direct confrontation, as Grant had done in 1864–65. Sherman's campaigns through Georgia and the Carolinas also had an impact, showing that the welfare, production, and morale of the enemy's society constituted vital military objectives.[10]

---

10. Weigley's *Eisenhower's Lieutenants*, 2–7, and *Towards an American Army*, 78–99, clearly show the acceptance of the idea of total warfare by Sherman, Sheridan, and twentieth-century thinkers.

In these respects, the Civil War's legacy cannot be ignored. It must be used to help explain the roots of U.S. strategy as expressed during the twentieth century, when massive numbers of volunteers swelled the military ranks, as their predecessors had done during the Civil War. But this connection between the Civil War and the wars of the twentieth century does not necessarily infer that principles used in these conflicts were applied without qualification to the Indian wars of the late nineteenth century. Instead, it points to the problems of attempting to establish a direct correlation between two very different conflicts, the civil and Indian wars. An apparent consensus among American strategists was not reached until after the First World War. Although Sherman and Sheridan influenced army policies, they believed that their Civil War experiences were applicable to warfare against enemies who used more conventional methods, rather than against American Indians. The two recognized that the country did not need to mount a full-scale war against Indians; thus they relied on the small regular establishment rather than on millions of volunteers.

Historians must carefully define the point at which military concern with Indian affairs ended. Many scholars conclude their studies with Wounded Knee in December 1890. There is some justification in doing so; this was indeed the last major violent confrontation between Indians and the army. It must be noted, however, that the regulars did not know this at the time. Annual reports from officers reflect continued uneasiness about Indian problems throughout the 1890s. Although no major conflicts rivaling those of earlier years broke out, nagging problems still worried army brass. The possibility of future violence particularly troubled veteran Indian fighter Nelson Miles. Only when he was forced to retire and the army command structure reorganized to meet new international responsibilities did the military's interest in shaping Indian policy wane significantly.

Were the long wars with the Indians after 1865 preventable? Probably not, considering the army's dim view of Indians, public distrust of the army, and the lack of an intelligently articulated

Indian policy. Few historical events can be labeled inevitable, but the mood of the republic in the nineteenth century offered little alternative to warfare, especially in light of the steadfast refusal by many tribes to accept the changes that whites demanded of them. Peaceful coexistence was acceptable to neither whites nor Indians. To complicate matters even further, neither side showed any proclivity to change its perception of how the land should best be used. Few either in the federal government or among the tribes could conceive of any means other than warfare to resolve the controversies arising along the western frontiers.

The problems confronting the army were similar to those facing the federal government as a whole. "The weakened spring of government" in the nineteenth century made it difficult for that government to handle the innumerable tasks assigned to it by the public. Society wanted subsidies without interference. As a result, many tasks of governing were left to private institutions and interest groups, whose selfishness and misbehavior often led to inequities, peculation, and injustice. The federal government's failure to define a clear, consistent Indian policy illustrates the dangers of such practices. The army, as part of that government and the society that created it, functioned in a similar fashion under similarly impossible demands. Political leaders wanted peace and budget reductions while at the same time wanting the Indians removed as a military threat. Unwilling either to pay for a crushing blow or to wait for reformers to "civilize" the Indians, the government dealt with Indians on a haphazard basis. Mismanagement, shortsightedness, and insensitivity thus characterized Indian-white relations.[11]

Were the army's Indian policies justified? Were they moral? Scholars and apologists have often criticized these policies as leading to the near extermination of the tribes. Such attacks have shown that the army's Indian warfare was inhumane, especially when considered from a twentieth- century context. However, the issue becomes more clouded if one considers conditions in the nineteenth-century Amer-

11. Farnham, "'The Weakened Spring of Government,'" 676–80.

ican West. Federal military and civilian policymakers of that age, along with their reform-minded rivals, had their own unique ideas about the world, the nation, and the West. They commonly perceived Indians as savage obstacles to the white man's inexorable advance. Only after first subjugating these barbarians, they believed, could they guide the tribes down the path of ultimate salvation.[12]

Yet an accurate understanding of the factors influencing Indian policy and the process by which that policy was made seems in the long run more valuable than judgments of right and wrong, which may change from generation to generation. In this spirit of historical discovery, the present study has attempted to explain the nation's strategic military policy—or lack thereof—against Indians between 1865 and 1903. A wide range of political and cultural factors influenced the formulation of that policy. The policy-making process itself was woefully lacking. Neither the federal government nor the army representing it organized institutions to examine Indian affairs in any comprehensive and systematic manner. The absence of detailed contemporary analysis sowed confusion, mistrust, and disinterest among those involved in making policy.

Similar problems affected purely military affairs. The army, viewing Indian affairs as a "fleeting bother," never took the trouble to reach a clear consensus on effective strategy against Indians.[13] Its structural flaws and lack of political acumen exacerbated the government's inability to establish orderly, consistent Indian policy. These failures regarding Indians prolonged the agony of the entire nation; in particular, it compounded the anguish of all those, citizens and soldiers, Indians and non-Indians, who lived in the western United States.

12. Gates, "Indians and Insurrectos," 59–68, provides a good overview of the individual commander's responsibility concerning morality.

13. Utley, "The Frontier and the American Military Tradition," in Tate, ed., *American Military on the Frontier*, 9.

Appendix

President	Secretary of War	Commanding General
Andrew Johnson (1865–69)	Edwin Stanton (1862–68) John M. Schofield (1868–69)	Ulysses S. Grant (1864–69)
U. S. Grant (1869–77)	John A. Rawlins (1869) William W. Belknap (1869–76) Alphonso Taft (1876) James D. Cameron (1876–77)	William T. Sherman (1869–83)
Rutherford B. Hayes (1877–81)	George W. McCrary (1877–79) Alexander Ramsey (1879–81)	
James A. Garfield (1881) Chester A. Arthur (1881–85)	Robert T. Lincoln (1881–85)	William T. Sherman retires 1883 Philip H. Sheridan (1883–88)

President	Secretary of War	Commanding General
Grover Cleveland (1885–89)	William C. Endicott (1885–89)	Philip H. Sheridan retires 1888 John M. Schofield (1888–95)
Benjamin Harrison (1889–93)	Redfield Proctor (1889–91) Stephen B. Elkins (1891–93)	
Grover Cleveland (1893–97)	Daniel S. Lamont (1893–97)	John M. Schofield retires 1895 Nelson A. Miles (1895–1903)
William McKinley (1897–1901)	Russell A. Alger (1897–99) Elihu Root (1899–1904)	
Theodore Roosevelt (1901–09)	Elihu Root retires 1904 William H. Taft (1904–08) Luke E. Wright (1908–09)	Nelson A. Miles retires 1903 Position abolished

Source: Adapted from Weigley, *History of the U.S. Army*, pp. 593–95.

Bibliography

A. Primary Sources

1. Manuscript Collections

Library of Congress (Washington, D.C.)
    William W. Belknap Papers
    Zachariah Chandler Papers (microfilm)
    Grover Cleveland Papers (microfilm edition, UT)
    Henry L. Dawes Papers
    Ulysses S. Grant Papers (microfilm edition, UT)
    Benjamin Harrison Papers (microfilm edition, UT)
    Joseph R. Hawley Papers
    Andrew Johnson Papers (microfilm edition, UT)
    August V. Kautz Papers
    Daniel S. Lamont Papers
    Henry W. Lawton Papers
    Robert Todd Lincoln Papers
    John Logan Papers
    Nelson A. Miles Collection (formerly Miles-Cameron Family Papers)
    John M. Schofield Papers
    Carl Schurz Papers (microfilm)
    Philip H. Sheridan Papers
    William T. Sherman Papers (microfilm edition, UT)
    John Coit Spooner Papers
    Edwin M. Stanton Papers (microfilm)

Alfred H. Terry Papers
Henry B. Wilson Papers
National Archives (Washington, D.C.)
Record Group 94: Records of the Adjutant General's Office
Letters Sent by the Office of the Adjutant General (microfilm)
Post Medical Returns, Fort Richardson (microfilm, Barker Archives)
Record Group 107: Records of the Secretary of War
Letters Sent by the Secretary of War Relating to Military Affairs
   (microfilm)
Record Group 393: Records of the U.S. Army Continental Commands
Letters Sent, Department of Arizona
Letters Sent, Department of the Columbia
Letters Sent, Department of Dakota
Letters Sent, Department of the Missouri
Letters Sent, Department of the Platte
Letters Sent, Department of Texas
Bancroft Library, University of California at Berkeley
Edward O. C. Ord Papers
Barker Archives, The University of Texas at Austin
J. F. Evans Papers
Bowdoin Library, Bowdoin College (Brunswick, Maine)
Oliver O. Howard Papers
Fort Concho Research Library (San Angelo, Texas)
Texas Letters of Benjamin Grierson (microfilm 16)
Fort Concho Post Returns (microfilm 89)
Hayes Library (Fremont, Ohio)
George Crook Papers
Illinois State Historical Library (Springfield, Illinois)
Christopher C. Augur Papers
Benjamin H. Grierson Papers
Minnesota State Historical Society (St. Paul, Minnesota)
Alexander Ramsey Correspondence and Miscellaneous Papers (microfilm)
Proctor Free Library (Proctor, Vermont)
Redfield Proctor Papers
Stanford University Library, Manuscripts Division (Stanford, California)
William Shafter Papers (microfilm edition, UT)
Texas State Archives (Austin, Texas)

Samuel B. Maxey Papers
U.S. Army History Research Collection (Carlisle Barracks, Pennsylvania)
Luther P. Bradley Papers
Crook-Kennon Papers
Winfield Scott Hancock Papers
Charles P. Hatfield, Order of Indian Wars Collection
Ranald S. Mackenzie Papers
Nelson A. Miles, Order of Indian Wars Collection
Stephen C. Mills Papers
Matthew F. Steele Papers
Samuel B. M. Young Papers
Western History Research Center, University of Wyoming (Laramie, Wyoming)
Frances E. Warren Papers (photostatic copies courtesy Dr. Lewis L. Gould, The University of Texas at Austin)

2. Government Documents

U.S. Congress. *American State Papers: Indian Affairs.* 2 vols. Washington, D.C.: Gales and Seaton, 1832–34.
U.S. Congress. *American State Papers: Military Affairs.* 7 vols. Washington, D.C.: Gales and Seaton, 1832–61.
U.S. Congress. *Congressional Globe,* 39th–42nd Congress (1866–73).
U.S. Congress. *Congressional Record,* 43rd–45th Congress (1873–78).
U.S. Congress. House and Senate Documents.
House Document, No. 311, 25th Congress, 2nd session, serial 329.
House Executive Document, No. 76, 39th Congress, 1st session, XII, serial 1263.
Senate Executive Document, No. 15, 39th Congress, 2nd session, II, serial 1277.
Senate Executive Document, No. 156, 39th Congress, 2nd session, serial 1279.
House Executive Document, No. 23, 39th Congress, 2nd session, VI, serial 1288.
House Executive Document, No. 45, 39th Congress, 2nd session, VII, serial 1289.

Senate Executive Document, No. 2, 40th Congress, 1st session, 1867, serial 1308.

Senate Executive Document, No. 13, 40th Congress, 1st session, 1867, serial 1308.

House Executive Document, No. 97, 40th Congress, 3rd session, 1869, serial 1337.

Senate Executive Document, No. 18, 40th Congress, 3rd session, 1869, serial 1360.

Senate Executive Document, No. 40, 40th Congress, 3rd session, 1869, serial 1360.

Senate Executive Document, No. 49, 41st Congress, 2nd session, II, serial 1406.

House Executive Document, No. 185, 41st Congress, 2nd session, VII, serial 1418.

House Executive Document, No. 240, 41st Congress, 2nd session, VII, serial 1425.

House Executive Document, No. 122, 43rd Congress, 1st session, IX, serial 1607.

House Report, No. 384, 43rd Congress, 1st session, 1874, serial 1624.

House Report, No. 240, 44th Congress, 1st session, II, 1876, serial 1708.

House Report, No. 354, 44th Congress, 1st session, II, 1876, serial 1709.

Senate Executive Document, No. 19, 45th Congress, 2nd session, I, serial 1780.

House Miscellaneous Document, No. 64, 45th Congress, 2nd session, VI, serial 1820.

House Report, No. 241, 45th Congress, 2nd session, I, serial 1822.

Senate Executive Document, No. 30, 46th Congress, 2nd session, I, serial 1882.

Senate Executive Document, No. 33, 50th Congress, 1st session, I, serial 2504

House Document, No. 369, 54th Congress, 1st session, pt. 1, LXIX, serial 3436.

Senate Miscellaneous Document, No. 119, 68th Congress, 1st session, II, serial 8254.

U.S. Secretary of the Interior. Annual Reports.

1866–House Executive Document, No. 1, 39th Congress, 2nd session, II, serial 1284.

1867–House Executive Document, No. 1, 40th Congress, 2nd session, III, serial 1326.

1868–House Executive Document, No. 1, 40th Congress, 3rd session, II, serial 1366.

1869–House Executive Document, No. 1, 41st Congress, 2nd session, III, serial 1414.

1870–House Executive Document, No. 1, pt. 1, 41st Congress, 3rd session, IV, serial 1449.

1871–House Executive Document, No. 1, pt. 1, 42nd Congress, 2nd session, III, serial 1505.

1872–House Executive Document, No. 1, pt. 1, 42nd Congress, 3rd session, III, serial 1560.

1873–House Executive Document, No. 1, pt. 5, 43rd Congress, 1st session, IV, serial 1601.

1874–House Executive Document, No. 1, pt. 5, 43rd Congress, 2nd session, VI, serial 1639.

1875–House Executive Document, No. 1, pt. 5, 44th Congress, 1st session, IV, serial 1680.

1876–House Executive Document, No. 1, pt. 5, 44th Congress, 2nd session, IV, serial 1749.

1877–House Executive Document, No. 1, pt. 5, 45th Congress, 2nd session, VIII, serial 1800.

1878–House Executive Document, No. 1, pt. 5, 45th Congress, 3rd session, IX, serial 1850.

1879–House Executive Document, No. 1, pt. 5, 46th Congress, 2nd session, IX, serial 1910.

1880–House Executive Document, No. 1, pt. 5, 46th Congress, 3rd session, IX, serial 1959.

1881–House Executive Document, No. 1, pt. 5, 47th Congress, 1st session, IX, X, serial 2017, 2018.

1882–House Executive Document, No. 1, pt. 5, 47th Congress, 2nd session, X, XI, serial 2099, 2100.

1883–House Executive Document, No. 1, pt. 5, 48th Congress, 1st session, X, XI, serial 2190, 2191.

1884–House Executive Document, No. 1, pt. 5, 48th Congress, 2nd session, XI, XII, serial 2286, 2287.

1885—House Executive Document, No. 1, pt. 5, 49th Congress, 1st session, XII, serial 2379.

1886—House Executive Document, No. 1, pt. 5, 49th Congress, 2nd session, VIII, serial 2467.

1887—House Executive Document, No. 1, pt. 5, 50th Congress, 1st session, X, XI, serial 2541, 2542.

1888—House Executive Document, No. 1, pt. 5, 50th Congress, 2nd session, X, XI, serial 2636, 2637.

1889—House Executive Document, No. 1, pt. 5, 51st Congress, 1st session, XI, XII, serial 2724, 2725.

1890—House Executive Document, No. 1, pt. 5, 51st Congress, 2nd session, XI, XII, serial 2840, 2841.

1891—House Executive Document, No. 1, pt. 5, 52nd Congress, 1st session, XIV, XV, serial 2933, 2934.

1892—House Executive Document, No. 1, pt. 5, 52nd Congress, 2nd session, XII, XIII, serial 3086, 3087.

1893—House Executive Document, No. 1, pt. 5, 53rd Congress, 2nd session, XIII, XIV, serial 3209, 3210.

1894—House Executive Document, No. 1, pt. 5, 53rd Congress, 3rd session, XIV, XV, serial 3305, 3306.

1895—House Document, No. 5, 54th Congress, 1st session, XIV, XV, serial 3381, 3382.

1896—House Document, No. 5, 54th Congress, 2nd session, XII, XIII, serial 3488, 3489.

1897—House Document, No. 5, 55th Congress, 2nd session, XII, XIII, serial 3640, 3641.

1898—House Document, No. 5, 55th Congress, 3rd session, XIV, XV, serial 3756, 3757.

1899—House Document, No. 5, 56th Congress, 1st session, XVII, XVIII, serial 3914, 3915.

1900—House Document, No. 5, 56th Congress, 2nd session, XXVI, XXVII, serial 4100, 4101.

1901—House Document, No. 5, 57th Congress, 1st session, XXII, XXIII, serial 4289, 4290.

1902—House Document, No. 5, 57th Congress, 2nd session, XVII, XVIII, serial 4457, 4458.

1902—House Document, No. 5, 58th Congress, 2nd session, XCIII, XIX, serial 4644, 4645.

U.S. Secretary of War. Annual Reports.

1850–House Executive Document, No. 1, 31st Congress, 2nd session, I, serial 595.

1851–House Executive Document, No. 2, 32nd Congress, 1st session, II, serial 633.

1852–House Executive Document, No. 1, 32nd Congress, 2nd session, I, serial 673.

1853–House Executive Document, No. 1, 33rd Congress, 1st session, I, serial 710.

1854–Senate Executive Document, No. 1, 33rd Congress, 2nd session, II, serial 747.

1855–Senate Executive Document, No. 1, 34th Congress, 1st session, I, serial 810.

1856–Senate Executive Document, No. 5, 34th Congress, 3rd session, II, serial 875.

1857–Senate Executive Document, No. 11, 35th Congress, 1st session, III, serial 920.

1858–Senate Executive Document, No. 1, 35th Congress, 1st session, I, serial 974.

1859–Senate Executive Document, No. 2, 36th Congress, 1st session, I, serial 1023.

1860–Senate Executive Document, No. 1, 36th Congress, 2nd session, I, serial 1078.

1866–House Executive Document, No. 1, 39th Congress, 2nd session, III, serial 1285.

1867–House Executive Document, No. 1, 40th Congress, 2nd session, II, serial 1324.

1868–House Executive Document, No. 1, 40th Congress, 3rd session, III, serial 1367.

1869–House Executive Document, No. 1, pt. 2, 40th Congress, 2nd session, II, serial 1413.

1870–House Executive Document, No. 1, pt. 2, 41st Congress, 3rd session, II, serial 1446.

1871–House Executive Document, No. 1, pt. 2, 42nd Congress, 2nd session, II, serial 1503.

1872–House Executive Document, No. 1, pt. 2, 42nd Congress, 3rd session, II, serial 1558.

1873–House Executive Document, No. 1, pt. 2, 43rd Congress, 1st session, II, serial 1597.

1874–House Executive Document, No. 1, pt. 2, 43rd Congress, 2nd session, II, serial 1635.

1875–House Executive Document, No. 1, pt. 2, 44th Congress, 1st session, II, serial 1674.

1876–House Executive Document, No. 1, pt. 2, 44th Congress, 2nd session, II, serial 1742.

1877–House Executive Document, No. 1, pt. 2, 45th Congress, 2nd session, II, serial 1794.

1878–House Executive Document, No. 1, pt. 2, 45th Congress, 3rd session, II, serial 1843.

1879–House Executive Document, No. 1, pt. 2, 46th Congress, 2nd session, II, serial 1903.

1880–House Executive Document, No. 1, pt. 2, 46th Congress, 3rd session, II, serial 1952.

1881–House Executive Document, No. 1, pt. 2, 47th Congress, 1st session, II, serial 2010.

1882–House Executive Document, No. 1, pt. 2, 47th Congress, 2nd session, II, serial 2091.

1883–House Executive Document, No. 1, pt. 2, 48th Congress, 1st session, II, serial 2182.

1884–House Executive Document, No. 1, pt. 2, 48th Congress, 2nd session, II, serial 2277.

1885–House Executive Document, No. 1, pt. 2, 49th Congress, 1st session, II, serial 2369.

1886–House Executive Document, No. 1, pt. 2, 49th Congress, 2nd session, II, serial 2461.

1887– House Executive Document, No. 1, pt. 2, 50th Congress, 1st session, II, serial 2533.

1888–House Executive Document, No. 1, pt. 2, 50th Congress, 2nd session, II, serial 2628.

1889–House Executive Document, No. 1, pt. 2, 51st Congress, 1st session, II, serial 2715.

1890–House Executive Document, No. 1, pt. 2, 51st Congress, 2nd session, II, serial 2831.

1891–House Executive Document, No. 1, pt. 2, 52nd Congress, 1st session, II, serial 2921.

1892–House Executive Document, No. 1, pt. 2, 52nd Congress, 2nd session, II, serial 3077.

1893–House Executive Document, No. 1, pt. 2, 53rd Congress, 2nd session, II, serial 3198.

1894–House Executive Document, No. 1, pt. 2, 53rd Congress, 3rd session, IV, serial 3295.

1895–House Document, No. 2, 54th Congress, 1st session, III, serial 3370.

1896–House Document, No. 2, 54th Congress, 2nd session, II, serial 3478.

1897–House Document, No. 2, 55th Congress, 2nd session, II, serial 3630.

1898–House Document, No. 2, 55th Congress, 3rd session, II, III, serial 3744, 3745.

1899–House Document, No., 2 56th Congress, 1st session, II, IV, V, VI, serial 3899, 3901, 3902, 3903.

1900–House Document, No. 2, 56th Congress, 2nd session, II, IV, V, VI, serial 4070, 4072, 4073, 4074, 4076.

1901–House Document, No. 2, 57th Congress, 1st session, II, IV, V, VI, serial 4269, 4271, 4272, 4273.

1902–House Document, No. 2, 57th Congress, 2nd session, IV, XII, serial 4443, 4451.

1903–House Document, No. 2, 58th Congress, 2nd session, II, IV, V, serial 4628, 4630, 4631.

1904–House Document, No. 2, 58th Congress, 3rd session, II, IV, V, serial 4781, 4783, 4784.

1905–House Document, No. 2, 59th Congress, 1st session, II, IV, V, serial 4942, 4944, 4945.

U.S. Statutes at Large, 14–26 (1866–91).

U.S. War Department. *The War of the Rebellion: A Compilation of the Official Records of the Union and Confederate Armies.* 128 vols. Washington, D.C.: U.S. Government Printing Office, 1880–1901.

3. Books

Adams, Henry, ed. *The Writings of Albert Gallatin.* 3 vols. 1872. Reprint. New York: Antiquarian Press, 1960.

Badé, William Frederic. *The Life and Letters of John Muir.* Vol. 2. Boston: Houghton Mifflin Co., 1924.

Ball, Eve. *Indeh: An Apache Odyssey.* Provo, Utah: Brigham Young University Press, 1980.

Bassett, John Spencer, ed. *Correspondence of Andrew Jackson.* 6 vols. 1927. Reprint. New York: Kraus Reprint Co., 1969.

Betzinez, Jason, with Nye, Wilber Sturtevant. *I Fought with Geronimo.* Harrisburg, Pa.: Stackpole Co., 1959.

Bigelow, John. *The Principles of Strategy, Illustrated Mainly from American Campaigns.* West Point Military Library. 1894. Reprint. New York: Greenwood Press, 1968.

Bourke, John G. *On the Border with Crook.* 1891. Reprint, Columbus: Long's College Book Co., 1950.

Callwell, C. E. *Small Wars: Their Principles and Practice.* 3rd ed. 1906. Reprint. West Yorkshire: EP Publishing, 1976.

————. *Tirah 1897.* Campaigns and Their Lessons. London: Constable and Co., 1920.

Carter, Clarence Edwin, and Bloom, John Porter, eds. *The Territorial Papers of the United States.* Vols. 10, 11, 12, 20, 21, 27, 28. Washington: U.S. Government Printing Office, 1942–75.

Carter, Robert G. *The Old Sergeant's Story: Winning the West from the Indians and Bad Men in 1870 to 1876.* New York: Frederick H. Hitchcock, 1926.

————. *On the Border with Mackenzie; Or Winning West Texas from the Comanches.* Washington: Eynon Printing Co., 1935.

Crane, Charles Judson. *Experiences of a Colonel of Infantry.* New York: Knickerbocker Press, 1923.

Davis, Britton. *The Truth about Geronimo.* Ed. Milo M. Quaife. 1929. Reprint. New Haven: Yale University Press, 1963.

Dixon, Joseph Kossuth. *The Vanishing Race: The Last Great Indian Council; A Record in Picture & Story of the Last Great Indian Council, Participated in by Eminent Indian Chiefs from Nearly Every Indian Reservation in the United States, Together with the Story of Their Lives as Told by Themselves—Their Speeches and Folklore Tales—Their Solemn Farewell and the Indians' Story of the Custer Fight.* Garden City, N.Y.: Doubleday, Page and Co., 1913.

Finerty, John C. *War-Path and Bivouac: The Big Horn and Yellowstone Expedition.* Ed. Milo M. Quaife. 1955. Reprint. Lincoln: University of Nebraska Press, 1966.

Hancock, Mrs. Winfield Scott. *Reminiscences of Winfield Scott Hancock by His Wife.* New York: Charles L. Webster and Co., 1887.

Hemphill, W. Edwin, Meriwether, Robert L., and Wilson, Clyde N., eds. *The Papers of John C. Calhoun.* Vol. 3. Columbia: University of South Carolina Press, 1959.

Howard, James H., trans. and ed. *The Warrior Who Killed Custer: The Personal Narrative of Chief Joseph White Bull.* Lincoln: University of Nebraska Press, 1968.

Howard, Oliver O. *My Life and Experiences among Our Native Indians: A Record of Personal Observations, Adventures, and Campaigns among the Indians of the Great West, with Some Account of Their Life, Habits, Traits, Religion, Ceremonies, Dress, Savage Instincts, and Customs in Peace and War.* 1907. Reprint. New York: Da Capo Press, 1972.

—————. *Nez Percé Joseph: An Account of His Ancestors, His Lands, His Confederates, His Enemies, His Murders, His War, His Pursuit and Capture.* Boston: Lee and Shepard, 1881.

Hyde, George E. *A Life of George Bent, Written from His Letters.* Ed. Savoie Lottinville. Norman: University of Oklahoma Press, 1968.

Jackson, Helen Hunt. *A Century of Dishonor: A Sketch of the United States Government's Dealings with Some of the Indian Tribes.* New York: Harper and Brothers, 1881.

Jameson, J. Franklin, ed. *Correspondence of John C. Calhoun.* Annual Report of the American Historical Association, 1899. Washington: U.S. Government Printing Office, 1900.

Kroeber, A. L. *(Black Wolf) Ethnology of the Gros Ventre.* Anthropological Papers of the American Museum of Natural History, I. 1908.

Linderman, Frank B. *Plenty-Coups, Chief of the Crow.* 1930. Reprint. New York: John Day Co., 1972.

Livermore, W. R. *The American Kriegsspiel: A Game for Practicing the Art of War upon a Topographical Map.* Boston: Houghton Mifflin and Co., 1882.

Logan, John A. *The Volunteer Soldier of America.* Chicago: R. S. Peale, 1887.

Long, E. B., ed. *Personal Memoirs of U.S. Grant.* New York: World Publishing Co., 1952.

McCreight, M. I. *Firewater and Forked Tongues: A Sioux Chief Interprets U.S. History.* Pasadena, Calif.: Trail's End Publishing Co., 1947.

McWhorter, Lucullus Virgil. *Yellow Wolf: His Own Story.* Caldwell, Idaho: Caxton Printers, 1940.

Michie, Peter Smith. *The Life and Letters of General Emory Upton, Colonel of the*

Fourth Regiment of Artillery, and Brevet Major-General, U.S. Army. New York: D. Appleton and Co., 1885.

Miles, Nelson A. *Personal Recollections and Observations of General Nelson A. Miles.* The American Scene, Comments and Commentators. 1896. Reprint. New York: Da Capo Press, 1969.

————. *Serving the Republic: Memoirs of the Civil and Military Life of Nelson A. Miles, Lieutenant-General, United States Army.* New York: Harper and Brothers, 1911.

Millis, Walter, ed. *American Military Thought.* American Heritage Series. New York: Bobbs-Merrill Co., 1966.

Morison, Elting E., ed. *The Letters of Theodore Roosevelt.* 8 vols. Cambridge: Harvard University Press, 1951–54.

Osgood, Ernest Staples, ed. *The Field Notes of Captain William Clark, 1803–1805.* Yale Western Americana Series, no. 5. New Haven: Yale University Press, 1964.

Perry, Clive, ed. *The Consolidated Treaty Series.* Dobbs Ferry, N.Y.: Oceana Publications, 1969.

Pratt, Richard Henry. *Battlefield and Classroom: Four Decades with the American Indian, 1867–1904.* Ed. Robert M. Utley. Yale Western Americana Series, no. 6. New Haven: Yale University Press, 1964.

Richardson, James D., comp. *A Compilation of the Messages and Papers of the Presidents, 1789–1897.* Vols. 6–9. Washington: U.S. Government Printing Office, 1897–98.

Root, Elihu. *Military and Colonial Policy of the United States: Addresses and Reports.* Collected and ed. Robert Bacon and James Brown Scott. Cambridge: Harvard University Press, 1916.

Schmitt, Martin F., ed. *General George Crook: His Autobiography.* 1946. Reprint. Norman: University of Oklahoma Press, 1960.

Schofield, John M. *Forty-six Years in the Army.* New York: Century Co., 1897.

Sheridan, Philip Henry. *Personal Memoirs of Philip Henry Sheridan.* 1888. Rev. ed. New York: D. Appleton and Co., 1902.

Sherman, William T. *Memoirs of General William T. Sherman, by Himself.* Civil War Centennial Series. Bloomington: Indiana University Press, 1957.

Syrett, Harold C., ed. *The Papers of Alexander Hamilton.* Vol. 23. New York: Columbia University Press, 1976.

Taylor, Joe F., comp. *The Indian Campaign on the Staked Plains, 1874–1875: Military Correspondence from War Department Adjutant General's Office, File 2815–1874.* Canyon: Panhandle-Plains Historical Society, 1962.

Thian, Raphael, comp. *Notes Illustrating the Military Geography of the United States, 1813–1880.* Ed. John M. Carroll. 1881. Reprint. Austin: University of Texas Press, 1979.

U.S. Army, Military Division of the Missouri. *Outline Descriptions of the Posts in the Military Division of the Missouri, Commanded by Lt. General P. H. Sheridan.* Chicago: Military Division of the Missouri, 1876.

————. *Record of Engagements with Hostile Indians within the Military Division of the Missouri, from 1868 to 1882, Lieutenant-General P. H. Sheridan, Commanding.* 1882. Reprint. Belleview, Neb.: Old Army Press, 1969.

Upton, Emory. *The Military Policy of the United States.* Washington: U.S. Government Printing Office, 1907.

Upton, Richard, ed. *The Indian as a Soldier at Fort Custer, Montana, 1890–1895: Lieutenant Samuel C. Robertson's First Cavalry Crow Indian Contingent.* El Segundo: Upton and Sons, 1983.

Wallace, Ernest, ed. *Ranald S. Mackenzie's Official Correspondence Relating to Texas, 1871–1873.* Lubbock: West Texas Museum Association, 1967.

Wilhelm, Thomas. *A Military Dictionary and Gazetteer. Comprising Ancient and Modern Military Technical Terms, Historical Accounts of All North American Indians, as Well as Ancient Warlike Tribes; Also Notices of Battle from the Earliest Period to the Present Time, with a Concise Explanation of Terms Used in Heraldry and the Offices Thereof.* Rev. ed. Philadelphia: L. R. Hammersly and Co., 1881.

Williams, T. Harry. *Hayes: The Diary of a President, 1875–1881. Covering the Disputed Election, the End of Reconstruction, and the Beginning of Civil Service.* New York: David McKay Co., 1964.

4. Articles

Army and Navy Journal. Vols. 6, 8, 11, 13, 14, 15, 17.

Athearn, Robert G., ed. "A Winter Campaign against the Sioux." *Mississippi Valley Historical Review* 35 (December 1948): 272–84.

————. "Major Hough's March into Southern Ute Country, 1879." *Colorado Magazine* 25 (May 1948): 97–109.

Bagley, Clarence B., ed. "Attitude of the Hudson's Bay Company during the Indian War of 1855–1856." *Washington Historical Quarterly* 8 (1917): 291–307.

Beaumont, Eugene P. "Over the Border with Mackenzie." *United Service Review* 12 (1885): 281–88.

Bloom, Lansing B., ed. "Bourke on the Southwest." *New Mexico Historical Review* 8 (1933): 1–30; 9 (1934); 33–77, 159–83, 273–89, 375–437; 10 (1935): 1–35, 271–322; 11 (1936): 77–102, 188–207, 217–82; 12 (1937): 41–77, 337–52; 13 (1938): 192–238.

Bourke, John G. "General Crook in the Indian Country." *Century Magazine* 41 (March 1891): 643–60.

————. "Mackenzie's Last Fight with the Cheyennes: A Winter Campaign in Wyoming and Montana." *Journal of the Military Service Institution of the United States* 53 (November-December 1913): 343–85.

Butler, E. "Our Indian Question." *Journal of the Military Service Institution of the United States* 2, no. 6 (1881): 183–221.

Crimmins, Martin L., ed. "Colonel Buell's Expedition into Mexico in 1880." *New Mexico Historical Review* 10 (April 1935): 133–42.

————. "Freeman's Report on the Eighth Military Department." *Southwestern Historical Quarterly* 51 (1947): 54–58; 167–74, 252–58, 350–57; 52 (1948): 100–8, 227–33, 349–53, 444–47; 53 (1949): 71–77, 202–8, 308–19, 443–73; 54 (1950): 204–18.

Crook, George. "The Apache Problem." *Journal of the Military Service Institution of the United States* 7 (September 1886): 257–69.

Davis, Jefferson. "The Indian Policy of the United States." *North American Review* 143 (November 1886): 436–46.

Davison, Stanley R., ed. "The Bannock-Paiute War of 1878: Letters of Major Edwin C. Mason." *Journal of the West* 11 (January 1972): 128–42.

Dorst, Joseph. "Ranald Slidell Mackenzie." *Journal of the U.S. Cavalry Association* 10 (December 1897): 367–82.

Dougherty, W. E. "The Recent Indian Craze." *Journal of the U.S. Cavalry Association* 12 (May 1891): 576–78.

Franklin, W. B. "National Defense." *North American Review* 137 (December 1883): 594–604.

Gibbon, John, "Arms to Fight Indians." *United Service* 1 (April 1879): 237–44.

———. "Hunting Sitting Bull." *American Catholic Quarterly Review* 2 (October 1877): 665–94.

———. "Last Summer's Expedition against the Sioux and Its Great Catastrophe." *American Catholic Quarterly Review* 2 (April 1877): 271–304.

———. "Our Indian Question." *Journal of the Military Service Institution of the United States* 2, no. 6 (1881): 101–22.

Godfrey, E. S. "Some Reminiscences Including an Account of General Sully's Expedition against the Southern Plains Indians, 1868." *Cavalry Journal* 36 (July, 1927): 417–25.

Hazen, W. B. "The Great Middle Region of the United States, and Its Limited Space of Arable Land." *North American Review* 120 (January, 1875): 1–34.

Howard, Oliver O. "Military Problems in South Africa." *North American Review* 170 (February 1900): 192–97.

Joseph, Chief. "An Indian's View of Indian Affairs." *North American Review* 128 (April 1879): 412–33.

King, Charles. "The Leavenworth School." *Harper's New Monthly Magazine* 76 (April 1888): 777–92.

Lyautey, Louis. "Du rôle colonial de l'armée." *Revue des Deux Mondes* 157 (1900): 308–28.

Mallery, Garrick. "The Burnside Army Bill." *Nation* 28 (January 16, 1879): 42–43.

Merritt, Wesley. "Important Improvements in the Art of War in the Last Twenty Years and Their Probable Effect on Future Military Operations." *Journal of the Military Service Institution of the United States* 4, no. 14 (1883): 172–87.

———. "Some Defects of Our Cavalry System." *United Service* 1 (October 1879): 557–61.

Miles, Nelson A. "The Indian Problem." *North American Review* 128 (March 1879): 304–14.

———. "My Forty Years of Fighting." *Cosmopolitan* 50 (1910–11): 206–18, 408–21, 546–57, 792–802; 51 (1911): 105–14, 249–62, 522–33, 637–50.

Potter, Reuban M. "The Red Man's God." *Journal of the Military Service Institution of the United States* 7 (March 1886): 61–71.

Schofield, J. M. "Notes on 'The Legitimate in War.'" *Journal of the Military Service Institution of the United States* 2, no. 5 (1881): 1–8.

Schurz, Carl. "Present Aspects of the Indian Problem." *North American Review* 133 (July 1881): 1–24.

Seaman, Louis Livingston. "Native Troops for Our Colonial Possessions." *North American Review* 171 (1900): 847–60.

Seymour, Charles G. "The Sioux Rebellion, the Final Review." *Harper's Weekly* 35 (February 7, 1891): 106.

Shipp, W. E. "Mounted Infantry." *Journal of the U.S. Cavalry Association* 5 (March 1892): 76–80.

Totten, Lieutenant C. A. L. "Strategos: The American Game of War." *Journal of the Military Service Institution of the United States* 1 (April 1880): 185–202.

Walker, Francis A. "The Indian Question." *North American Review* 116 (April 1873): 329–88.

Welsh, Herbert. "Indian Question, Past and Present." *New England Magazine*, n.s. 3 (October 1890): 257–66.

———. "The Meaning of the Dakota Outbreak." *Scribner's Magazine* 9 (April 1891): 439–52.

Whittaker, F. "The American Army." *Galaxy* 24 (September 1877): 390–98.

Williams, R. "Army Organization in the United States." *Galaxy* 24 (November, 1877): 594–602.

———. "The Staff of the United States Army." *Atlantic Monthly* 41 (March 1878): 376–84.

Wood, C. E. S. "Our Indian Question." *Journal of the Military Service Institution of the United States* 2, no. 6 (1881): 123–82.

"The Zulu War." *United Service* 1 (April, 1879): 297–300.

B. Secondary Sources

1. Books

Adams, Michael C. C. *Our Masters the Rebels: A Speculation on Union Military Failure in the East, 1861–1865.* Cambridge: Harvard University Press, 1978.

Altschuler, Constance Wynn. *Chains of Command: Arizona and the Army, 1856–1875.* Tucson: Arizona Historical Society, 1981.

Ambrose, Stephen E. *Crazy Horse and Custer: The Parallel Lives of Two American Warriors*. Garden City, N.Y.: Doubleday and Co., 1975.

―――. *Duty, Honor, Country: A History of West Point*. Baltimore: Johns Hopkins Press, 1966.

―――. *Halleck: Lincoln's Chief of Staff*. Baton Rouge: Louisiana State University Press, 1962.

―――. *Upton and the Army*. Baton Rouge: Louisiana State University Press, 1964.

Andrist, Ralph K. *The Long Death: The Last Days of the Plains Indian*. New York: Macmillan Co., 1964.

Armstrong, David A. *Bullets and Bureaucrats: The Machine Gun and the United States Army, 1861–1916*. Contributions in Military History, no. 29. Westport, Conn.: Greenwood Press, 1982.

Athearn, Robert G. *Forts of the Upper Missouri*. Englewood Cliffs, N.J.: Prentice-Hall, 1967.

―――. *William Tecumseh Sherman and the Settlement of the West*. Norman: University of Oklahoma Press, 1956.

Bailey, Joun Wendell. *Pacifying the Plains: General Alfred Terry and the Decline of the Sioux*. Contributions in Military History, no. 17. Westport, Conn.: Greenwood Press, 1979.

Beal, Merrill D. *I Will Fight No More Forever: Chief Joseph and the Nez Percé War*. Seattle: University of Washington Press, 1963.

Berkhofer, Robert F., Jr. *The White Man's Indian: Images of the American Indian from Columbus to the Present*. New York: Alfred A. Knopf, 1978.

Berthrong, Donald J. *The Southern Cheyennes*. Norman: University of Oklahoma Press, 1963.

Billington, Ray Allen. *America's Frontier Heritage*. Histories of the American Frontier. Albuquerque: University of New Mexico Press, 1974.

Boatner, Mark. *Civil War Dictionary*. New York: David McKay Co., 1959.

Bond, Brian. *The Victorian Army and the Staff College, 1854–1914*. London: Eyre Metheun, 1972.

Bowman, John S., ed. *The Civil War Almanac*. New York: Bison Books, 1982.

Branch, E. Douglas. *The Hunting of the Buffalo*. New York: D. Appleton and Co., 1929.

Bradley, James H. *The March of the Montana Column: A Prelude to the Custer Disaster*. Norman: University of Oklahoma Press, 1961.

Brown, Dee. *Bury My Heart at Wounded Knee: An Indian History of the American West*. New York: Holt, Rinehart and Winston, 1971.

Brumble, H. David. *An Annotated Bibliography of American Indian and Eskimo Autobiographies*. Lincoln: University of Nebraska Press, 1981.

Burgess, Larry E. *The Lake Mohonk Conference of Friends of the Indian*. Library of American Indian Affairs. New York: Clearwater Publishing Co., 1975.

Capps, Benjamin. *The Warren Wagontrain Raid: The First Complete Account of an Historic Indian Attack and Its Aftermath*. New York: Dial Press, 1974.

Carpenter, John A. *Sword and Olive Branch: Oliver Otis Howard*. Pittsburgh: University of Pittsburgh Press, 1964.

Carriker, Robert C. *Fort Supply, Indian Territory: Frontier Outpost on the Plains*. Norman: University of Oklahoma Press, 1970.

Casdorph, Paul. *A History of the Republican Party in Texas*. Austin: Pemberton Press, 1965.

Cate, Wirt Armistead. *Lucius Q. C. Lamar: Secession and Reunion*. Chapel Hill: University of North Carolina Press, 1935.

Chappell, Gordon. *The Search for the Well-Dressed Soldier, 1865–1890*. Museum Monograph, no. 5. Tucson: Arizona Historical Society, 1972.

Clarke, Dwight L. *William Tecumseh Sherman: Gold Rush Banker*. San Francisco: California Historical Society, 1969.

Clendenen, Clarence C. *Blood on the Border: The United States Army and the Mexican Irregulars*. Wars of the United States. New York: Macmillan Co., 1969.

Connelly, Thomas Lawrence, and Jones, Archer. *The Politics of Command: Factions and Ideas in Confederate Strategy*. Baton Rouge: Louisiana State University Press, 1973.

Cooper, Jerry M. *The Army and Civil Disorder: Federal Military Intervention in Labor Disputes, 1877–1900*. Contributions in Military History, no. 19. Westport, Conn.: Greenwood Press, 1980.

Cosmas, Graham A. *An Army for Empire: The United States Army in the Spanish-American War*. Columbia: University of Missouri Press, 1971.

Cresap, Bernarr. *Appomattox Commander: The Story of General E. O. C. Ord*. New York: A. S. Barnes and Co., 1981.

Cunliffe, Marcus. *Soldiers and Civilians: The Martial Spirit in America, 1775–1865*. 1968. Reprint. New York: Free Press, 1973.

Dillon, Richard H. *Burnt-Out Fires: California's Modoc Indian War.* Englewood Cliffs, N.J.: Prentice-Hall, 1973.

Dippie, Brian W. *The Vanishing American: White Attitudes and U.S. Indian Policy.* Middletown, Conn.: Wesleyan University Press, 1982.

Doenecke, Justus D. *The Presidencies of James A. Garfield and Chester A. Arthur.* American Presidency Series. Lawrence: Regents Press of Kansas, 1981.

Dunlay, Thomas W. *Wolves for the Blue Soldiers: Indian Scouts and Auxiliaries with the United States Army, 1860–90.* Lincoln: University of Nebraska Press, 1982.

Eisenschiml, Otto. *The Celebrated Case of Fitz John Porter: An American Dreyfus Affair.* Indianapolis: Bobbs Merrill, 1950.

Ellis, Richard N. *General Pope and U.S. Indian Policy.* Albuquerque: University of New Mexico Press, 1970.

Emmett, Chris. *Fort Union and the Winning of the Southwest.* Norman: University of Oklahoma Press, 1965.

Faulk, Odie B. *The Geronimo Campaign.* New York: Oxford University Press, 1969.

Foote, Shelby. *The Civil War: A Narrative.* Vol. 3, *Red River to Appomattox.* New York: Random House, 1974.

Frazer, Robert W. *Forts of the West: Military Forts and Presidios and Posts Commonly Called Forts West of the Mississippi River to 1898.* Norman: University of Oklahoma Press, 1965.

Fritz, Henry E. *The Movement for Indian Assimilation, 1860–1890.* Philadelphia: University of Pennsylvania Press, 1963.

Gates, John Morgan. *Schoolbooks and Krags: The United States Army in the Philippines, 1898–1902.* Contributions in Military History, no. 3. Westport, Conn.: Greenwood Press, 1973.

George, Mary Karl. *Zachariah Chandler: A Political Biography.* East Lansing: Michigan State University Press, 1969.

Glatthaar, Joseph T. *The March to the Sea and Beyond: Sherman's Troops in the Savannah and Carolinas Campaigns.* New York: New York University Press, 1985.

Goetzmann, William H. *Army Exploration in the American West 1803–1863.* Yale Publications in American Studies, no. 4. New Haven: Yale University Press, 1959.

Goff, John S. *Robert Todd Lincoln: A Man in His Own Right.* Norman: University of Oklahoma Press, 1969.

Gooch, John. *The Plans of War: The General Staff and British Military Strategy c. 1900–1916.* New York: John Wiley and Sons, 1974.

Gould, Lewis L. *The Presidency of William McKinley.* American Presidency Series. Lawrence: Regents Press of Kansas, 1980.

————. *The Spanish-American War and President McKinley.* Lawrence: University Press of Kansas, 1982.

————. *Wyoming: A Political History, 1868–1896.* New Haven: Yale University Press, 1968.

Gray, John S. *Centennial Campaign: The Sioux War of 1876.* Fort Collins, Colo.: Old Army Press, 1976.

Greene, Jerome A. *Slim Buttes, 1876: An Episode in the Great Sioux War.* Norman: University of Oklahoma Press, 1982.

Grinnell, George Bird. *The Fighting Cheyennes.* 1915. Reprint. Norman: University of Oklahoma Press, 1955.

Hagan, William T. *Indian Police and Judges: Experiments in Acculturation and Control.* New Haven: Yale University Press, 1966.

Haley, James L. *The Buffalo War: The History of the Red River Uprising of 1874.* Garden City, N.Y.: Doubleday and Co., 1976.

Hampton, H. Duane. *How the U.S. Cavalry Saved Our National Parks.* Bloomington: Indiana University Press, 1971.

Hart, B. H. Liddell. *Sherman: Soldier, Realist, American.* New York: Frederick A. Praeger, 1958.

Hattaway, Herman, and Jones, Archer. *How the North Won: A Military History of the Civil War.* Urbana: University of Illinois Press, 1983.

Heitman, Francis B. *Historical Register and Dictionary of the United States Army, from Its Organization, September 29, 1789, to March 2, 1903.* Washington: U.S. Government Printing Office, 1903.

Higham, Robin, ed. *A Guide to the Sources of United States Military History.* Hamden, Conn.: Archon Books, 1975.

Hill, Forest G. *Roads, Rails, and Waterways: The Army Engineers and Early Transportation.* Norman: University of Oklahoma Press, 1957.

Hitsman, J. Mackay. *Safeguarding Canada, 1763–1871.* Toronto: University of Toronto Press, 1968.

Hoig, Stan. *The Battle of the Washita: The Sheridan-Custer Indian Campaign of 1867–69.* Garden City, N.Y.: Doubleday and Co., 1976.

Horton, Louise. *Samuel Bell Maxey: A Biography.* Austin: University of Texas Press, 1974.

Huntington, Samuel P. *The Soldier and the State: The Theory and Politics of Civil-Military Relations*. Cambridge: Harvard University Press, 1957.

Hutton, Paul Andrew. *Phil Sheridan and His Army*. Lincoln: University of Nebraska Press, 1985.

Hutton, Paul Andrew, ed. *Soldiers West: Biographies from the Military Frontier*. Lincoln: University of Nebraska Press, 1987.

Hyde, George. *Red Cloud's Folk: A History of the Oglala Sioux Indians*. Norman: University of Oklahoma Press, 1937.

Jackson, Donald. *Custer's Gold: The United States Cavalry Expedition of 1874*. New Haven: Yale University Press, 1966.

James, Lawrence. *The Savage Wars: British Campaigns in Africa, 1870–1920*. New York: St. Martin's Press, 1985.

Jesup, Philip C. *Elihu Root*. 2 vols. New York: Dodd, Mead and Co., 1938.

Johnson, Allen, and Malone, Dumas, eds. *Dictionary of American Biography*. 1931. Reprint. New York: Charles Scribner's Sons, 1960.

Johnson, Virginia Weisel. *The Unregimented General: A Biography of Nelson A. Miles*. Boston: Houghton Mifflin Co., 1962.

Jones, James Pickett. *John A. Logan: Stalwart Republican from Illinois*. Tallahassee: University Presses of Florida, 1982.

Jones, Oakah L. *Pueblo Warriors and Spanish Conquest*. Norman: University of Oklahoma Press, 1966.

Josephy, Alvin M. *The Nez Percé Indians and the Opening of the Northwest*. Yale Western Americana Series, no. 10. New Haven: Yale University Press, 1965.

Keller, Robert H., Jr. *American Protestantism and United States Indian Policy, 1869–82*. Lincoln: University of Nebraska Press, 1983.

Kemble, C. Robert. *The Image of the Army Officer in America: Background for Current Views*. Contributions in Military History, no. 5. Westport, Conn.: Greenwood Press, 1983.

Kenner, Charles L. *A History of New Mexican–Plains Indian Relations*. Norman: University of Oklahoma Press, 1969.

King, James T. *War Eagle: A Life of General Eugene A. Carr*. Lincoln: University of Nebraska Press, 1963.

Knight, Oliver. *Life and Manners in the Frontier Army*. Norman: University of Oklahoma Press, 1978.

Kroecker, Marvin E. *Great Plains Command: William B. Hazen in the Frontier West*. Norman: University of Oklahoma Press, 1976.

Kvasnicka, Robert M., and Viola, Herman J., eds. *The Commissioners of Indian Affairs, 1824–1977.* Lincoln: University of Nebraska Press, 1979.

Lamar, Howard R. *Dakota Territory, 1861–1889: A Study of Frontier Politics.* New Haven: Yale University Press, 1956.

———. *The Far Southwest: A Territorial History.* New Haven: Yale University Press, 1966.

Lambert, Oscar Doane. *Stephen Benton Elkins.* Pittsburgh: University of Pittsburgh Press, 1955.

Lane, Jack C. *America's Military Past: A Guide to Information Sources.* American Government and History Information Guide Series, no. 7. Detroit: Gale Research Co., 1980.

Leckie, William H. *The Military Conquest of the Southern Plains.* Norman: University of Oklahoma Press, 1963.

Leckie, William H., and Leckie, Shirley A. *Unlikely Warriors: General Benjamin H. Grierson and His Family.* Norman: University of Oklahoma Press, 1984.

Leonard, Thomas C. *Above the Battle: War-Making in America from Appomattox to Versailles.* New York: Oxford University Press, 1978.

Leopold, Richard W. *Elihu Root and the Conservative Tradition.* Library of American Biography, ed. Oscar Handlin. Boston: Little, Brown and Co., 1954.

Lewis, Lloyd. *Sherman: Fighting Prophet.* 1932. Reprint. New York: Harcourt, Brace and Co., 1958.

Luvaas, Jay. *The Education of an Army: British Military Thought, 1815–1940.* Chicago: University of Chicago Press, 1964.

Mahon, John K. *History of the Militia and the National Guard.* The Wars of the United States. New York: Macmillan Co., 1983.

———. *History of the Second Seminole War, 1837–1842.* Gainesville: University of Florida Press, 1967.

Mardock, Robert. *The Reformers and the American Indian.* Columbia: University of Missouri Press, 1971.

Marquis, Thomas B. *Wooden Leg: A Warrior Who Fought Custer.* Minneapolis: Midwest Co., 1931.

Marshall, S. L. A. *Crimsoned Prairie: The Indian Wars on the Great Plains during the Winning of the West.* New York: Charles Scribner's Sons, 1972.

Matloff, Maurice, ed. *American Military History*. Army Historical Series. Washington: U.S. Government Printing Office, 1969.

McDonough, James L. *Schofield, Union General in the Civil War and Reconstruction*. Tallahassee: Florida State University Press, 1972.

McElwee, William. *The Art of War: Waterloo to Mons*. Bloomington: Indiana University Press, 1974.

McFeely, William S. *Grant: A Biography*. New York: W. W. Norton and Co., 1981.

Mearns, David Chambers. *The Lincoln Papers: The Story of the Collection with Selections to July 4, 1861*. Garden City, N.Y.: Doubleday and Co., 1948.

Merrill, James M. *William Tecumseh Sherman*. Chicago: Rand McNally, 1971.

Miller, Stuart Creighton. *"Benevolent Assimilation": The American Conquest of the Philippines, 1899–1903*. New Haven: Yale University Press, 1982.

Millett, Allan R., and Maslowski, Peter. *For the Common Defense: A Military History of the United States of America*. New York: Free Press, 1984.

Mishkin, Bernard. *Rank and Warfare among the Plains Indians*. Vol. 3. Monographs of the American Ethnological Society. New York: J. J. Augustin, 1940.

Monaghan, Jay. *Custer: The Life of George Armstrong Custer*. Lincoln: University of Nebraska Press, 1959.

Moorhead, Max L. *The Apache Frontier: Jacobo Ugarte and Spanish-Indian Relations in Northern New Spain, 1769–1791*. Norman: University of Oklahoma Press, 1968.

Morgan, H. Wayne. *From Hayes to McKinley: National Party Politics, 1877–1896*. Syracuse: Syracuse University Press, 1969.

Murphy, James B. *L. Q. C. Lamar: Pragmatic Patriot*. Southern Biography Series. Baton Rouge: Louisiana State University Press, 1973.

Murray, Keith A. *The Modocs and their War*. Norman: University of Oklahoma Press, 1959.

Murray, Robert A. *Military Posts on the Powder River Country of Wyoming, 1865–1874*. Lincoln: University of Nebraska Press, 1968.

Neidhardt, W. S. *Fenianism in North America*. University Park: Pennsylvania State University Press, 1975.

Nenninger, Timothy K. *The Leavenworth Schools and the Old Army: Education,*

Professionalism, and the Officer Corps of the United States Army, 1881–1918. Contributions in Military History, no. 15. Westport, Conn.: Greenwood Press, 1978.

Nichols, David A. *Lincoln and the Indians: Civil War Policy and Politics.* Columbia: University of Missouri Press, 1978.

Ogle, Ralph Hedrick. *Federal Control of the Western Apaches, 1848–1886.* 1940. Reprint. Albuquerque: University of New Mexico Press, 1970.

Palmer, Williston Birkimer. *The Evolution of Military Policy in the United States.* Carlisle Barracks, Pa.: Army Information School, 1946.

Preston, Richard A. *The Defence of the Undefended Border: Planning for War in North America 1867–1939.* Montreal: McGill-Queen's University Press, 1977.

Priest, Loring B. *Uncle Sam's Stepchildren: The Reformation of United States Indian Policy, 1865–1887.* New Brunswick: Rutgers University Press, 1942.

Prucha, Francis Paul. *American Indian Policy in Crisis: Christian Reformers and the Indian, 1865–1900.* Norman: University of Oklahoma Press, 1976.

———. *Broadax and Bayonet: The Role of the United States Army in the Development of the Northwest, 1815–1860.* Madison: University of Wisconsin Press, 1953.

———. *Indian Policy in the United States: Historical Essays.* Lincoln: University of Nebraska Press, 1981.

———. *The Sword of the Republic: The United States Army on the Frontier, 1783–1846.* The Wars of the United States. New York: Macmillan Co., 1969.

Rickey, Don. *Forty Miles a Day on Beans and Hay: The Enlisted Soldier Fighting the Indian Wars.* Norman: University of Oklahoma Press, 1963.

Rippy, J. Fred. *The United States and Mexico.* New York: Alfred A. Knopf, 1926.

Rister, Carl C. *Border Command: General Phil Sheridan in the West.* Norman: University of Oklahoma Press, 1944.

Roth, Russell. *Muddy Glory: America's "Indian Wars" in the Philippines, 1899–1935.* West Hanover, Mass.: Christopher Publishing House, 1981.

Rothman, David J. *Politics and Power: The United States Senate, 1869–1901.* Cambridge: Harvard University Press, 1966.

Sandoz, Mari. *The Buffalo Hunters: The Story of the Hide Men.* American Procession Series. New York: Hastings House, 1954.

Secoy, Raymond. *Changing Military Patterns on the Great Plains (17th Century through Early 19th Century).* Vol. 21. Monographs of the American Ethnological Society, ed. Esther S. Goldfrank. Locust Valley, N.Y.: J. J. Augustin, 1953.

Sefton, James E. *The United States Army and Reconstruction, 1865–1877.* Baton Rouge: Louisiana University Press, 1967.

Sheehan, Bernard W. *Seeds of Extinction: Jeffersonian Philanthropy and the American Indian.* Chapel Hill: University of North Carolina Press, 1973.

Smith, Henry Nash. *Virgin Land: The American West as Symbol and Myth.* Cambridge: Harvard University Press, 1950.

Sonnichsen, C. L. *The Mescalero Apaches.* Norman: University of Oklahoma Press, 1958.

Stampp, Kenneth M. *The Era of Reconstruction, 1865–1877.* New York: Alfred A. Knopf, 1965.

Stedman, Raymond W. *Shadows of the Indian: Stereotypes in American Culture.* Norman: University of Oklahoma Press, 1982.

Stegner, Wallace. *Beyond the Hundredth Meridian: John Wesley Powell and the Second Opening of the West.* Lincoln: University of Nebraska Press, 1953.

Stewart, Edgar Irving. *Custer's Luck.* Norman: University of Oklahoma Press, 1955.

Stohlman, Robert F. *The Powerless Position: The Commanding General of the Army of the United States, 1864–1903.* Manhattan: MA/AH Publishing, 1980.

Tate, James P., ed. *The American Military on the Frontier: The Proceedings of the 7th Military History Symposium.* Washington: Office of Air Force History, 1978.

Taylor, George Rogers, ed. *The Turner Thesis concerning the Role of the Frontier in American History.* 3rd ed. Lexington, Mass.: D. C. Heath and Co., 1972.

Thomas, Emory M. *The American War and Peace.* Englewood Cliffs, N.J.: Prentice-Hall, 1973.

Thompson, Erwin N. *Modoc War: Its Military History and Topography.* Sacramento: Argus Books, 1971.

Thompson, Gerald. *The Army and the Navajo.* Tucson: University of Arizona Press, 1976.

Tolman, Newton F. *The Search for General Miles.* New York: G. P. Putnam's Sons, 1968.

Trafzer, Clifford E. *The Kit Carson Campaign: The Last Great Navajo War.* Norman: University of Oklahoma Press, 1982.

Trask, David R. *The War with Spain in 1898.* The Wars of the United States. New York: Macmillan Co., 1981.

Trefousse, Hans L. *Carl Schurz: A Biography.* Knoxville: University of Tennessee Press, 1982.

Trennert, Robert A., Jr. *Alternative to Extinction: Federal Indian Policy and the Beginnings of the Reservation System, 1846–51.* Philadelphia: Temple University Press, 1975.

Turner, Frederick Jackson. *Frontier and Section: Selected Essays of Frederick Jackson Turner.* Englewood Cliffs, N.J.: Prentice-Hall, 1961.

Turner, John P. *The North West Mounted Police, 1873–1893.* 2 vols. Ottawa: Ed Cloutiers, King's Printer and Controller of Stationery, 1950.

Turney-High, Harry H. *Primitive War: Its Practice and Concepts.* Columbia: University of South Carolina Press, 1949.

Unruh, John D., Jr. *The Plains Across: The Overland Emigrants and the Trans-Mississippi West, 1840–60.* Urbana: University of Illinois Press, 1979.

Utley, Robert. *Custer and the Great Controversy: Origin and Development of a Legend.* Los Angeles: Westernlore Press, 1962.

———. *Frontier Regulars: The United States Army and the Indian, 1866–1891.* The Wars of the United States. New York: Macmillan Co., 1973.

———. *Frontiersmen in Blue: The United States Army and the Indian, 1848–1865.* The Wars of the United States. New York: Macmillan Co., 1967.

———. *The Indian Frontier of the American West, 1846–1890.* Histories of the American Frontier. Albuquerque: University of New Mexico Press, 1984.

———. *The Last Days of the Sioux Nation.* Yale Western Americana Series, no. 3. New Haven: Yale University Press, 1963.

Van Creveld, Martin L. *Command in War.* Cambridge: Harvard University Press, 1985.

Vaughn, J. W. *The Reynolds Campaign on Powder River.* Norman: University of Oklahoma Press, 1961.

Wallace, Andrew. *Gen. August V. Kautz and the Southwestern Frontier.* Tucson: Privately printed, 1967.

Walton, George. *Sentinel of the Plains: Fort Leavenworth and the American West.* Englewood Cliffs, N.J.: Prentice-Hall, 1973.

Warner, Donald F. *The Idea of Continental Union: Agitation for the Annexation of Canada to the United States 1849–1893.* Lexington: University of Kentucky Press, 1960.

Webb, Walter P. *The Texas Rangers: A Century of Frontier Defense.* Boston: Houghton Mifflin Co., 1935.

Weigley, Russell Frank. *The American Way of War: A History of United States Military Strategy and Policy.* The Wars of the United States. New York: Macmillan Co., 1973.

————. *Eisenhower's Lieutenants: The Campaign of France and Germany 1944–1945.* Bloomington: Indiana University Press, 1981.

————. *History of the United States Army.* The Wars of the United States. New York: Macmillan Co., 1967.

————. *Towards an American Army: Military Thought from Washington to Marshall.* New York: Columbia University Press, 1962.

Whinah, Donald R. *A History of the United States Weather Bureau.* Urbana: University of Illinois Press, 1961.

White, Leonard D. *The Republican Era, 1869–1901: A Study in Administrative History.* New York: Macmillan Co., 1958.

Williams, T. Harry. *The History of American Wars from 1745 to 1918.* New York: Alfred A. Knopf, 1981.

————. *Lincoln and the Radicals.* Madison: University of Wisconsin Press, 1941.

Young, Otis E. *The West of Philip St. George Cooke, 1809–1895.* Western Frontiersman Series, no. 5. Glendale Calif.: Arthur H. Clark Co., 1935.

2. Articles

Altshuler, Constance Wynn. "Men and Brothers." *Journal of Arizona History* 19 (Autumn 1978): 315–22.

Anderson, Harry. "A Sioux Pictorial Account of General Terry's Council." *North Dakota History* 22 (July 1955): 92–116.

Anderson, Harry H. "A Challenge to Brown's Indian Wars Thesis." *Montana, the Magazine of Western History* 12 (January 1962): 40–49.

Athearn, Robert G. "War Paint against Brass: The Army and the Plains Indians." *Montana, the Magazine of Western History* 6 (Summer 1956): 11–22.

Ball, Eve. "The Apache Scouts: A Chiricahua Appraisal." *Arizona and the West* 7 (Winter 1965): 315–28.

Baur, John E. "The Senator's Happy Thought." *American West* 10 (January 1973): 34–39, 62–63.

Berthrong, Donald J. "Cattlemen on the Cheyenne-Arapaho Reservation, 1883–1885." *Arizona and the West* 13 (Spring 1971): 5–32.

Blackburn, Forrest R. "Fort Leavenworth: Logistical Base for the West." *Military Review* 53 (December 1973): 3–12.

Bond, Brian. "Doctrine and Training in the British Cavalry, 1870–1914." In *The Theory and Practice of War*, ed. Michael Howard. Bloomington: Indiana University Press, 1965.

———. "The South African War, 1880–1." In *Victorian Military Campaigns*, ed. Brian Bond. New York: Frederick A. Praeger, 1967.

Boylan, Bernard L. "The Forty-Fifth Congress and Army Reform." *Mid-America* 41 (July, 1959): 173–86.

Brinckerhoff, Sidney B., and Chamberlin, Pierce. "The Army's Search for a Repeating Rifle: 1873–1903." *Military Affairs* 32 (1968): 20–30.

Brinsfield, John M. "The Military Ethics of General William T. Sherman: A Reassessment." *Parameters: The Journal of the U.S. Army War College* 12 (June 1982): 36–48.

Brinton, Crane, et al. "Jomini." In *Makers of Modern Strategy: Military Thought from Machiavelli to Hitler*, ed. Edward Mead Earle. 1943. Reprint. Princeton: Princeton University Press, 1971.

Brown, Mark H. "A New Focus on the Sioux War." *Montana, the Magazine of Western History* 11 (October 1961): 76–85.

Burlingame, Merrill Gildea. "The Military-Indian Frontier in Montana, 1860–1890." Abstract, Ph.D. diss., University of Iowa, 1936. University of Iowa Studies in the Social Sciences, *Abstracts in History* 3, no. 10 (February 1938): 59–69.

Carpenter, John A. "General Howard and the Nez Percé War of 1877." *Pacific Northwest Quarterly* 49 (October 1958): 129–45.

Carriker, Robert C. "Mercenary Heroes: The Scouting Detachment of the Indian Territory Expedition, 1874–1875." *Chronicles of Oklahoma* 51 (Fall 1973): 309–24.

Catton, Bruce. "Sheridan at Five Forks." *Journal of Southern History* 21 (August 1955): 305–15.

Chaput, Donald. "Generals, Indian Agents, Politicians: The Doolittle Survey of 1865." *Western Historical Quarterly* 3 (July 1972): 269–82.

Clow, Richmond L. "General Philip Sheridan's Legacy: The Sioux Pony Campaign of 1876." *Nebraska History* 57 (Winter 1976): 461–77.

Cohen, William B. "Malaria and French Imperialism." *Journal of African History* 24, no. 1 (1983): 23–36.

Cooney, Charles F. "At the Trial of the Lincoln Conspirators: The Reminiscences of General August V. Kautz." *Civil War Times Illustrated* 12 (August 1973): 22–31.

Crimmins, Colonel M. L. "General Mackenzie and Fort Concho." *West Texas Historical Association Year Book* 10 (1934): 16–31.

Cutler, Lee. "Lawrie Tatum and the Kiowa Agency, 1869–1873." *Arizona and the West* 13 (Autumn 1973): 221–44.

Dawson, Joseph G., III. "The Alpha-Omega Man: General Phil Sheridan." *Red River Valley Historical Review* 3 (Spring 1979): 147–63.

D'Elia, Donald J. "The Argument over Civilian or Military Indian Control, 1865–1880." *Historian* 24 (February 1962): 207–25.

Dunlay, Thomas W. "General Crook and the White Man Problem." *Journal of the West* 18 (April 1979): 3–10.

Ellis, Richard N. "Copper-Skinned Soldiers: The Apache Scouts." *Great Plains Journal* 5 (Spring 1966): 51–67.

———. "The Humanitarian Generals." *Western Historical Quarterly* 3 (April 1972): 169–78.

———. "The Humanitarian Soldiers." *Journal of Arizona History* 10 (Summer 1969): 53–66.

Ewers, John C. "Intertribal Warfare as the Precursor of Indian-White Warfare on the Northern Great Plains." *Western Historical Quarterly* 6 (October 1975): 397–410.

Fisher, Vincent J. "Mr. Calhoun's Army." *Military Review* 37 (September 1957): 52–58.

Fite, Gilbert. "The United States Army and Relief to Pioneer Settlers, 1874–1875." *Journal of the West* 6 (January 1967): 99–107.

Forman, Sidney. "Why the United States Military Academy Was Established in 1802." *Military Affairs* 29 (Spring 1965): 16–28.

Fritz, Henry E. "The Making of Grant's 'Peace Policy.'" *Chronicles of Oklahoma* 37 (Winter 1959–60): 411–32.

Garfield, Marvin H. "The Indian Question in Congress and in Kansas." *Kansas Historical Quarterly* 2 (February 1933): 29–44.

Gates, John M. "The Alleged Isolation of U.S. Army Officers in the Late 19th Century." *Parameters: The Journal of the U.S. Army War College* 10 (September 1980): 32–45.

———. "General George Crook's First Apache Campaign (The Use of Mobile, Self-Contained Units against the Apache in the Military Department of Arizona, 1871–1873)." *Journal of the West* 6 (April 1967): 310–20.

———. "Indians and Insurrectos: The U.S. Army's Experience with Insurgency." *Parameters: The Journal of the U.S. Army War College* 13 (March 1983): 59–68.

Gottmann, Jean. "Bugeaud, Gallieni, Lyautey: The Development of French Colonial Warfare." In *Makers of Modern Strategy: Military Thought from Machiavelli to Hitler*, ed. Edward Mead Earle. 1943. Reprint. Princeton: Princeton University Press, 1973.

Gould, Lewis L. "Francis E. Warren and the Johnson County War." *Arizona and the West* 9 (Summer 1967): 131–42.

Greene, Jerome A. "The Crawford Affair: International Implications of the Geronimo Campaign." *Journal of the West* 2 (June 1972): 143–53.

Griess, Thomas E. "A Case Study in Counterinsurgency: Kitchener and the Boers." In *New Dimensions in Military History: An Anthology*, ed. Russell F. Weigley. San Rafael, Calif.: Presidio Press, 1975.

Guentzel, Richard. "The Department of the Platte and Western Settlement, 1866–1877." *Nebraska History* 56 (Fall 1975): 389–418.

Hacker, Barton C. "The U.S. Army as National Police Force: The Federal Policing of Labor Disputes 1877–1892." *Military Affairs* 33 (April 1969): 255–64.

Hackett, Charles W. "The Recognition of the Diaz Government by the United States." *Southwestern Historical Quarterly* 28 (July 1924): 41–55.

Hagan, William T. "Kiowas, Comanches, and Cattlemen, 1867–1906: A Case Study of the Failure of U.S. Reservation Policy." *Pacific Historical Review* 40 (August 1971): 333–55.

Hansen, Anne Carolyn. "The Congressional Career of Senator Francis E. Warren from 1890 to 1902." *Annals of Wyoming* 20 (January 1948): 3–49.

Harte, John Bret. "Conflict at San Carlos: The Military-Civilian Struggle for Control, 1882–1885." *Arizona and the West* 15 (Spring 1973): 27–44.

Hedren, Paul L. "An Infantry Company in the Sioux Campaign, 1876." *Montana, the Magazine of Western History* 33 (Winter 1983): 30–39.

Hewes, James. "The United States Army General Staff, 1900–1917." *Military Affairs* 38 (April 1974): 67–72.

Highland, John. "Sheridan's 'Hell and Texas' Remark." *Southwestern Historical Quarterly* 45 (October 1941): 197–98.

Holden, W. C. "Frontier Defense in Texas during the Civil War." *West Texas Historical Association Year Book* 4 (1928): 16–31.

Horsman, Reginald. "Scientific Racism and the American Indian in the Mid-Nineteenth Century." *American Quarterly* 27 (May 1975): 152–68.

Hoxie, Frederick B. "The End of the Savage: Indian Policy in the United States Senate, 1880–1900." *Chronicles of Oklahoma* 55 (Summer 1977): 157–79.

Huntington, Samuel P. "Equilibrium and Disequilibrium in American Military Policy." *Political Science Quarterly* 76 (December 1961): 481–502.

Hutchins, James S. "Mounted Riflemen: The Real Role of Cavalry in the Indian Wars." In *Probing the American West: Papers from the Santa Fe Conference*, ed. K. Ross Toole et al. Santa Fe: Museum of New Mexico, 1962.

Hutton, Paul Andrew. "The Indians' Last Stand: A Review Essay." *New Mexico Historical Review* 59 (July 1984): 311–18.

———. "Phil Sheridan's Pyrrhic Victory: The Piegan Massacre, Army Politics, and the Transfer Debate." *Montana, the Magazine of Western History* 32 (Spring 1982): 32–43.

Jacobs, Wilbur R. "The Fatal Confrontation: Early Native-White Relations on the Frontiers of Australia, New Guinea, and America—A Comparative Study." *Pacific Historical Review* 40 (August 1971): 283–309.

Jones, Oakah L., Jr. "Pueblo Indian Auxiliaries and the Reconquest of New Mexico, 1692–1704." *Journal of the West* 2 (July 1963): 257–80.

———. "Pueblo Indian Auxiliaries in New Mexico, 1763–1821." *New Mexico Historical Review* 37 (April 1962): 81–109.

Karsten, Peter. "Armed Progressives: The Military Reorganizes for the

American Century." In *The Military in America: From the Colonial Era to the Present*, ed. Peter Karsten. New York: Free Press, 1980.

Keegan, John. "The Ashanti Campaign, 1873–4." In *Victorian Military Campaigns*, ed. Brian Bond. New York: Frederick A. Praeger, 1967.

Keenan, Gerald. "The Seventeenth of June." *North Dakota History* 26 (January 1959): 25–31.

Kelsey, Harry. "William P. Cole and Mr. Lincoln's Indian Policy." *Journal of the West* 10 (July 1971): 484–92.

Keuchel, Edward F. "Chemicals and Meat: The Embalmed Beef Scandal of the Spanish-American War." *Bulletin of the History of Medicine* 98 (Summer 1974): 249–64.

Killingray, David. "The Idea of a British Imperial African Army." *Journal of African History* 20, no. 3 (1979): 421–36.

King, James T. " 'A Better Way'; General George Crook and the Ponca Indians." *Nebraska History* 50 (Fall 1969): 239–54.

———. "General George Crook at Camp Cloud Peak: 'I Am at a Loss What to Do.' " *Journal of the West* 11 (January 1972): 114–27.

———. "George Crook: Indian Fighter and Humanitarian." *Arizona and the West* 9 (Winter 1967): 333–48.

———. "Needed: A Reevaluation of General George Crook." *Nebraska History* 45 (September 1964): 223–35.

Langellier, J. Phillip. "Camp Grant Affair, 1871: Milestone in Indian Policy?" *Military History of Texas and the Southwest* 15, no. 2 (1979): 17–30.

Langley, Lester D. "The Democratic Tradition and Military Reform 1878–1885." *Southwestern Social Science Quarterly* 48 (September 1967): 192–200.

Leckie, William H. "Buell's Campaign." *Red River Valley Historical Review* 3 (Spring 1978): 186–93.

———. "The Red River War 1784 [*sic*]–1875." *Panhandle-Plains Historical Review* 29 (1956): 78–100.

Long, E. B. "John A. Rawlins: Staff Officer Par Excellence." *Civil War Times Illustrated* 12 (January 1974): 4–9, 43–46.

Luvaas, Jay. "European Military Thought and Doctrine, 1870–1914." In *The Theory and Practice of War*, ed. Michael Howard. Bloomington: Indiana University Press, 1965.

Mahon, John K. "Anglo-American Methods of Indian Warfare, 1676–

1794." *Mississippi Valley Historical Review* 45 (September 1958): 254–75.

Mardock, Robert Winston. "Alfred Love, Indian Peace Policy, and the Universal Peace Union." *Kansas Quarterly* 3 (Fall 1971): 64–71.

Mattison, Ray H. "The Army Post on the Northern Plains, 1865–1885." *Nebraska History* 35 (March 1954): 17–43.

———. "The Indian Reservation System on the Upper Missouri, 1865–1890." *Nebraska History* 36 (September 1955): 141–72.

———. "The Military Frontier on the Upper Missouri." *Nebraska History* 37 (September 1956): 159–82.

Matzo, John A. "President Theodore Roosevelt and Army Reform." *Proceedings of the South Carolina Historical Association* (1973): 30–40.

Millbrook, Minnie Dubbs. "The West Breaks in General Custer." *Kansas Historical Quarterly* 36 (Summer 1970): 113–48.

Monaghan, Jay. "Custer's Last Stand—Trevilian Station, 1864." *Civil War History* 8 (September 1962): 245–58.

Morris, Ralph C. "The Notion of a Great American Desert East of the Rockies." *Mississippi Valley Historical Review* 13 (September 1956): 190–200.

Morris, Robert E. "Custer Made a Good Decision: A Leavenworth Appreciation." *Journal of the West* 16 (October 1977): 5–11.

Morrison, James L., Jr. "Educating the Civil War Generals: West Point, 1833–1861," *Military Affairs* 38 (October 1974): 108–11.

Morton, Desmond. "Cavalry or Police: Keeping the Peace on Two Adjacent Frontiers, 1870–1900." *Journal of Canadian Studies* 12 (Spring 1977): 27–37.

———. "Comparison of U.S./Canadian Military Experience on the Frontier." In *The American Military on the Frontier: Proceedings of the 7th Military History Symposium*, ed. James P. Tate. Washington: Office of Air Force History, 1978.

Nelson, Harold L. "Military Roads for War and Peace—1791–1836." *Military Affairs* 19 (Spring 1955): 1–14.

Newcomb, W. W. "A Re-examination of the Causes of Plains Warfare." *American Anthropologist* 52 (July-September, 1950): 317–30.

Nichols, Roger L. "The Army and Early Perceptions of the Plains." *Nebraska History* 56 (Spring 1975): 121–35.

———. "The Army and the Indians 1800–1830—A Reappraisal: The

Missouri Valley Example." *Pacific Historical Review* 41 (May 1972): 151–68.

O'Conner, Richard. "Sherman: Imaginative Soldier." *American Mercury* 67 (November 1948): 555–64.

Parker, Watson. "The Majors and the Miners: The Role of the U.S. Army in the Black Hills Gold Rush." *Journal of the West* 11 (January 1972): 99–113.

Partridge, Frank C. "Redfield Proctor, His Public Life and Services." *Vermont Historical Society Proceedings* (1913): 59–104.

Penrod, Mike. "The Big Horn Expedition of 1876." *Kansas Quarterly* 10 (Summer 1978): 79–90.

Pomeroy, Earl. "Toward a Reorientation of Western History: Continuity and Environment." *Mississippi Valley Historical Review* 41 (March 1955): 579–600.

Porter, Kenneth Wiggins. "The Seminole Negro-Indian Scouts 1870–1881." *Southwestern Historical Quarterly* 55 (January 1952): 358–77.

Preston, Richard A. "Comments on Desmond Morton, 'Comparison of U.S./Canadian Military Experience on the Frontier.' " In *The American Military on the Frontier: Proceedings of the 7th Military History Symposium*, ed. James P. Tate. Washington: Office of Air Force History, 1978.

Quinn, Joan Corbett. "A Mountain Charade: The Sheepeater Campaign—1879." *Montana, the Magazine of Western History* 28 (January 1978): 16–27.

Ranson, Edward. "Nelson A. Miles as Commanding General, 1895–1903." *Military Affairs* 29 (Winter 1965–66): 179–200.

Rattan, Donald V. "Counterguerilla Operations: A Case Study from History." *Military Review* 40 (May 1960): 23–27.

Reid, Jasper B., Jr. "Russell A. Alger as Secretary of War." *Michigan History* 43 (June 1959): 225–39.

Remington, Frederic. "Indians as Irregular Cavalry." *Harper's Weekly* 34 (December 27, 1890): 1004–6.

Rickey, Don. "The Battle of Wolf Mountain." *Montana, the Magazine of Western History* 13 (Spring 1963): 44–54.

Rister, Carl Coke. "The Significance of the Destruction of the Buffalo in the Southwest." *Southwestern Historical Quarterly* 33 (July 1929): 34–49.

————. "The Significance of the Jacksboro Indian Affair of 1871." *Southwestern Historical Quarterly* 29 (January 1926): 181–200.

Robertson, Francis B. " 'We Are Going to Have a Big Sioux War': Colonel David S. Stanley's Yellowstone Expedition, 1872." *Montana, the Magazine of Western History* 34 (Autumn 1984): 2–15.

Rolak, Bruno J. "General Miles' Mirrors: The Heliograph in the Geronimo Campaign of 1886." *Journal of Arizona History* 16 (Summer 1975): 145–60.

Rothfels, H. "Clausewitz." In *Makers of Modern Strategy: Military Thought from Machiavelli to Hitler*, ed. Edward Mead Earle. 1943. Reprint. Princeton: Princeton University Press, 1973.

Schott, Christine. "Gustave Schleicher: A Representative of the Early German Emigrants in Texas." *West Texas Historical Association Year Book* 28 (October 1952): 50–70.

Skelton, William B. "Army Officers' Attitudes toward the Indians, 1830–1860." *Pacific Northwest Quarterly* 67 (July 1976): 113–24.

————. "The Commanding General and the Problem of Command in the United States Army, 1821–1841." *Military Affairs* 34 (December 1970): 117–22.

Smith, Marian W. "The War Complex of the Plains Indians." *American Philosophical Society, Proceedings* 78 (1937): 425–61.

Spiller, Roger J. "Calhoun's Expansible Army: The History of a Military Idea." *South Atlantic Quarterly* 79 (Spring 1980): 189–203.

Stacey, C. P. "Fenianism and the Rise of National Feeling in Canada at the Time of Confederation." *Canadian Historical Review* 12 (September 1931): 238–61.

————. "The Military Aspect of Canada's Winning of the West, 1870–1885." *Canadian Historical Review* 21 (March 1940): 1–24.

Stegmaier, Robert M. "Artillery Helped Win the West." *Kansas Quarterly* 10 (Summer 1978): 59–74.

Svingen, Orlan J. "The Case of Spotted Hawk and Little Whirlwind: An American Dreyfus Affair." *Western Historical Quarterly* 15 (July 1984): 281–97.

Tate, Michael L. "John P. Clum and the Origins of an Apache Constabulary, 1874–1877." *American Indian Quarterly* 3 (Summer 1977): 99–120.

————. "The Multi-purpose Army on the Frontier: A Call for Further

Research." In *The American West: Essays in Honor of W. Eugene Hollon*, ed. Ronald Lora. Toledo: University of Toledo Press, 1980.

———. "Soldiers of the Line: Apache Companies in the U.S. Army, 1891–1897." *Arizona and the West* 16 (Winter 1974): 343–64.

Taylor, Morris F. "The Carr-Penrose Expedition: General Sheridan's Winter Campaign, 1868–1869." *Chronicles of Oklahoma* 51 (Summer 1973): 159–76.

Thomas, Donna. "Ambrose E. Burnside and Army Reform, 1850–1881." *Rhode Island History* 37 (February 1978): 3–13.

Trennert, Robert A. "A Grand Failure: The Smithsonian Indian Exhibition of 1876." *Prologue: The Journal of the National Archives* 6 (Summer 1974): 118–29.

———. "Popular Imagery and the American Indian: A Centennial View." *New Mexico Historical Review* 51 (July 1976): 215–32.

Unrau, William E. "The Civilian as Indian Agent: Villain or Victim?" *Western Historical Quarterly* (October 1972): 405–20.

Utley, Robert M. "The Frontier and the American Military Tradition." In *The American Military on the Frontier: Proceedings of the 7th Military History Symposium*, ed. James P. Tate. Washington: Office of Air Force History, 1978.

Wade, Arthur P. "The Military Command Structure: The Great Plains, 1853–1891." *Journal of the West* 15 (July 1976): 5–22.

Wallace, Andrew. "General August V. Kautz in Arizona, 1874–1878." *Journal of Arizona History* 4 (Winter 1963): 54–66.

Wallace, Ernest, and Anderson, Adrian S. "R. S. Mackenzie and the Kickapoos: The Raid into Mexico in 1873." *Arizona and the West* 7 (Summer 1965): 105–26.

Waltmann, Henry G. "Circumstantial Reformer: President Grant and the Indian Problem." *Arizona and the West* 13 (Winter 1971): 323–42.

Watson, Elmo Scott. "The Last Indian War, 1890–91—A Study of Newspaper Jingoism." *Journalism Quarterly* 20 (September 1943): 205–19.

Weigley, Russell R. "The Military Thought of John M. Schofield." *Military Affairs* 23 (Summer 1959): 77–84.

Welty, Raymond L. "The Army Fort of the Frontier (1860–1870)." *North Dakota Historical Quarterly* 2 (April 1928): 155–67.

———. "The Indian Policy of the Army, 1860–1870." *Cavalry Journal* 36 (July 1927): 367–81.

White, Lonnie J. "General Sully's Expedition to the North Canadian, 1868." *Journal of the West* 11 (January 1972): 75–98.

————. "Winter Campaigning with Custer and Sheridan: The Expedition of the Nineteenth Kansas Volunteer Cavalry." *Journal of the West* 6 (January 1967): 68–98.

White, W. Bruce. "The American Indian as Soldier, 1890–1919." *Canadian Review of American Studies* 7 (Summer 1975): 15–25.

Woodward, Arthur. "Sidelights on Fifty Years of Apache Warfare." *Journal of Arizona History* 2 (Fall 1961): 3–14.

Wooster, Robert. "Military Strategy in the Southwest, 1848–1860." *Military History of Texas and the Southwest* 15, no. 2 (1979): 5–15.

Worcester, Donald E. "The Apaches in the History of the Southwest." *New Mexico Historical Review* 50 (January 1975): 25–43.

3. Theses and Dissertations

Bell, Rodney Ellis. "A Life of Russell Alexander Alger, 1836–1907." Ph.D. diss., University of Michigan, 1975.

Bowie, Chester Winston. "Redfield Proctor: A Biography." Ph.D. diss., University of Wisconsin–Madison, 1980.

Cox, Merlin Gwinn. "John Pope, Fighting General from Illinois." Ph.D. diss., University of Florida, 1956.

DeMontravel, Peter R. "The Career of Lieutenant General Nelson A. Miles from the Civil War through the Indian Wars." Ph.D. diss., St. John's University, 1982.

Denton, Edgar. "The Formative Years of the United States Military Academy, 1775–1833." Ph.D. diss., Syracuse University, 1964.

Griess, Thomas E. "Dennis Hart Mahan: West Point Professor and Advocate of Military Professionalism, 1830–1871." Ph.D. diss., Duke University, 1968.

Malone, Patrick Mitchell. "Indian and English Military Systems in New England in the Seventeenth Century." Ph.D. diss., Brown University, 1971.

Roberts, Larry Don. "The Artillery with the Regular Army in the West from 1866 to 1890." Ph.D. diss., Oklahoma State University, 1981.

Roberts, William R. "Loyalty and Expertise: The Transformation of the Nineteenth-Century American General Staff and the Creation of the Modern Military Establishment." Ph.D. diss., Johns Hopkins University, 1980.

Sexton, Donal Jones. "Forging the Sword: Congress and the American Naval Renaissance, 1880–1890." Ph.D. diss., University of Tennessee, 1976.

Wooster, Robert. "Military Strategy in the American West, 1815–1860." M.A. thesis, Lamar University, 1979.

Index